ENGENDERING ECONOMICS

Between 1950 and 1975, the percentage of women receiving economic doctorates in the United States sunk to a new low. This book consists of a series of interviews with some of the few women who did attain this status during that period – a pioneering group who paved the way for the revival of later years.

Engendering Economics demonstrates that women's experiences in economics not only differ from those of men, but from those of each other. Amongst those interviewed are Marianne Ferber, Alice Rivlin, Barbara Bergmann, Ingrid Rima, and Lourdes Benería. The result provides a rich picture of the sociology of the economics profession and the vital contributions made to it by women economists.

The study will be invaluable to all those working in feminist economics, the history of economic thought, and social and institutional economics. It should also prove to be an eye-opener to the profession as a whole, male-dominated as it continues to be.

Paulette I. Olson is Associate Professor of Economics at Wright State University. **Zohreh Emami** is Professor of Economics at Alverno College and Associate Dean for Academic Affairs at Alverno College.

ENGENDERING ECONOMICS

Conversations with women economists
in the United States

Paulette I. Olson and Zohreh Emami

London and New York

First published 2002
by Routledge
11 New Fetter Lane, London EC4P 4EE

Simultaneously published in the USA and Canada
by Routledge
29 West 35th Street, New York, NY 10001

Routledge is an imprint of the Taylor & Francis Group

© 2002 Paulette I. Olson and Zohreh Emami

Typeset in Goudy by Taylor & Francis Books Ltd
Printed and bound in Great Britain by Biddles Ltd, Guildford and King's Lynn

British Library Cataloguing in Publication Data
A catalogue record for this book is available from the British Library

Library of Congress Cataloging-in-Publication Data
Olson, Paulette, I., 1949–
Engendering economics: conversations with women economists in the United States/
Paulette I. Olson and Zohreh Emami
Includes bibliographical references and index.
1. Women economists–United States–Biography. 2. Feminist economics.
I. Emami, Zohreh, 1954– II. Title.
HB74.8 .O45 2002
330'.082'0973–dc21   2001048405

ISBN 0–415–20555–7 (hbk)
ISBN 0–415–20556–5 (pbk)

To the memory of Michèle Pujol who inspired and encouraged me to pursue this project, and to all the women economists who were not included in this book, but should have been. PIO

To my mother, Mahligheh Khamseh, and daughter, Leila Emami Davis, for keeping me grounded in current reality while hopeful for a better future. ZE

CONTENTS

PLATES

ABBREVIATIONS AND ACRONYMS

AAUP	American Association of University Professors ·
AB	Bachelor of Arts
ABD	All but dissertation
AEA	American Economic Association
AER	*American Economic Review*
AFDC	Aid to Families with Dependent Children
AFEE	Association for Evolutionary Economics
AFIT	Association for Institutional Thought
AHA	American History Association
AID	Agency for International Development
AIESEC	Association Internationale des Etudiants en Sciences Economiques et Commerciales
ASA	American Sociological Association
ASSA	Allied Social Science Association
AT&T	American Telephone and Telegraph Company
BA	Bachelor of Arts
BLS	Bureau of Labor Statistics
Caltech	California Institute of Technology
CBO	Congressional Budget Office
Co-ed	Co-educational
Coop	Cooperative
COPEC	Conference on Problems of Economic Change
CPI	Consumer Price Index
CSWEP	Committee on the Status of Women in the Economics Profession
CUNY	City University of New York
CV	Curriculum Vitae
EEA	Eastern Economic Association
EEOC	Equal Employment Opportunity Commission
FDR	Franklin D. Roosevelt
Fed	Federal Reserve System
FEMECON	Discussion list for feminist economists
GAO	General Accounting Office

GDP	Gross Domestic Product
GGC	Gender and Global Change program at Cornell University
GI	A member or former member of the US Army, especially an enlisted person
GNP	Gross National Product
GRE	Graduate Record Examination
GS-5	Government ranking for salaried employees: Grade level 5
The Hill	Capitol Hill in Washington, DC
HUD	Department of Housing and Urban Development
IAFFE	International Association for Feminist Economics
IBM	International Business Machines (a multinational corporation)
ILO	International Labour Organization
IMF	International Monetary Fund
IS–LM	A theoretical framework for illustrating the effects of fiscal policy; the IS curve represents aggregate spending (the real sphere) and the LM curve represents liquidity preferences (the financial sphere)
IWPR	Institute for Women's Policy Research
JEI	*Journal of Economic Issues*
JPE	*Journal of Political Economy*
MA	Master of Arts
MBA	Master of Business Administration
MIT	Massachusetts Institute of Technology
NAACP	National Association for the Advancement of Colored People
NAFTA	North American Free Trade Agreement
NASA	National Aeronautics and Space Administration
NEA	National Economics Association
NIE	National Institute of Education
NLS	National Longitudinal Surveys
NSF	National Science Foundation
NYC	New York City
NYU	New York University
OMB	Office of Management and Budget
PCs	Personal Computers
PEW	Charitable trust named after the Pew family
PhD	Doctor of Philosophy
PTA	Parent Teacher Association
RFF	*Resources for the Future*
SAT	Standard Aptitude Test
SNCC	Student Non-violent Coordinating Committee
TA	Teaching Assistant
UCLA	University of California at Los Angeles
UN	United Nations

UNICEF	United Nations International Children's Fund
URPE	Union for Radical Political Economics
USIA	United States Information Agency
WASP	White Anglo-Saxon Protestant
WTO	World Trade Organization
YMCA	Young Men's Christian Association
YWCA	Young Women's Christian Association

ACKNOWLEDGMENTS

Work of any kind is often a collective endeavor, reflecting the many contributions of its collaborators. This is especially true for this volume. First and foremost, our heartfelt thanks go to the women who shared their stories with us. Their courage and generosity as oral history pioneers in the field of economics, as well as their enormous patience in waiting for this book to be published, are greatly appreciated. We would also like to thank Alison Kirk for believing in the project, Barbara Duke for her valuable assistance in preparing the manuscript and Robert Langham for his continuous encouragement and prodding, and for shepherding the book to its fruition.

A special thanks goes to Chris Snyder who artfully created the collages from a host of photographs of different shapes, sizes, and colors. We would also like to express our gratitude to the Archival Division of the Oklahoma Historical Society for granting permission to reprint the photographs of Barbara Jones in 1958 during the civil rights movement in Oklahoma City.

More personally, Paulette is indebted to the many women in her life who provide affirmation, inspiration, laughter, traveling companionship, and the permission to party. She is particularly grateful to her mother, Isabelle, for being, loving, and teaching her the art of good cooking. And one could not have better friends and colleagues than Anna, Barbara, Catherine, Dell, Kelli, Lois, Maggie, Nancy, Pamela, and Peggy. Paulette is also grateful for faculty development grants provided by Dean Rishi Kumar and Wright State University's Research and Sponsored Programs to subsidize the preparation of the manuscript.

Zohreh would like to thank John Davis and Leila Emami Davis for their encouragement, patience, and unwavering practical and moral support; John Davis and Donna Engelmann for their generous reading and camaraderie; Jean Acken and Janis Wells for all their help when she really needed it; Sara Mason for her feedback; and her students for attempting to change the rules and keeping her optimistic. She would also like to thank her colleagues at Alverno College for working to create a collaborative community where many of the issues still plaguing institutions of higher education are being constructively addressed.

INTRODUCTION

> We have claimed the historical realities of our lives as the places
> from which our thought and politics not only *do* begin, but also
> *should* begin. It has also taken courage to claim these identities for
> such purposes when the fathers of our intellectual traditions have
> insisted for centuries that we are exactly *not* the kinds of persons
> whose beliefs can ever be expected to achieve the status of
> knowledge. They still claim that only the impersonal, disinter-
> ested, socially anonymous representatives of human reason – a
> description that refers to themselves, of course – are capable of
> producing knowledge. Mere opinion is all that folks like us can
> hope to produce. ... So, it is an extraordinary achievement of
> feminist thought to have shown ... that the unselfconscious
> perspective that claims universality is in fact not only partial but
> also distorting in ways that go beyond its partiality.
>
> (Harding 1991: 100–1)

In recent years, feminist economists have generated an impressive literature
illuminating the various levels of exclusionary practices within the discipline of
economics. At one level, feminist historians of economic thought have docu-
mented how the profession excluded women from the discipline of economics
and, thereby, from the production of economic knowledge. At another level,
they have examined the social construction of knowledge within the profession,
and have discovered the multiple ways in which women's contributions to
economics have been systematically ignored, misrepresented, and/or marginalized. In this process, they have also begun the formidable task of unearthing the
rather extensive contributions of women economists during the eighteenth,
nineteenth, and early twentieth centuries (Pujol 1992; Groenewegen 1994;
Dimand *et al.* 1995; Albelda 1997). Together this research suggests that the
invisibility of women's scholarly achievements stems more from systematic
methods of burial than from their collective lack of scholastic ability or non-
participation in the profession. At a third level, feminist theorists have exposed
the androcentric bias inherent in economic theories, assumptions, discourse,
methods, and methodologies. In addition, Eurocentricism (Grapard 1995) and

1

the intersecting social categories of race (Simms and Malveaux 1986; Williams 1993), class (Folbre 1982; Benería and Roldán 1987), sexual identity (Badget 1995; Gluckman and Reed 1997), age (Olson 1990; Shaw 1988), and ethnicity (Amott and Matthaei 1996) have increasingly received attention. Clearly, the latter categories will receive greater attention as global membership in the International Association for Feminist Economics increases.

This book is an attempt to contribute to this important feminist research agenda. However, our approach is somewhat different from most. We present the oral histories of contemporary women economists who received their doctorates in the United States between 1950 and 1975. The approach is "somewhat different" in the sense that oral history is not considered a legitimate tool for data collection in the discipline of economics. Therefore, it is rarely used even among feminist economists. While we do not claim to be the first in the field to use oral history as a research method (see King and Saunders 1999; Olmsted 1997), we hope that our book will encourage the discussion of methodological issues in feminist economics in particular, and the profession in general.

There are essentially three motivations for this volume, stemming from the broader feminist agenda of developing a feminist understanding of economics and contributing to progressive change in the economics profession. First, we want to document for future generations the variety of experiences and interests of mature women economists at the turn of the twenty-first century. Oral history gives contextual meaning to those experiences and interests. Through oral history, we discover how individuals within a particular historical and cultural context interpret and understand their multifaceted lives as students, researchers, teachers, care givers, and persons with intersecting social identities. Second, we want to highlight the advantages of using oral history as an additional method of inquiry within economics. By allowing us to ask new and qualitatively different questions, oral history allows us to challenge orthodox ways of knowing and to create new material about women. Third, this volume represents an initial attempt to develop a much richer understanding of the sociology of the economics profession from the perspective of women economists. The women included in this project are repositories of historical knowledge. They have a wealth of information and experience as students, professionals, and creators of formal and informal networks and organizations. They explain why they were attracted to economics; how they chose their graduate programs; how they were trained; what institutional constraints they faced; what strategies they used to navigate the profession; and what changes they have observed in the profession, among other things. Their collective memory and knowledge contributes to a more complete understanding of the history of the economics profession, its practices, how it operates, and what specifically is required for its improvement. In general, we hope that this collection will encourage similar oral history projects incorporating the voices, experiences, interests, and insights of various generations of women economists from around the world.

The case for oral history research in economics

In their work to reclaim women's contributions to the field of economics, feminist historians of economic thought have noted the limitations of historical and bibliographic research and have underscored the need for biographical research including oral history (Dimand *et al.* 1995: xi). As they point out, most of the scholarship on women economists of the past relies on bibliographical data. Researchers must examine scholarly publications, association records, newspaper accounts, letters, diaries, and other archival data in an effort to piece together as complete an account of women's contributions to the profession and accomplishments as possible. This type of archival research is not only quite difficult, it often lacks contextual meaning. Consequently, bibliographical and historical data can provide a picture of a complex past, but oral history allows for a dynamic and nuanced view of the past by giving the speaker explanatory power. For instance, the women in our study explain why they wrote what they did, when they did. In this way oral history reveals the complex constructions of self, motivation, and meaning. It allows us to understand how childhood and family relationships, social identities, personal experiences of inequality, political affiliations, support networks, and feelings associated with all of these aspects of their lives have operated to shape career choices, research agendas, teaching pedagogies, and the creation of new kinds of relationships in families, in communities, and in the profession. By allowing women to represent themselves rather than be represented, oral history gives legitimacy to feminist knowledge.

Feminist economists have also highlighted the androcentric bias and limitations of using traditional data collection techniques within economics (MacDonald 1995; Pujol 1997). Simply put, economists are uncomfortable with being labeled "social scientists." In their effort to take the "social" out of social science, they construct highly abstract, formalized, and deductive models and privilege quantitative analysis over qualitative analysis to demonstrate their "objectivity" and "value neutrality." The goal is to distance themselves as far away from the object of analysis as possible and to pretend that their values have nothing to do with what they want to know. Indeed, the quintessential economist – male or female – is the econometrician who "objectively" interprets the results of a computer printout. What is conveniently ignored, among other things, is the considerable amount of qualitative work that goes into the development of data sets. As feminist economists have pointed out, there is nothing inherently "objective" in the design and collection of economic statistics. Instead, data points are based on metaphoric and narrative constructions and definitions which are arbitrary, contingent, and subjective. More important, available quantitative data are often inadequate for providing answers which would help inform policy making from a feminist perspective. To the extent that economic statistics are value laden, therefore, the hierarchy between "hard facts" and "soft" approaches to science breaks down.

The point, however, is not to reverse the hierarchical dualism and claim the superiority of qualitative research over quantitative research. Instead, what is required to further the feminist goals of scientific inquiry is the explicit recognition of the underlying assumptions and priorities that guide research questions. As Sandra Harding has argued, the ideal of value neutrality has weakened objectivity because it denies that there are "contextual values" guiding scientific inquiry (Harding 1995). Explicit and systematic identification of values and priorities, on the other hand, strengthens objectivity and leads to what Harding has called "strong objectivity" or greater understanding. By embedding our research in women's lives and allowing for multiple and complex interpretations of social life, oral history research has the advantage of moving us from the modernist conception of "objectivity" to a feminist understanding of "strong objectivity." Through our conversations with women economists, the contextual values and priorities informing the conceptual frameworks of those we interviewed are revealed. Abstract and androcentric assumptions about human behavior are replaced with concepts and interpretations which are concrete and grounded in women's experiences, which are diverse, complex, and unpredictable. Thus, oral history, as a self-conscious technique for collecting data, broadens and deepens the range and focus of economic research.

Oral history also reveals our values and priorities as researchers. Many of the questions that we ask are admittedly shaped by our feminist values and social identities, including our position as women economists. The key feminist value that guides our investigation is openness of information and inquiry. In this way, our research supports the work of other feminist economists who are interested in improving the science of economics. One of the central goals is the demystification of economics as a profession. Not unlike other scientists who study the natural or physical world, feminist economists want to study the social world of economics. Oral history, as a feminist tool, opens up for examination and understanding the internal workings of the economics profession just as biochemical information opens the living cell for examination.

As feminist economists, we are committed to economic justice and social change. This feminist quest, however, is not an individual act, but a collective endeavor. To this end, we join other feminist scholars in a variety of disciplines who are using oral history as a method of documenting the historical sociology of their respective professions (see Laslett and Thorne 1997; Boris and Chaudhuri 1999). Oral history is a "feminist tool" to the extent that it allows feminist scholars to explore how power relations are organized, maintained, and experienced within the various disciplines. Understanding the structural barriers that constrain individual agency moves us closer to challenging the various systems of power that operate within academia.

The historical significance of our cohort

Women in the United States have a long history in economics, dating back before its inception as an academic discipline in the latter part of the nineteenth century. Their early contributions to the development of economic thought are found in such journals as the *American Economic Review*, the *Journal of Political Economy*, *Economic Journal*, the *Journal of the American Statistical Association*, *Economica*, among others. Before the founding of "economic" journals, their theoretical work was published in books, periodicals, pamphlets, and magazines. They also wrote numerous papers and monographs which were never published, and collaborated on numerous books but were rarely acknowledged (Dimand 1995). Moreover, during the progressive era, women played an important role in the social and economic reform debates by gathering and reporting data for government agencies and private think tanks and testifying before Congress. And although women with PhDs were a distinct minority in a male-dominated profession, they were active members and officers in the American Economic Association and presented papers at national meetings. But because of their gender, they were excluded from the prestigious universities and confined to jobs in women's colleges and state universities with heavier teaching loads (Albelda 1997: 25–6).

During the 1920s, women's active participation in the profession came to an abrupt halt. As economics began to define the boundaries of the discipline in an effort to gain professional status, women were simultaneously excluded. According to Randy Albelda (1997: 14), women were excluded in three basic ways. First, access to PhDs and academic jobs in PhD programs was restricted, thereby limiting the number of women who could become "experts" in the field. Second, the adoption of a positivist methodology rendered feminist, institutionalist, and radical analyses as "not economics." Third, with increased specialization, women's "special interests" were marginalized by the profession. As a result, by 1920, the percentage of dissertations in economics written by women hit a record peak (Forget 1995: 26–7). But while the percentage of women doctorates in all other disciplines continued to climb until 1930, then leveled off until 1940, and then declined for the next thirty years, the trend in economics followed a different path (Forget 1995: 26). After the percentage peak in the 1920s, there was a clear downward trend. By the 1950s, the percentage of all economic doctorates awarded to women dropped below 5 percent, where it remained until the late 1960s. Not until the late 1970s did it finally surpass the 1920 percentages (Albelda 1997: 13, 25). In 1979, a little over 7 percent of all economists with PhDs were women (Albelda 1997: 37). This, in part, explains the focus of our book. We are primarily interested in the experiences of women who received their doctorates between 1950 and 1975 when the percentage of women economists hit a new record low. This cohort, we believe, constitutes a unique group of women because they represent the postwar pioneers who have charted the way for future generations of women economists.

Another reason for our focus is that, at least to our knowledge, there is no systematic study of women economists in this cohort. It was not until after the establishment of the Committee on the Status of Women in the Economics

Profession (CSWEP) in 1971 that data began to be collected on women's status in the profession. Several papers using this early data were subsequently published in the *American Economic Review*. Each study supports some of the findings in this volume. For instance, Carolyn Shaw Bell (1973), the first chair of CSWEP, reported the low representation of women in the profession. Alice Amsden and Collette Moser (1975) noted the barriers to academic employment and promotion despite the establishment of affirmative action programs in the late 1960s. Barbara Reagan (1975) identified men's attitudes about their female colleagues as a significant variable restricting women's advancement up the promotional ladder and hence their relatively low wages. And Myra Strober (1975) found that women were attracted to economics because of their interest in the subject matter, and/or because they wanted to use their mathematical skills and to solve social problems. Although the CSWEP newsletter continues to track the status of women economists and regularly publishes biographies of the deceased, there remains a dearth of information on women in the economics profession between 1950 and 1975. One exception is the information that can be gleaned from Margaret Rossiter's *Women Scientists in America* which focuses on women scientists in general, and their experience in academia in particular.

As Rossiter and others have pointed out, this was a period in which women experienced further retrenchment within academia. Following World War II, returning soldiers who attended college received government subsidies under the Servicemen's Readjustment Act (or GI Bill) of 1944. Comparable resources were not available to women until the passage of the National Education Act of 1958 (Gatlin 1987: 17). Moreover, as the Cold War heated up, scientific research assumed greater value in institutions of higher learning. As Margaret Rossiter notes, this was the golden age of science, with record growth in money spent, people trained, jobs created, articles published, and Nobel prizes won (Rossiter 1995: xv). But women scientists were underutilized, marginalized, or eventually forced out of academic positions. According to Rossiter, much of the retrenchment was tied to the antinepotism rules which prohibited the hiring of relatives in the same department or university (Rossiter 1995: 123). Whereas single women were not taken seriously because they were expected to get married and leave, faculty wives were often prevented from continuing their careers. Overt discrimination was the rule rather than the exception. Despite their credentials, many women scientists worked for decades as "emergency" or "volunteer" instructors before gaining tenure track positions. Others worked for years as research assistants for male faculty. Still others left academia altogether and took jobs with the federal government or created positions for themselves in non-profit organizations. Most, however, found work in the female ghetto of home economics (Rossiter 1995: 129–48). But by the early 1960s, even the former female bastions of women's colleges, teachers colleges, and colleges of home economics began replacing women deans, chairs, and faculty with young men with far less experience. Men, it was argued, would improve the prestige of the colleges and the ability to attract good students (Rossiter 1995: 184–6).

During the 1950s and 1960s, the discriminatory practices in academia were part of a much larger pattern affecting women's employment nationwide. These exclusionary practices together with women's marginalization within the various political movements of the late 1960s essentially fueled what became known as the women's movement. By the late 1960s, the civil rights movement which had begun with sit-ins in the South in the 1950s moved northward. Antiwar protests against the draft and universities' involvement in ROTC and military research heated up on campuses across the United States. As women began to reflect on their marginalized status, especially within social movements, they joined forces and began to collectively pressure for political change. They formed consciousness-raising groups, signed petitions, joined marches, offered courses on women's issues, collected data and prepared reports, and in general raised awareness of women's secondary status. As a result of these collective efforts, between 1968 and 1972, there was a legal revolution in women's education and employment rights. It was within this historical and political context that the women in our study sought and obtained a PhD in economics.

This volume supports a growing feminist scholarship that re-examines the postwar era and challenges the well-entrenched stereotype that all American women, especially during the 1950s, were passive, home-bound, suburban housewives (Coontz 1992; Meyerowitz 1994). While these scholars do not deny the cultural constraints imposed on women by the domestic ideal or the Cold War conservatism of the 1950s and 1960s, they argue that the unrelenting focus on the suburban housewife obscures both the gender ambiguities embedded in the postwar culture and the complexity of women's lives and commitments. Clearly, not all women were white, middle-class housewives, and of those who were, they were neither wholly domestic nor quiescent (Meyerowitz 1994: 1–2). Millions of women worked outside the home, and were actively involved in the civil rights, peace, labor, and women's movements of that era. Indeed, many of the women in this volume talk about their activism and political commitments in working for social change. Thus we join other scholars in presenting a more nuanced interpretation of women's lives during the postwar years by illustrating how women of that generation were both shaped by and actively resisted the cultural stereotypes and social pressures of the postwar era.

The approach

The range of our inquiry is limited in three major ways. First, we were specifically interested in women who received their doctorates in economics between 1950 and 1975 for the reasons discussed above. Second, the study is restricted to women economists who received their PhDs in the United States. Third, only eleven women are included in the study. The reasons for the limitations are straightforward. Significant time and resource constraints restricted both the number of women we could interview and the geographic distance we could travel for the interviews. In fact, the study was not expanded until we were able to pool our resources and pursue the project together.

Originally, one of the most difficult tasks confronting us was the selection of women economists to be included in the study. Again, because of our limited time and resource constraints, the selection process was not random. We essentially identified our cohort through our professional associations and other less formal networks of acquaintances, keeping a diversity criterion in mind. We wanted to include a diverse group of women who would reflect the heterogeneity of the female population in the United States as well as the different career paths and philosophical perspectives within the economics profession. Although the original list of women was much longer, a variety of unforeseen circumstances mitigated against the inclusion of many women. Sometimes coordinating our schedules became impossible, and in one case, a woman withdrew from the project early on, while another woman withdrew after the final revisions.

During her sabbatical in 1996–7, Zohreh began interviewing Marianne Ferber and Suzanne Helburn. In 1998, she interviewed Lourdes Benería, Ingrid Rima, Lois Shaw, and Myra Strober. Likewise, Paulette interviewed Heidi Hartmann, Barbara Jones, Anne Mayhew, and Alice Rivlin during her sabbatical in 1997–8. During our trip to Washington, DC, in February of 1998, we both interviewed Barbara Bergmann, Suzanne Helburn, and Margaret Simms.

Those who are included in our study vary to some degree along the lines of race, ethnicity, and class origin. Most, however, are white and have middle- to upper-class backgrounds, although a few are immigrants and women of color, and some have working-class roots. Their ethnic heritage conforms with most Americans. A majority have ethnic roots in Northern and Eastern Europe. One is from Southern Europe (Spain). Two have ethnic backgrounds in Africa and several are of Jewish descent. They are single, married, divorced, mothers, aunts, grandmothers, and presumably all are heterosexual. A significant cluster grew up in the northeast, primarily New York. But there is diverse regional representation. Whereas some spent their childhoods in the Mid-West or the South, one grew up on the west coast in San Diego. Although the majority grew up in urban areas of the United States, three spent their childhoods in rural areas in such divergent places as Texas, Spain, and Canada.

The women in our study have also chosen different career paths at academic, governmental, research, and consulting institutions. They range in age from their mid-fifties to mid-seventies, a range of twenty years. Some are near retirement, while others are officially "retired," although not from scholarship. Some continue to write books and articles, while others have recently begun new jobs or embarked on new professional challenges.

Finally, the women in this collection also embrace diverse theoretical perspectives, representing different schools of thought within contemporary economics. They represent institutionalism, Marxism, Keynesianism, post-Keynesianism, social economics, and socialist feminism. Interestingly, only one woman in our group identified herself as a "modified" neoclassical while two others with neoclassical proclivities described themselves as "eclectic" economists. Most, though certainly not all, consider themselves feminists. Among those who do, there is considerable variation in the ways they define feminism. This supports the feminist contention that feminism is not monolithic; that it allows for multiple identities.

After agreeing to participate in the project, each of the eleven women were sent a list of questions (see the Appendix). The questions were designed to serve as semi-structured conversation guides. We hoped that this approach would jar memories and inspire thought and reflection about their specific life experiences. We were not looking for specific answers to specific questions. Rather, the main objective was to encourage a dialogue around a few central themes that would help create a richer picture of their lives as family members, students, and professionals. As the reader will discover, certain sections of each narrative will vary in length and detail, depending on the significance of the experience for each woman. Consequently, the tone and direction of the conversation often guided the questions.

The first theme we chose was family genealogy. Information about the ethnic and class background of their families and the educational attainment of their parents often generated important insights about the development of their social identities, value systems, and interests, as well as their educational and career trajectories. Likewise, questions about their educational experience as undergraduates and graduates tell us something about how they were socialized by institutions outside the family. We were particularly interested in why they chose economics over other academic disciplines and whether they had role models and/or mentors that influenced their decision to pursue economics. Questions about their training in economics and their interaction with professors provided additional historical and social context for understanding what it was like to be a woman and/or an African–American in economics during this period. The third theme focused on the ability to balance their family and professional lives. That is, what specific constraints did they face and what types of strategies did they use to survive the demands of both family and career? Not surprisingly, issues of child care were of paramount concern among women with children. The fourth theme was a bit broader, focusing on their experiences as professional economists. This set of questions was designed to encourage reflections about their career paths in particular and changes in the economics profession in general.

The choice of when and where the conversations took place was largely left to the discretion of the women in our study. However, our scarce time and resource constraints quickly defined the boundaries of this choice. The conversations were tape-recorded, and this was followed by the arduous task of transcribing the tapes verbatim. In the first round of editing, we focused on grammatical changes, and little else. The intention was to keep the editing to a minimum. But whatever the intent, editing admittedly reshapes the conversation because it is governed by two simultaneous forces: by our own experience as participants and listeners in the conversation, and by our audience to whom we must display a degree of scholarly competence (Gluck and Patai 1991; Reinharz 1992).

In the next step of the editing process, we solicited feedback about our interpretation and representation of the interview. Each woman was invited to edit, and to add or subtract information. The objective was to get further clarification, explanation, and/or the meaning of particular words, phrases, or thoughts. To preserve the character of the chapters as conversations, we asked them to avoid autobiography. We wanted the readers to feel the flavor of the conversations, and to picture the women through the expressions they used, the stories they told, and their sense of humor. The next step included phone and Internet conversations between ourselves and the participants about the final product. Here we asked for further information and/or clarification in order to fill in the holes. Finally, we requested a set of pictures from each woman which they thought would best represent the different stages of their lives. As a result, each chapter contains a one-page collage which provides another dimension in the self-construction of their identities.

Needless to say, this experience has greatly enhanced our appreciation of the work of oral historians. Given our heavy teaching and administrative loads throughout the year and the process of communicating back and forth with our participants who also have considerable demands on their time, it has taken close to five years to complete this project. There are eleven chapters that follow, each highlighting the life and work of the different women in our study. To provide historical continuity, the chapters are organized chronologically according to when each received their PhD. We begin each chapter with a short biography, followed by a brief overview of the context within which the individual conversations took place. A list of acronyms and associated terms is included as a convenient reference for those unfamiliar with the discipline, and the interview questions are found in the Appendix. The Bibliography contains not only references cited in the Introduction, but selected articles and books mentioned in the conversations, and the major publications of the featured women economists.

In what follows we offer some general observations about the commonalities and differences among the women in our study. Our observations, however, are not intended to be all inclusive. Each of us will take away from these stories different impressions, insights, and interpretations that make particular sense to us. One story may resonate more strongly with our experiences and interests than another. But this should not render the other stories in this volume any less significant to our understanding of what we want to know and discover about our collective history. As a feminist project, the goal is to expand the production of knowledge and to strive for "strong objectivity." To this end, we invite the readers of this text to compare and contrast their interpretations with ours, explicitly acknowledging the underlying assumptions, interests, and priorities that make these interpretations possible.

Observations

All of the women in this volume appear to have understood from an early age that they would eventually attend college. From grade school onward, they were all high academic achievers. Many talk about the recognition they received from teachers and peers for their intellectual acumen in the form of awards, scholarships, and other types of support. But central to their decisions to attend college were the high expectations of their parents. This is consistent across all the women regardless of the income status and educational backgrounds of their parents. A few of the women talked about their parents' financial difficulties, working through college, and/or their feelings of insecurity around wealthy children in school. But compared to family income, the educational backgrounds of their parents is much more diverse. At least four of the women grew up in families in which neither parent attended college. At the other end of the spectrum, two women come from families in which both parents had college degrees, and an additional two had fathers with college diplomas. What is notable, however, is that three additional women had mothers who were college-educated. This is notable because few women of their parents' generation attended college. But it is equally interesting to note that the majority of their mothers worked for pay at some time during their lives. And not unexpectedly, they all worked in traditional female jobs such as domestic work, elementary school teaching, secretarial work, stenography, social work, etc. Thus, at least for this small group of women, parental expectations, coupled with the educational and work experience of their mothers, might in part explain their educational achievements.

For some of the women the attraction to economics began in high school, for others it began in college, but none of the women began their college careers as economics majors. Four were enrolled in interdisciplinary programs in which economics was a part. The hook for the rest was an economics course with an excellent teacher and/or an affinity to mathematics. One woman took a double major in math and economics, while four others thought that they would major in math but decided to switch to economics. In retrospect, many point out how classroom economics was less quantitative and abstract as compared to today. Indeed, for most of the women the main attraction of economics over math was its focus on relevant policy issues and the pursuit of knowledge. As one woman explains, "I shifted away from math as my major. It wasn't because I couldn't do it. It just wasn't interesting to me because I couldn't figure out how … it could be useful to me." This explanation supports the claims of other women who felt that economics compared to other disciplines offered "better tools" for understanding their immediate family circumstances as well as larger social and political issues.

For most, but not all, the decision to attend graduate school in economics was serendipitous rather than a conscious career move. Only three entered PhD programs immediately after receiving their Bachelor's degree. Some were encouraged by colleagues, professors, and/or husbands. Some chose economics for financial reasons: "as a way to get a decent job;" or for expeditious reasons: "I didn't want to start a whole new discipline." For others, it was completely unintended. A significant number of women followed their husbands to a job or graduate school and found themselves without alternatives, or saw their particular circumstances as their only chance to continue their education. But regardless of their reasons, the overwhelming majority received their PhDs from some of the nation's top-ranked universities such as Harvard, Stanford, and MIT.

Almost all of the women experienced the pressures and constraints of patriarchy in their graduate programs, although not all of them recognized it as discriminatory at the time. They recalled their graduate programs as "incredibly male places" where "women scholars were not taken seriously." Indeed, all but two were in departments in which there were no women faculty members. Some remember how infuriated they were at the paternalistic and racist ways in which they were treated and ignored by the faculty, and expressed resentment at the institutionalized ways in which they were tracked as people of color and as women. Many recall the extremely competitive conditions of the prestigious programs and the basic lack of time and energy to challenge, much less think about, discriminatory practices. For most, the main objective was survival. As one woman puts it, "I think we felt lucky to be there at all."

At the dissertation stage, most of the women noted the complete lack of faculty assistance and/or mentoring with the exception of Lois Shaw, who had a woman faculty advisor. This contrasts sharply with the experiences of men in roughly the same cohort (1944–75) who attended similar institutions. For instance, in Arjo Klamer's book, *Conversations with Economists*, many of the men recall their close personal relationships with male mentors and the professional networks that helped to propel their work into the public limelight.

Another gender difference highlighted in our conversations is the disproportionate share of family responsibilities primarily borne by women. Of the women in our study, 73 percent were wives, close to 64 percent were mothers, and 54 percent had children during their graduate years. As primary care givers, they had two basic options – they could either stay home with their children or find alternative care. Whereas some used child care centers, others did stay home. But the majority hired child care providers who often worked as housekeepers as well. This reveals something about the relatively low cost of child care during this time period, and the relatively high class status of women who become economists.

Today, graduate women in economics would never attempt to enter the job market without a few publications in addition to a PhD. In contrast, the majority of women in our cohort entered the job market before finishing their dissertations. Several mention the prevalence of jobs for college teachers while simultaneously noting the difficulties they encountered finding their first jobs and/or tenure track positions. More than half discussed their experiences dealing with discriminatory behavior and practices while they were on the job market – ranging from distinct "no women" policies and discriminatory questions during interviews to outright hostility. Some admit to naivete in their job search strategies while others express feelings of powerlessness and the need "to go with the flow" to survive. Not unexpectedly, most of the women emphasized the significance of having personal connections to secure employment.

Most who held positions in academia recall a variety of gender and/or racial biases in the workplace. Among other things, they discuss the higher standards required for tenure, their relatively low salaries, their exclusion from economic seminars, and the overall feeling of marginalization for simply teaching courses and/or conducting research on discrimination, poverty, and other topics of marginal concern to the discipline.

When asked for their current evaluation of economics, almost all complained about the discipline's increasing irrelevance as it has become more abstract, theoretical, mathematical, and less policy-oriented over time. Compared to the past, many also consider economics more exclusionary, insular, and resistant to alternative perspectives. This has essentially made the discipline hostile to any historical and institutional analyses especially of race and gender issues since this kind of work is considered subjective and unscientific. Asked whether they would encourage young women to pursue a career in economics, they had three general responses. A third of the women do not and would not encourage women to enter economics. Approximately another third would advise women to study economics, to do what is necessary to succeed, to mentor younger women for success, and to critique mainstream economics from a position of strength within the discipline. Another third urge women to be passionate about the economic issues they have chosen to study, including feminist issues. According to this group, the key to survival within the profession is to find a support group – a group to work with and to help transform the character of the discipline.

Despite their critical evaluation of the discipline, the serendipitous ways in which their careers progressed, and the difficulties they faced as pioneers in the profession, most of the women in this study seem content and fulfilled with the development of their careers. They have all developed a niche reflecting their theoretical and political commitments without compromising their personal and professional values. The wide range of their work on questions of equity and justice, poverty and income distribution, institutional structure and culture, and education and pedagogy has indeed broadened and enriched the discipline.

Plate 1   Top left: Ingrid Rima at age 22. Top right: Ingrid with family, dancers, and tour guide at a dinner theater, Bangkok (1974). Main portrait: Receiving Lindback Award for distinguished teaching at Temple University (1998). Right middle: Ingrid with Temple University colleague Lou Harms. Bottom right: Ingrid at age 16.

1

INGRID HAHNE RIMA

Intellectually I see the phenomenon of income distribution as the most challenging problem in economics. Many of us have discarded the marginal productivity theory of income distribution, but we have not really replaced it. We don't have a handle on how to explain either the wage structure in the US, or income sharing among different countries in the world.

(Ingrid Rima, 1998)

A consummate theoretician, Ingrid has written numerous books and over thirty articles. Her books on the history of economic thought and Joan Robinson's legacy in economics are particularly noteworthy. She has consistently explored the hard theoretical questions and has grounded her own interests and theoretical contributions in the history of our discipline. Her work on contemporary economic issues such as labor markets, global restructuring, and sectoral changes in employment have all been informed by a sophisticated understanding of the historical debates as well as her own contributions to the fundamental questions of measurement, quantification, and time in economic analysis. As the Editor of the *Eastern Economics Journal*, Ingrid made substantial contributions to providing a fair and scholarly venue for young economists, including those interested in asking heterodox questions. Among her many accomplishments, Ingrid has received several teaching awards, has served as the President of the History of Economics Society, and was a Fulbright Distinguished Professor of Economics at Lingnan College, Zhongshan University, the People's Republic of China. Currently she is a Professor of Economics at Temple University. She graduated cum laude with a BA in economics (1945) from Hunter College. She received her MA (1946) and PhD (1951) from the University of Pennsylvania.

We spent several hours with Ingrid during the World Congress of Social Economics in Chicago in July of 1998. It was indeed a pleasure listening to Ingrid's story over lunch and afternoon coffee. She was always animated and never dull. It was a particularly amusing affair when we were forced to change our clothes for lunch because of the dress code at the hotel restaurant.

Ingrid, can you tell us about your family genealogy? Well, it's certainly no secret that I am a first-generation American. In fact, I was not born in this country. I was born in the German city of Barmen, not far from Cologne. My mother was from Berlin. Coming to this country, my parents were economic rather than political refugees. Much of the wealth of the German business and commercial classes was wiped out by inflation. Towards the beginning of the 1930s, when the handwriting was somewhat on the wall that Germany would confront economic hardship and political instability, my father thought that he would either return to Sweden, which was his adopted homeland, or possibly go to America. My father had lived in Malmo, Sweden, for many years; it was a textile center outside of Stockholm. Ultimately, he decided instead to visit Australia. But first he went to visit his mother in Barmen, their home city. While he was there, he met my mother who worked as a purchasing agent for the largest iron and steel manufacturer. So he never got to Australia [*laughter*]. Instead he opened a textile factory near the border city of Aachen (Aix-la-Chapelle). They spent four or five years there until they decided, because of Germany's instability, to look elsewhere for economic security. It was my mother's facility with English that made her aware of the employment opportunities for engineers in America.

My mother, who was probably less oriented to homemaking than most women of her generation, persuaded her fiancé to seek a superintendency in a large woven label mill in Patterson, New Jersey. He made numerous trips back and forth to Germany, not at all convinced that it would be a good match culturally. Meanwhile my "arrival" was postponed. Birth control was readily available in Germany unlike the US. Eventually they concluded that America offered better opportunities for their future. But understandingly, my mother found the prospect of a week-long sea voyage unattractive, so I was born in Germany. It was close to a year before my mother and I arrived in New York, bound for the textile city of Patterson, New Jersey.

Was your father already established in the US? My father was already established in the sense that he was running a good-sized textile mill and was quite comfortable in terms of income. At least from an economic point of view, their situation was more stable than it would have been in Germany, where measures to overcome rampant inflation precipitated severe unemployment.

Then how would you classify your parents in terms of their class position? I would say middle class.

What kind of educational background did your parents have? My father had an engineering diploma and my mother had training in the humanities beyond what we would call high school. Remember, in Germany, high school ended at age 14. My mother was probably in school for three or four years beyond that. She had a very good education in literature and languages. Both of my parents were very good linguists. My father spoke five languages fluently and my mother spoke three. But that was not unusual among educated Europeans, either then or now.

Did you grow up knowing your grandparents? We visited them in Berlin, but once we left for America I never saw them again. My father had become a naturalized citizen, which conferred citizenship on me. My mother was anxious to visit her parents, but my father was concerned because I was German-born, and Hitler's youth movement was in full swing. It was a risk for me. So a return visit never materialized. The combination of Hitler's maniacal behavior and the arrival of my American-born siblings made it quite clear to my parents that they had made the right choice in coming to America.

My mother was home with me. My sister arrived when I was three. My brother arrived a year and a half later. By this time my father was working in Brooklyn for the Union Label Company as a textile engineer. They made ribbons and labels for women's hats and clothing. One of my very earliest passions as a girl (around the age of 12) was to go to the factory and look at the very elegant four-color labels. These were the end product of designs. They were works of art. My father plotted them onto semi-log graph paper as a pattern to be replicated by a machine. As I approached my teens, I had become acquainted with the activities of Manhattan's Seventh Avenue. I learned how to stitch the labels into my clothing in a very professional way. My jackets and coats may have been sewn at home or may have come from Sears, but they invariably had a designer label. I soon learned to drape it so that the elegant label would show [*laughter*].

What was your life like growing up in Brooklyn? My Brooklyn was a beautiful place. It was a borough of neighborhoods with something of a small town aura that probably no longer exists.

What kind of neighborhood did you live in? Well, that's kind of interesting because, as relative newcomers to America, we knew very little about neighborhoods. One of the first neighborhoods I can recall was an Irish–Italian parish attached to a Catholic church. The parish didn't have a school, so my siblings and I went to the neighborhood public school with children whose backgrounds were different from our own. Coming from a part of Germany that was historically Protestant, there was not much of a cultural fit for us except for Christmas and Easter, which my family observed as secular holidays. Indeed, to my childish mind I thought it was a big advantage that we got to celebrate Christmas eve in the style of North Germany. We didn't have to wait until Christmas morning for our presents like the Catholics.

My parents were not churchgoers, and early on I had little appreciation for religion. I didn't know anyone in my immediate neighborhood (by which I mean a six- to eight-block radius) who wasn't Catholic. So my early inference was that all Americans were Catholic. It wasn't until I ventured a few blocks further from home on my beautiful Silver King two-wheeler that I realized that there were other Protestants as well as Jewish families not too far away.

My first contact with a church was after I joined Girl Scouts. I was about 12 years old. Every fourth Sunday of the month was "Girl Scout Sunday." The girls were encouraged to invite their parents. My parents did come to the church service. They came to view it as an opportunity for me to learn about different religions by visiting others for comparison. I'm sure I brought home a great deal of misinformation to my parents who equated Protestantism with the Lutheran church (the state religion in Germany when they grew up). It provided me with an opportunity to learn about the Reformation and made good conversation around the dinner table. At my house we were a family of talkers. We were expected to relate our daily experiences and what we had learned.

What was your social life like when you were growing up? As I look back, in many ways it was lonesome. I only had my nuclear family. I had no cousins and only one unmarried aunt. My social life when I was old enough to date was very difficult. Many young men were excluded for one reason or another.

I remember one Jewish boy that I was very taken with. But there was no way I could have dated him. Growing up in a non-religious household, what he told me was quite beyond my understanding. His mother would die if he ever dated me.

So your first teenage romance was not to be? That's right. But I don't think that I pined for very long. We moved frequently, so I always made new friends, both boys and girls. In fact, we moved almost every other year. My mother was always in search of a better school, especially for me, because I was the eldest. The quality of schools in New York was very good, yet some were better than others in providing language instruction in fourth or fifth grade. This was the grade I started Spanish. So my mother and I looked at schools, and then we looked for an apartment.

I also experienced economics in action. There were always lots of vacant apartments, no doubt related to the high rate of job loss before the outbreak of World War II. Eager landlords would offer one or even two months of rent concession for signing a year's lease. This provided a real incentive for renters to move.

Moving to a new neighborhood and sometimes to a new school was something of an adventure for me. The school that I particularly remember as "my school" was one that had an IPC (international progress) program. This meant that a child would move along different achievement levels during a given year. This is exactly what happened to me. I entered school in the second grade. During the year I was moved into a combined second and third grade. By the time school ended in June, I had been promoted to the fourth grade.

Did your parents have high educational expectations of you and your siblings? We were all expected to be high achievers, but the schools had their own ideas about the academic focus for girls as compared to boys. I was one of the few girls to enter a college prep track in high school. When I graduated from eighth grade, we were asked what type of program we would prefer in high school. I believe I was the only girl who checked the academic program. The academic program was distinguished by two things: languages and math. Those who were college-bound (under the laws of New York State Regents Board) were required to take at least three years of one language and two years of another as well as a math and science requirement. It was a rigid requirement and not one that most families opted for as far as their daughters were concerned. My teachers recommended the "commercial courses" for the girls so we would qualify for the good secretarial jobs – jobs to which most girls aspired before they were married. Although my parents did not seem to share the American ideal of raising daughters to be good wives and mothers, I also had less social freedom than many of my friends.

Did you get much resistance from the school when you decided to opt for the academic program? Not really resistance, but certainly not a lot of encouragement either. After all, girls were supposed to be secretaries or nurses until they got married. Yet I was not reared that marriage was something to plan and strive for as an achievement. I was encouraged to do anything I thought I would enjoy doing and to excel. As long as I showed evidence of willingness to work and some degree of natural talent, I was encouraged.

There were two other things that I undertook to do as a young girl. I started piano lessons, practiced diligently, and really liked playing the piano. I also took ballet lessons and perhaps had more talent here than I did for music, partly because I was small and physically quite strong. So I was quite good at ballet because it requires considerable physical endurance. When I went to college at 16, I was studying ballet seriously enough to think in terms of a ballet career.

Where did you go to college? I went to Hunter College in New York City. Hunter College in those days was very competitive. I began in what was called an "exploratory major" which also enabled me to schedule dance classes. One of the courses I ended up taking was a course in economics, where I encountered price theory. I did very well in the course. It probably helped that my instructor was a handsome young PhD just out of Harvard. I also loved all those graphs that looked so beautiful and orderly, and thought market equilibrium was quite an extraordinary phenomenon. I decided I would major in economics. I thought all I would have to do was draw graphs and shift demand and supply curves in accordance with various scenarios. I was enchanted with the geometry of economics, and the subsequent possibility of economic planning in a politically democratic system. You can only imagine the new avenue of conversations with my father. He was a great admirer of European socialist scholars. When I was invited to take honors in economics and assigned Marshall's *Principles* and Joan Robinson's *Imperfect Competition*, I knew I was on the right track. I thought that the most beautiful concepts in the world were marginal cost and marginal revenue [*laughter*]. Then we read the *General Theory* and I learned about involuntary unemployment and equilibrium at less than full employment. By this time I was a senior. I was awarded a scholarship that took me into the PhD program in economics at the University of Pennsylvania.

How many women were in your class at Hunter? There were some 400 women. Maybe fifty were in economics.

Did any of your teachers become your mentor? Oh, yes. One was Dorothy Lampen, whose book *Adam Smith's Daughters* was highly regarded. It has recently been revisited (for want of a better word) by Betty Polkinghorn. Dorothy was both my mentor and honors supervisor. Another equally influential woman at Hunter was Dr Hazel Roberts. Her work on Marshall Vauban, an early physiocrat, is still recognized among economic historians. I was very impressed with her as a role model for women. She was elegantly groomed and well spoken.

There were also several men who are remembered today as outstanding scholars. Carroll Daugherty was a well-known labor economist. There were also several European scholars such as Hans Neisser, whose work on employment theory is still cited.

Do you think there is a place for women's colleges today? Women's colleges still have a very real role to play in educating women. They are places where women don't have to feel that they have to be non-achievers to be attractive to men. When women are not competing with men, they can be nurtured to recognize that they can make it in any environment. They can gain confidence in their abilities. I suspect it's more difficult under other circumstances. In retrospect, the education and confidence that I received at Hunter College made graduate school at the University of Pennsylvania much easier. I did it in three years. I was the only woman in my graduate class, and I had read many things that my male peers had never even heard about. But remember, men were held back by military service. As a result, I was far better prepared for graduate education than many of the men of my generation.

Did you always know you were going to graduate school? No, not really.

What made you decide on graduate school, and did you know from the start that you wanted to get your PhD? When I went to college at Hunter I found myself in a college largely comprised of upper middle-class women. They were all very committed to higher learning. A number of women were thinking about graduate school. As they sent for graduate school materials and filled out various applications, so did I. Radcliffe, the University of Pennsylvania, and Clark University in Massachusetts all offered me scholarships. My father wanted me to attend Columbia University, but my mother insisted that it was time to cut the silver cord. So we picked the University of Pennsylvania because it was only 90 miles [145 km] from New York City which was a short train ride.

Why did you not attend Radcliffe? I didn't want to attend a women's graduate school. I decided I was ready for the world, which included men.

What was your experience like in graduate school? My areas of specialization were monetary and international theory and what passed for labor economics, which was really industrial relations. I was primarily interested in theory. I was the only woman taking economic theory. There were some other women who came later, but only one went for a doctorate.

Were you friends? Yes, we eventually became quite good friends. She eventually became a Professor of Social Economics at the University of Pennsylvania. She wrote a well-known book in the field of poverty.

Did you have a group of peers with whom you had an intellectual involvement? No, and this is despite the fact that I am an extrovert socially, intellectually, and professionally. I have always been a loner, and I am to this day.

Did you have any mentors among the faculty at Penn? Yes: Sidney Weintraub in the economics department, and Charles Whittelsey in the finance department. However, I took Weintraub's teaching a lot more seriously than he took me as a student and as a potential scholar. In general, women scholars were not taken seriously.

Were there any women faculty members at Penn? No, there were none in the economics department while I was a student. It is only recently that appointments were made, and it is still disproportionately small. Overall, the University of Pennsylvania has been slow about advancing the status of women in the economics department. This probably reflects the early overlap between the Graduate School in economics and the Wharton School as an institution for training business leaders.

Can you talk about your Master's thesis and dissertation, and the kind of support you had while you worked on it? My Master's thesis was on the theory of the equilibrium rate of exchange. I worked under Charles Whittelsey. I was very interested in the pressing post-Bretton Woods issues, in particular the question of the relative fixity of exchange rates. My doctoral dissertation took me into a very different field: public utility rate making. This followed from my interest in the problems of pricing, particularly differential pricing. I worked under Professor Joe Rosen, who consulted with the public utility commission. He was a very supportive dissertation advisor. In fact, at that point I thought I would get a law degree because of my interest in regulatory pricing. I had wonderful advisors. I experienced no major battles or horror stories during my graduate education.

When did you enter the job market? I was offered a job as I was completing my Master's. Professor Whittelsey arranged an interview for me at the Federal Reserve Bank in Philadelphia. I was offered a position in their research department. They would have paid for the rest of my PhD education, but I declined the offer. I had been taking a course in price theory from Raymond Bye. He had written a well-known principles book. I helped with the revisions. In fact, I learned to write by helping him. Anyway, he told me that Temple University was expanding and hiring instructors, and that he would be happy to write a recommendation. So instead of taking the research job with the Federal Reserve Bank, I took the teaching position at Temple. I taught five courses. I taught a course in the history of economic thought, which I inherited from someone who quit. I used Eric Roll's classic text, which I knew from my undergraduate days. But my interest was in theory. Roll's descriptive approach, which characterized the history of economic thought then, seemed less systematic than the principles courses using Samuelson. So I developed notes using a more analytical approach. Eventually the notes grew into handouts and the handouts grew into a book, *Development of Economic Analysis*, first published in 1967.

How would you describe your life as a professional economist? And feel free here to interject the personal side of your story. I have been a visiting professor at several universities, but I've never been anywhere other than Temple on a permanent basis, which suits me.

What is the department like? When I started, the department was maybe twelve or fifteen people. It has grown every year along with an expansion of young people in the college. In the late 1950s and the early 1960s, college students came in droves. The Temple during that era was uncompromisingly a teaching institution. Returning GIs after the Korean War were eager to learn and hardworking. I became an assistant professor a year after I received my doctorate. By the time I went for tenure I was fully committed to teaching. I went up for tenure after seven years, which was the law. I was tenured, but not promoted. So I remained an assistant professor for twelve years.

Why didn't you get promoted? I guess I didn't knock on the door. It took me a while to get a sense of entitlement. Also, I had gotten married in 1956 and became a mother. I became involved in the balancing act that all women go through who want a career and a marriage. But I had an advantage. I had the good sense to delay marriage. I didn't even date when I was in graduate school because I was literally afraid of becoming sidetracked. I was always able to imagine the worst possible scenario. I am not a risk taker by nature. I devoted 99 percent of my attention to scholarship until I felt that I was positioned to allow myself to embark on the next stage of my life. I got married *after* I got my degree and was reasonably well along toward tenure.

How did you meet your husband? Through my brother, who was his instructor at the Naval Advanced Electronics School in Memphis. My brother was in the navy; Philip was in the Marine Corps. I met Philip coming home from an ASSA meeting in Chicago. My brother did not get leave for Christmas so Philip drove from the base to say hello to my mother. She was living in eastern Pennsylvania. Well, my mother was quite taken with Philip and she invited him to stay as a houseguest. I arrived in Easton in the middle of a snow-storm, and as I was getting out of the taxi I fell into a huge snow bank. Philip came running down the steps of our house to pull me out [*laughter*]. That's how I met my husband. The bells rang and the whistles blew as I was rescued by this enchanting man. I have been enchanted ever since.

When was this? In 1954. He transferred from Memphis to a marine squadron stationed at Atsugi, Japan. We corresponded. In December of 1955 he was rotated back to the States and was stationed at Cherry Point, North Carolina. He got a leave for Easter vacation (1956), and we met in Florida where my mother was living. We were married the following June in Philadelphia. This is what I mean when I say that we didn't date. It was prob-ably not too different from an arranged marriage [*laughter*]. We had very brief meeting intervals, and usually my family was around all the time. After the wedding I returned to Cherry Point with him until it was time to go back to school. He drove 500 miles [800 km] every weekend to be with me in Philadelphia.

How long before you had children? Two years.

How many children do you have? Two. They are four years apart. I wanted each to have the nurturing they needed. This meant that each baby had me to himself until he was ready for nursery school.

Who stayed with the baby while you were teaching? I was lucky. I engaged a wonderful caretaker who also helped with housekeeping.

What was Philip doing during this time? Philip was what we called a weekend warrior [*laughter*]. Incredibly lucky for us, his final duty station was Willow Grove Naval Air Station, a reserve training base that maintains a core of regular marine and naval personnel. Philip worked Saturday and Sunday as an electronics instructor for the reserves. He was off Monday and Tuesday, which became his days with the baby. The housekeeper was also off. By the time Eric was born, David was in nursery school. By then Philip was eligible for retirement from the Marine Corps.

When you received tenure at Temple, were there other women in your department? There was one other woman, a graduate of the University of Illinois. She was many years my senior, and had come to Temple as an assistant professor. I would have liked to have done research with her because she was also interested in macroeconomics. But Temple gave us little encouragement to do research. The teaching load was fifteen hours. I taught history of thought every semester, and my book in history of thought was in process. By 1965 or 1966 the book was under contract. I was ready to knock on the door, but I got promoted to associate professor.

How long did it take before you were promoted to full professor? Not too long afterwards we got a new dean who had been a labor economist in Washington, DC, and served in the State Department during the Kennedy administration. Somehow during his travels abroad he had the occasion to see my book, *Development of Economic Analysis*, at several foreign universities. So when he arrived at Temple he was familiar with my name. For reasons I did not quite understand, he decided that I should be the chair of the department. In those days departments did not elect their chairs; the deans appointed them. This was in 1967–8. By that time I had become aware of salary differentials. After quite a bit of thought I agreed to become chair on condition that I would be promoted to full professor, and would receive an appropriate raise. I became the first woman chair, and the first woman professor in Temple University's School of Business. But it had taken close to twenty years to arrive at this juncture.

I was reminded of what my father used to say when I told him that I wanted to be a great ballerina. By age 35 my legs would give out; my dancing career would be over. However, if I studied political economy (which is what he called it), I might be taken seriously by 35. Perhaps father was right. In 1967 I became a full professor. This is one of the few dates I have in the informational material about myself. In a sense, 1967 is when my life as an economist began. The only date that really counts is 1967 [*laughter*]. Until then nobody took me seriously.

How many years were you chair? For only three years. I didn't like administrative work and the guys in my department were not enamored of me as chair. But since then I have had some twenty-five years of warm congeniality.

Were your colleagues supportive of you? Oh, yes. Until relatively recently the ongoing development of the graduate program in economics has been very rewarding. But, in the last decade our PhD program, along with those of most universities, has fallen on sad times. We still have a large department of more than thirty, including four women. But the status of economics as a discipline has declined at Temple, much as it has elsewhere, especially in schools of business. Our MBA program is flourishing. Our PhD program is attracting fewer American students, although we have a substantial number of good foreign students.

You were the editor of the *Eastern Economic Journal* and involved in the Eastern Economic Association for a long time. What can you tell us about that experience? When I accepted the editorship of the *Eastern Economic Journal*, the Association itself had been in existence for five years. It was the last of the regional economics associations to be established. Unlike its national counterpart, the American Economic Association, the objective of the Eastern Economic Association was to be inclusive. Whereas the annual meetings of the AEA were largely comprised of planned sessions and invited papers which were presented by established scholars and their protégés, the EEA had an open call for papers. The objective was to facilitate not only broad participation, but also a broad representation of alternative approaches to economics. Its founding members felt that we needed greater opportunities for publication, presentation, and discussion on the east coast, particularly by younger and less well-established scholars. By contrast, the AEA was more receptive to proposals from scholars whose credentials and approach reflected their mainstream connections.

Our spirit of dissent is reminiscent of the rebellion of the younger generation of American economists, such as Richard T. Ely and Edwin R. A. Seligman who, in 1885, organized the AEA in an effort to break the dominance of orthodox doctrine. Thus, there was ample historical precedence at the time the EEA was organized. What was needed in the economics profession was a new organization that would hold conferences and establish a journal whose venue would be reflective of both heterodox economic doctrines and the neoclassical tradition which flourished at the most prestigious PhD-granting institutions. Although the EEA came very late to the ball, we enjoyed an incredible degree of support from the profession's luminaries, including MIT's Robert Solow and Paul Samuelson, Yale's James Tobin, and Lawrence Klein of the University of Pennsylvania. They were all present at our first meeting in Albany in 1974. Theodore Schultz (Chicago), Daniel Fusfeld (University of Michigan), and

Robert Heilbroner (The New School; who described himself as part of the eastern dis-establishment) gave us reason to hope that their simultaneous presence at the first conference would provide support for an eclectic journal.

The founders of the Association focused on serving the needs of the young and rapidly growing professorate of the 1960s, 1970s, and 1980s. Most of these new PhDs brought with them a training in mathematical economics and econometrics that was, by then, characteristic of any well-regarded doctoral program. It was also an era of large undergraduate enrollments. Many new PhDs gained employment at new four-year colleges and universities or new community colleges and technical institutions. The very growth of the economics profession brought with it a demand for journal space to accommodate the burgeoning number of new submissions by tenure track appointees. They were working at institutions that were trying to establish themselves as "research" institutions. Their needs created a large gap between the demand for and the supply of journal space. In particular, a rich source of new eastern talent came from the universities of Michigan and Wisconsin. Much to my surprise and delight, many of the new members came from beyond the Mid-West; from Canada, Germany, Italy, and the UK. Thus, the membership of the EEA was international.

Did you develop a particular style of editing to fulfill what you perceived to be the responsibilities of your editorship? My style of editing, if I may call it that, was to provide double blind review for every paper outside my several areas of expertise. In an ASSA breakfast meeting with the other journal editors, I learned that this practice was generally viewed as unnecessary, or worse, inappropriate. Yet, I was convinced that double blind reviewing was the proper thing to do. After my initial screening, I sent the papers that were not rejected outright to reviewers who, in addition to their technical expertise, also shared the author's paradigmatic perspective. I chose this procedure because I instinctively believe, partly from personal experience, that papers are often rejected simply because they are not from "the right place" or the "right person." Editors, even those familiar with multiple fields, serve their readers and authors more effectively with "double blind" reviewing. Orley Ashenfelter's recent Report of the Editor in the *American Economic Review* acknowledges that the AEA Board recently voted to adopt double blind refereeing. The *Eastern Economic Journal* led the way. I pursued the job of editing with all the energy, enthusiasm, commitment, and, I hope, good judgment I could muster.

In editing the *Eastern Economic Journal* were you being guided primarily by your concerns that heterodox economists be represented? No, that would be an overstatement. The *Eastern* was intended to be a general journal aimed at maintaining high technical excellence at a level consistent with the subject. The perceived need for a new journal stemmed not from the identification of subdisciplines that were less than well satisfied by existing journals, nor was it dictated (as was the case with URPE) by ideological considerations. It was instead substantially dictated by the needs of a rapidly growing professorate whose futures were contingent on the publication of between four and seven articles within three to six years in refereed journals.

My editorial board and I were technically able to review and publish articles that conformed to the mainstream paradigm. But we also provided new publication opportunities for articles related to heterodox issues and approaches, and the history of economic thought. Although the latter was served by specialized journals, publication opportunities remained limited, especially in view of the relentless tick of the tenure clock.

Ingrid, if you could do it over again would you have changed anything? If I could have written a script, I would do it just the way it happened.

Let's talk about your perspective as an economist. How would you describe yourself as an economist? I would describe myself as an eclectic. By this, I mean there are few areas of economics which I have not seriously studied and tried to integrate into my thinking. Part of my broad perspective is the very fortuitous legacy of having been an editor of a general journal. I felt it was important to read every paper that came across my desk. If I didn't have a minimal level of understanding, I felt it was important to get enough so that I could send the paper to an appropriate reviewer. This meant that I had to learn more about both contemporary neoclassical economics and heterodoxy.

My own predilection runs strongly in the direction of post-Keynesianism. I have also learned a lot about radical economics, institutional economics, and other non-orthodox approaches. I think of myself as an eclectic economist in the sense that I see many areas of genuine truth and insight in every paradigm. I hope that I am sufficiently mature intellectually to combine insights from different paradigms in ways that are useful in illustrating and helping us to understand what Heilbroner calls the "human condition."

Can you explain why your sympathies lie with the post-Keynesian traditions? Intellectually, I see the phenomenon of income distribution as the most challenging problem in economics. Many of us have discarded the marginal productivity theory of income distribution, but we have not really replaced it. We don't have a handle on how to explain either the wage structure in the US, or income sharing among different countries in the world. While I am not primarily concerned with policy, I do see policy as the ultimate objective of economic theorizing. But you cannot make policy until you have an understanding of causality. This is why I struggle for a better understanding of labor market outcomes. The post-Keynesians have spent much time analyzing the monetary sector, and I have learned a lot from their analysis. But my current focus, as far as contemporary theory is concerned, is on labor markets. This has been neglected by both the mainstream (which focuses on household choice) and the post-Keynesians. I have tried different approaches and have written several papers exploring the sectoral changes in employment in an attempt to address the phenomenon of income distribution. Joan Robinson was really the first person to articulate the perspective that the "other half" of the Keynesian revolution is the theory of income distribution. Although many people of

Keynes's generation, even those who were critical of him, were in favor of policies that dealt with the problem of unemployment, Robinson noted that it did
not dawn on them that Keynes's real message was the problem of income distribution. This is the main problem we are struggling with, isn't it?

What attracted you to study the work of Joan Robinson? At first it was the
theory of imperfect competition and those beautiful diagrams [*laughter*]. As I
told you earlier, I started out as a price theorist. I was very much taken by the
orderliness of price theory. But I had also studied institutional economics.
Imperfect competition provided a theoretical explanation for what institutional
economists observed about the economy.

Although I entered economics in a time of considerable prosperity, I nevertheless remember my father talking about the Depression. I became quite
interested in business cycles; later in Keynes and the *General Theory*. But by the
time I studied Keynesian economics in graduate school, there was utter confusion in my mind. It took me a while to realize that macroeconomics had been
reduced to IS–LM. This, in effect, removed Keynes's discussion of the problem
of involuntary unemployment. Hicks and Hansen had reinterpreted Keynes's
concept of underemployment equilibrium to make it consistent with the notion
of market clearing. Once again I turned my attention to micro theory. It seemed
to be on much firmer ground. I pursued questions of rate making and pricing to
establish optimum outputs and fair rates of return.

My renewed interest in macro coincided with the arrival of Sidney
Weintraub who transferred to the University of Pennsylvania from St Johns. He
had written a book on price theory, but soon after he began his reconstruction
of Keynes's aggregate supply function which challenged the monetarist hypothesis of the inevitable "trade-off" between inflation and unemployment. His
reasoning became the basis for an alternative paradigm – post-Keynesian
economics. This rekindled my interest in macroeconomics, in particular in
labor markets.

Although my article on the respecified labor supply curve was published in
Journal of Post Keynesian Economics, my idea about the need to respecify the
classical labor supply curve has drawn little discussion or attention. This is, in
part, attributable to the fact that, currently, unemployment is not considered a
problem. But it is surely a problem elsewhere in the world, and it is likely to
become a problem in the future. Moreover, post-Keynesians don't focus on
unemployment. Instead they focus on the role of money in the market. I have
no disagreement on the centrality of monetary matters. But it does not offer an
entrée into the problem of income distribution and sectoral changes in employment, topics of particular concern to me as a post-Keynesian.

**When in your career did you become disenchanted with neoclassical
economics? Given your interest in price theory, you must have been contented
with it?** When Joan Robinson and her book, which I so greatly admired, were
disowned, I began to ask questions. I was introduced to the writings of Shackle
and the notion of uncertainty. So I began to think in terms of how we might

conceptualize non-equilibrium systems. Then, during the fiftieth anniversary of Keynes's *General Theory*, I rediscovered the Swedish school and became very interested in Gunnar Myrdal's early writings on the monetary system and the notion of *ex ante/ex post* as a vehicle for dealing with the phenomenon of time. I was also interested in the way that Dennis Robertson conceptualized the importance of time in thinking about decision making today, and what happens tomorrow as a result of decisions made today. It became increasingly apparent that a major problem in economics from a methodological standpoint is how to handle the difference between logical time and historical time. My interest in "time" is reflected in some of my current work.

Could you talk about your current work? As I've said, my major intellectual concern is with the sharing of income; not so much the sharing of wealth, but the disparities in the distribution of wage and salary income, both domestically and globally. I am also concerned about sectoral changes in employment. I have tried to find a conceptual vehicle within which I can harness my thinking. I think that I have found a theoretical anchor in a systems approach to economics. Partly, this is derived from some consulting work that I did quite a number of years ago, first on the B-52 bomber program and later on several of the Apollo Moon missions. I was hired as an IBM consultant to teach marginal analysis to systems engineers.

During the postwar McNamara era, IBM received an edict that they had to incorporate a cost-effectiveness requirement in every proposal that came from the Defense Department (and NASA). Cost-effectiveness was something engineers did not have a clue about, and, of course, neither did economists. A problem was posed to me by an IBM engineer. He had to engineer a bombing system that would allow military aircraft to achieve what they called "target kill." This meant hitting a target with some percentage of effectiveness. Simultaneously, he had a budget constraint. He had a gut feeling that this was an insoluble problem, but could not define the source of its insolubility. I put his problem into the context of indifference curves. I sketched out a family of indifference curves to represent alternative possibilities of target kill. I put system maintainability on one axis and reliability on the other. Then I added a budget constraint to demonstrate the possibilities. He could achieve either a given level of target kill or spend a certain amount of dollars. So I suggested that the military needed to tell him the level of target kill to be engineered into his aircraft and leave the budget to the engineers, or they had to tell him how much the Department of Defense was prepared to spend. From this the engineers could determine the level of target kill. Shortly thereafter I was invited to teach indifference curves to engineers, which they easily understood, given their knowledge of topography.

When was this? This was 1963–5.

I learned, but I didn't realize it at the time, the notion of systems interdependence: either the system functions and all the parts contribute to the achievement of a goal, or nothing works. I began to think of business firms as systems. More recently, given our social problems, I have become cognizant that households, schools, and religious organizations are systems. Together they can be conceptualized as an anthropogenic system, a system engaged in producing human competencies. This is a perspective I have borrowed from the late Alfred Eichner.

While sociologists, theologians, and ethicists are concerned with anthropogenic models and policies, this is a link that escapes most economists. Neoclassical economics conceives of households as utility maximizers who make decisions about such things as how much to invest in education and training, or whether to participate in the labor force. In this view, it is within the province of the individual to create competencies and to supply them to employers. Thus there is an ongoing reason to understand the role of aggregate demand. This is why I'm currently exploring the interactions between the production and anthropogenic subsystems. I recognize the need for a theoretical framework that can incorporate in a meaningful way a feedback among the sociological and human systems and the economy's production systems.

Could you say something about the changes you have observed in the profession over the years? Economists have increasingly become technicians. They are very capable in manipulating numbers to confirm their theories. As technicians, economists have become brilliantly competent, but I am not sure that I would call them economists any more. They are steeped in technique to the point that they are unable to define the relevant questions confronting us. I blame a lot of this on the computer revolution which made it possible. It also reflects the nature of the publication requirements for tenure and promotion. Although seven years seems like a long time to achieve a publication record for tenure, the delays associated with the review and printing processes make seven years too short a time period. The time constraint for economists to realize the return on their human capital investment, I think, has compromised the nature of their work. The easiest way to get an article accepted for publication is to do an econometric study. If you use a different data set to confirm a previous conclusion, it's publishable in the eyes of many editors. This may be one of the reasons why young people entering our profession have such a narrow approach to the discipline. It's a survival technique. It's very difficult for a young economist to be creative. If it's true that people are most productive until they are 35–45 years old, then most economists do not use their peak years to create new ideas, but to stay alive professionally.

I think this process might actually be somewhat different for women. Even if they never actually withdraw from the workforce, most women nevertheless lead bifurcated lives. This means that women in the profession have a maturity, particularly after they turn 40, that is more consistent with creativity. It is such a wonderful thing that women are living as long as they are because there is much to life after menopause [*laughter*]. A woman who is lucky enough to have good and robust health, and the freedom from family responsibilities, is more likely to unleash her creativity which might have been stultified when she was younger.

Then why do you think that more women are not attracted to economics? Women have unquestionably become discouraged by the barriers and the impediments to academic achievement. There are many more successful women economists from my generation in government service. But beyond that, perhaps young women today are more realistic. They recognize that the practice of economics is not solving problems, so they choose other fields where they can be truly productive in the sense that they do not need to work outside of a paradigm to which they cannot commit. It is incredibly difficult to work outside of the mainstream paradigm in economics and survive, let alone prosper.

Do you think that feminist economics has anything to offer to our profession? I'm not sure I understand what feminist economics is. I am separated by a generation from those who call themselves feminist economists. My own feeling is that as a group these women have an important contribution to make to the profession. However, it is my guess that as individuals they would fare better if they did not make this distinction. It gives the profession a basis for assigning "feminist economists" to a separate category that is perhaps not considered on par with men. They would do far better if they just worked on economic problems of interest to them. The problem might very well be women in the labor market. But there is nothing that makes research on women in the labor market "feminist." On the other hand, feminist economics is an important subdiscipline because it has a broadening effect on the profession. But a talented woman economist would do better to be an expert in some other field in economics than in feminist economics.

Do you have any advice for women in economics? I am reluctant to give advice of a general nature to anyone. I think advice should always be related to something specific.

Let me ask you something a bit more specific then. Let's say a young woman enters economics as a professional. She has chosen economics because of a concern for human welfare and doesn't really accept the mainstream theoretical framework. How can she get tenured and survive in the profession long enough to have enough security to do meaningful and creative work? Well, I think the first thing that she ought to do is to be very knowledgeable about neoclassical economics. I don't think it is possible to reject the mainstream out of hand. It's important to know what it is about the mainstream paradigm that is objectionable. I don't think it serves young people well when senior professors begin by teaching heterodox economics. First you have to have a firm foundation in the basics of the neoclassical paradigm. Only then is it possible to understand why it has problems and to begin thinking creatively about how to alter the paradigm. It can also be mind-opening to study other social sciences including demography, anthropology, sociology, and history. But ultimately it is important, first and foremost, to remember that you are an economist.

Ingrid, is there anything you would like to add to our conversation? I have nothing to add except to say thank you for asking me. I am flattered that you thought I had something to contribute.

2

MARIANNE ABELES FERBER

For the first couple of years I was the only woman faculty on the committee and I was very conscious of the fact that when I opened my mouth they did not hear me, Marianne Ferber. What they heard was "the woman."

(Marianne Ferber, 1997)

Marianne received her BA from McMaster University in 1944, a Master's from the University of Chicago in 1946, and a PhD from the University of Chicago in 1954. She began teaching as a visiting professor at the University of Illinois in the mid-1950s and remained a visiting professor at a starting assistant professor salary for over fifteen years. It was not until the early 1970s that she was brought on board as an assistant professor. This was also a time when Marianne's scholarship began to bloom. Since the mid-1970s Marianne has co-authored five books, and has published numerous articles, chapters, reviews, and comments in scholarly books and journals. She became a Professor of Economics in 1979, and also served as the Director of Women's Studies at the University of Illinois. Since 1993 she has been Professor Emerita and subsequently honored as a Distinguished Alumna at McMaster University and has served as a Matina S. Horner Distinguished Visiting Professor at Radcliffe College. Marianne is also a former President of the International Association for Feminist Economics and former President of the Midwest Economic Association.

Marianne was one of the first people we interviewed for the project. For several days, she was a very generous host at her home. After the first interview, we made several modifications to the manuscript, including changes in the focus of our questions. Accordingly, we have had many subsequent discussions with Marianne to obtain more of her story. Through it all, Marianne has been a patient and most gracious collaborator as well as an especially enthusiastic supporter of this project. We thank you.

Plate 2   Clockwise from top left: Marianne Ferber in Alaska on a raft trip (1997); rowing in Jackson Park, Chicago (1945); main portrait (1975); with 9-year-old son Don, and 5-year-old daughter Ellen (1957); with mother Elsa Ornstein Abeles, father Karl Abeles, and sister Wilma Abeles Iggers (1937); with husband Bob in Rocky Mountain National Park (1970); at age 22 (1945).

Let's begin with your family genealogy. What can you tell us about your parents?
Well, my father was a farmer, as were a lot of people in my family. His father
had been in part a farmer and in part a cattle dealer. His father (my great grandfather) was a cattle dealer in the days when Jews could not own land, but my
grandfather was permitted to own land. So he bought a little bit because it was a
good complement to being a cattle dealer. Depending on cattle prices, he could
raise feed and keep cows or horses for a while. So by the time my father became
an adult, many of his generation in our family were full-time farmers. Most were
doing quite well, and my father, who was quite a brilliant man despite never
having gone beyond high school, was also doing very well. In the little town of
3,000 where we lived, we were considered upper class. In any case, we lived
there very comfortably and would have never thought of leaving if Hitler and
the Nazis had not invaded Czechoslovakia.

Tell us about your mother. My mother was a very intelligent person. She
briefly attended a commercial school after high school. But she was a traditional
housewife and very conformist.

How old was she when she married your father? She was 19 or 20 years of
age, which was more or less average in those days. They must have been married
around 1919, because my sister was born in 1921. My mother was something of
an intellectual. She had a collection of good books and was interested in
theater, concerts, and ballet. When we had a chance to go into the city, she was
the one to initiate it. As I already mentioned, my father was a brilliant guy, but
he wasn't especially interested in that sort of thing.

Marianne, how old were you when you left Czechoslovakia for Canada? I
was 15.

What kind of experiences did you have as an immigrant? In those days
Canada was very Anglo-Saxon. Undoubtedly there may have been a bit of paranoia on the part of my fairly large extended family, but our paranoia was not
altogether unwarranted. For example, the adults didn't want us to speak
German or Czech too loudly on the bus for fear people would recognize that we
were refugees. There were still signs in the windows that showed what kind of
people businesses were looking to hire. They said "British stock only."

Did you work or go to school? At first, I worked on the farm for a year. Then
I had a job stuffing advertisements into envelopes for another year. During that
time I tried to save up a bit of money so I could go back to high school. When I
left Czechoslovakia I was three years short of graduating from high school. We
had eight years of gymnasium there.

When I went to see the high school principal in Canada, he suggested that
I speak to someone at McMaster University in order to help him make a decision about where I should be placed. My older sister graduated from a Canadian
high school the first year we arrived and was attending McMaster already. So I
went to McMaster to find out my status. The registrar asked if I had as much
schooling in Europe as my sister did. I told him that I had one year less. He
apparently took no interest in the fact that she graduated from a Canadian high

school. After thinking for a minute, he said "We'll try an experiment; what would you like to major in?" Just like that!

So you went to college before you finished high school when you were 16? Seventeen. I was out of school for two years. Needless to say, I wasn't going to let on that I had never thought of that. I was delighted I did not have to go back to high school. But when it came to a major, I didn't want to major in German, in part because I was not very good at languages and in part because my sister's major was German. She is very bright and especially good at languages, and I wasn't going to compete with her on her turf. I also knew I'd better not major in anything that I would be expected to know from high school like math or history. So I asked for a catalog as a sort of a stall tactic and started leafing through it. In those days, McMaster was a very small university and it didn't have many esoteric majors, so it didn't take me long to find economics. I was pretty sure no one took it in high school. I thought – great, I'll start out even. I also remember thinking that I would see how things went and would switch later on. That's how I chose economics. When I told my parents, they were of course amazed that I would be going to college. And when I told them that my major was economics, they asked, "What's that?" I told them that I would tell them as soon as I found out [*laughter*].

As it turned out, I liked economics from the beginning. We were given homework related to the chapter we were reading, and were supposed to write up something. I was sufficiently interested, but worried about not "making it." I studied very hard and often read several chapters ahead. Once, early in the semester, my writing clearly indicated some knowledge well beyond what was covered in the assigned chapters. The professor called me to his office and asked whether my parents were economists, what kind of education they had, and so forth. It took me a while, but I caught on. He thought I hadn't done the homework myself. I guess it never occurred to him that I would read chapters that were not assigned. But luckily, he took my word for it. I told him that my parents were definitely not economists and I wrote the paper all by myself. In any case, from the beginning, I was pretty happy with my choice of major.

Why did you like it so much? In recent years, I have asked myself what other fields I might feel comfortable with if I had to do it over again. The answer is clearly a social science. I'm more interested in people than in anything else. I can, for instance, get interested in reading a fascinating article about astronomy or geology or something, but I wouldn't want to devote my life to those types of disciplines. What I really liked about economics is that, at least at that time, you learned something about human behavior. This has become somewhat debatable in the rigorous, mathematical version of contemporary economics. It is interesting, but at that time I was unaware that math had anything to do with economics. I only found out about the love affair with math among economists when I went to the University of Chicago. I don't know precisely how much of that can be attributed to the smallness of McMaster or how much of it can be attributed to the period.

What kind of courses did you take as an undergraduate? Pretty routine courses; the first one was introductory micro, which was a full-year course. I also had a course in economic history. There were also requirements in accountancy and commercial law. Those were not fields that especially appealed to me, and they also happened to be very poorly taught. The course in international trade was far more interesting. In general, I took a routine kind of undergraduate curriculum with none of the esoteric specialities.

How big was the department? This was a university with 600 students and the department had a total of sometimes two or three faculty.

And how many majors? Well, in my year, there were four majors. And this gets to the question of how I felt about being in a man's field. I guess I wasn't especially aware that it was a man's field. With only four of us, I never thought about being the only woman. Now that I think of it, there probably weren't many women majoring in economics in the other years either. There were so few majors, it wasn't much of an issue. Nor was I disturbed by the fact that all of the economics professors were male. The faculty as a whole was predominantly male. I simply thought that was the way college was. I started in 1940 and between 1940 and 1944, to the best of my recollection, there were altogether maybe three or four women faculty.

In the entire college? In the whole college.

Out of approximately how many? It wasn't a huge faculty. You know, I never tried to add that up. But with 600 students, there could have been 40–60 faculty.

Did you attend McMaster for four years? Yes.

Do you think you received a good education? In many ways I had a very good education. McMaster was a good little university. Incidentally, it has become much bigger since then. It was also a Baptist school. It has since become a public school.

What year did you go to the University of Chicago for graduate school? In 1944. My very first class was with Jacob Viner. He was a superb teacher. He taught the introductory micro course for graduate students. He walked into the first class and said, "Those of you who don't know more math than I do by the end of the first year will flunk out." I cheerfully tell people that I proved him wrong.

I had an interesting assortment of instructors that first semester. In addition to Viner, I had Frank Knight and Oscar Lange. They really made you think. They overlapped a good bit in their lectures, but each had a totally different point of view. Knight was profoundly conservative. Unlike the present-day Chicago people, he did not believe that markets work perfectly, but he was deeply convinced that the government would only make it worse. Viner didn't go nearly that far. They were in different fields as well. Knight was primarily a history of thought person as well as a theorist. Viner was primarily in international trade. I majored in trade. Lange, of course, was a Marxist. I believe to this day that his little piece on market socialism is a masterpiece of exposition. It has some really good ideas if only people would pay attention. I had my students read it when I taught comparative economic systems. Lange was also a good econometrician (although econometrics didn't do much for me). Although he was not a fascinating teacher and a bit plodding, he was very systematic and easy to follow. With Viner, I could always see ten minutes ahead, where he was trying to go. But with Knight, it took me for ever to figure out where he was going. Knight was beyond any doubt a brilliant man, but I don't know if he was just difficult to follow or if I had difficulty following him because he and I didn't quite think the same way.

I worked as a research assistant for Lawrence Klein while he was working on his first macro model. He was working for the Cowles Commission. After they moved the Commission to Yale, it was called the Cowles Foundation. I did regressions for him on a manual computer.

Who were some of your contemporaries? Oh, there were some interesting people there. Possibly the best known was Don Patinken. He was a good friend. Another student who had been there for some time was Leo Hurwicz. There were also a couple of interesting women I became good friends with. One was Anita Summers; Anita Arrow then. She was there my second year. She took a Master's and left. The other woman friend I had was Margie Reuss. She was married, but her husband was away in the army. She and her child were living with her parents and commuted. She recently told me that I was the only student she got to know. After the war, her husband ran for Congress and was in Congress until the middle to late 1980s when he retired. She also got her Master's at Chicago. Later she got a PhD at one of the schools in the Washington, DC area and taught there for many years.

Were there women faculty in the economics department? Oh heavens no! Certainly not in the economics department. But surprisingly, I didn't give it much thought. I've always been a feminist in the sense that I thought women ought to be able to do whatever they want and are as capable on average as men, but that was the world as I knew it.

In Chicago, did you have a role model? No, actually I didn't.

Did you have a mentor? Well, in truth, I didn't have a mentor either. To an extent, some of the older students I mentioned were my mentors. By the way, when we talked about students, I forgot to mention the one that was most important in my life: my future husband, Bob Ferber. He had come to Chicago two years before me. He was my senior, and very helpful to me in many ways for the rest of his life.

How would you describe your overall experience at the University of Chicago? What are your memories of the place? I remember a couple of episodes at Chicago which really infuriated me. Although in some ways I wasn't treated that badly. In my second year, I received the second-largest fellowship in the department. Mind you, this was during World War II, when the ratio of men to women was much lower than normal. In any case, I received this fellowship for $1,000 and I thought the millennium had arrived! On the day I found out, I bumped into Lloyd Mints. I had taken two or three courses from him and had gotten As. He stopped me in the hall and congratulated me. Then he volunteered that he had voted against me. I wasn't that surprised he voted against me, but I was amazed that he chose to tell me. So I asked him why. He said, "Why should we invest our scarce resources in women who are only going to get married and have babies?" I remember saying to myself, "I'm going to prove that guy wrong." And from then on, every time I was tempted to chuck my dissertation, which was frequently, I said "Oh, no!" But that was an unconscionable thing for him to do. Incidentally, there is a good part to this story. There was obviously a majority in the department who felt differently, because I did get the fellowship.

The other episode occurred when Viner was leaving for the Princeton Advanced Institute. This was 1946, about the time I was leaving. I asked him to write a letter of recommendation, which of course I didn't see. However, the department head thought I would be pleased to know what Viner had written. He shared that Viner had written that I was the best woman student he had ever had. I was furious. As far as anyone knew, I was possibly the only woman student he ever had! The implication is that I was not compared to my fellow male students, I was in a different class. This reminds me of a book I read some years ago about the status of women in academia in the olden days. The authors suggest that it was not so much that women had low status as they were outside the status system altogether. That was exactly what was going on in Chicago.

The world has not changed as much as you might think. I told this story in the mid-1980s to my brother-in-law, a historian and, at that time, the department head at the State University of New York, Buffalo. He said he had recently received a similar letter of recommendation for a woman. Now, mind you, in history departments it is more likely that there would be lots of women. You wouldn't think she was the only one.

Still, I was really shaken by the Viner incident. On the other hand, I was treated well at the Cowles Commission. They gave me an assistantship when I desperately needed income to make ends meet. It was also a good way to learn and get to know people.

What did you write your dissertation on? Well, my whole career, as you have already gathered, is so esoteric and so unreasonable that it hardly makes for a good model for anyone. I must say that when I chose a dissertation topic I had no advice from anyone. The faculty in Chicago didn't tend to mentor anyone, either man or woman. Anyway, in choosing a topic, I was also confronted with the fact that the department required two major languages. I knew two other languages besides English. I was raised on German and to a lesser extent Czech. While German was considered a major language, Czech was not. But I found out that if you could prove that you needed a minor language for your dissertation, it would count. So I carefully chose a topic that required Czech. This wasn't as unreasonable as it might sound. My major field was trade, and my secondary field was money and banking. And there was an interesting episode in Czechoslovakia after World War I, which I knew a little bit about. People still talked about it. As you know, after World War I there was major run-away inflation in both Germany and Austria. Prices moved up pretty rapidly, the value of their currencies deteriorated, and Czech currency moved right along with it. Czechoslovakia was closely linked economically with Austria even after the war. During this period the Czech finance minister, a very brilliant and determined guy, instituted a rather draconian monetary reform which managed to greatly reduce the economic links with Austria. I wrote my dissertation about this episode.

Who served on your dissertation committee? When I requested a dissertation committee, they gave me people, probably by mistake rather than intentionally, who I never took a course from or had contact with. And I was too stupid to question this! I just assumed I had to accept whatever committee I was assigned. My committee consisted of Gale Johnson in agricultural economics – a subject quite unrelated to my dissertation. Another member was Lloyd Metzler. He was a very brilliant and nice man, but we had never had any contact. The third one was Earl Hamilton, an economic historian. This might have made a certain amount of sense, except it wasn't the kind of economic history he did.

Who did you work with? Johnson. He was never nasty, but he wouldn't answer the mail I sent him. You see I left Chicago in 1946, ABD. I had finished all my course work and my prelims. Bob had left ABD in 1945. By then we had pretty much decided to get married. We agreed that I would stay long enough to finish my course work and prelims, and I would work on the dissertation after I left. So everything had to be done long distance, which was extremely common in those days. There were few people who stayed on campus to finish their dissertations, but people were often hired ABD.

As I already mentioned, Johnson wouldn't answer my correspondence. Eventually, I had to phone him, but long-distance calls were not as common as they are now, and Bob and I couldn't especially afford them. I received absolutely no help; no support of any sort. But, again, I don't take this personally. This is the way these people tended to behave. One hears many horror stories about Chicago dissertations, and not just in economics, but about all departments.

Where did you move in 1946? I moved to New York because Bob had taken a job there. Bob was from New York. He was an only child and his parents desperately wanted him to live there. He hated the place, but he thought he should give it a try. So in 1946 I moved to New York. I tried very hard to find a teaching job and got some lovely rejections. Many people wanted to teach in New York so it was difficult getting a position without a PhD. Finally, I started looking for a non-academic job. I didn't especially want to work for a business, so I tried the Federal Reserve Bank. I would have been happy to work there. They were interested, but they said they could not make a decision until the next meeting of their board. I wasn't a citizen and they had to wait to get special approval to make me an offer. Well, I couldn't afford to wait very long because I was running out of money, and Bob hadn't accumulated much. A company called Standard Oil New Jersey (now known as Exxon) had just created an economics research section. They had tried to hire Bob, but they found out about me and made me an offer. I believe it paid $4,500 a year; high enough for me to think the millennium had arrived! Not normally my cup of tea, it turned out to be an interesting situation. They hired four or five guys, all of them from Harvard, and three women from Chicago. I knew the other women quite well. One was Anita Arrow, and the other was Sophie Gogek. She worked at Standard Oil New Jersey for some years. We are good friends to this day.

I remember having lively discussions with the guys from Harvard about the merits of segregated schools. I particularly remember a conversation when one of them said, "But you can't concentrate on your work when there are women in the library." I responded that anyone who couldn't work in the presence of women shouldn't go to college; they should go to a psychiatrist instead. I also pointed out that in Chicago men were able to study in the library with women around. He responded that the women at Chicago were dogs!

Incidentally, when we were leaving for Illinois in 1948, these same guys invited Bob and me for drinks at the Harvard Club in New York. When we arrived, we had to use the back door.

Why? Because of me! Women couldn't use the front door. I must admit, when I was working at Radcliffe from 1993 to 1995, I took great pleasure in occasionally eating at the Harvard Club. The food was good and inexpensive, and every time I walked in the front door I thought to myself – there *has* been some improvement.

Why did you leave New York? The decision to leave New York was mainly Bob's. I didn't mind New York, and kind of enjoyed it in a way. But I certainly didn't mind leaving either. While my job at Standard Oil was a good job, I wasn't interested in working for a business. It wasn't what I wanted to do with my life.

What did you do for Standard Oil? I worked in their international economics research section using my background in international trade. We did what they called "country studies," focusing on countries that Standard Oil had an interest in, which covered a lot of territory. But, as I mentioned earlier, I tried to get a teaching job. And, ironically, after I took the job at Standard Oil, Hunter College offered me the opportunity to teach a course in the evening. I jumped at the chance, because it gave me some teaching experience. This slowed down the progress on my dissertation. I had a full-time job plus a teaching job. Even so, it wasn't a bad idea because it reconfirmed my belief that I really wanted to teach.

So you moved to Illinois. Did you have a job lined up? The year we moved to Illinois, a new dean, Howard Bowen, had just been hired. He was building up the economics department by hiring all kinds of really good people. I had good recommendations from Chicago and my grades were certainly above reproach so I had reason to believe that, sooner or later, something would come up for me. As luck would have it, I was eight months pregnant when we moved, so I didn't mind not having a job right away. I hoped to be offered something a year later. However, by the following year, his position was somewhat shaky. By the following year there was a famous blowout and he was gone. The department became incredibly conservative, which led Martin Bronfenbrenner to claim publicly that Illinois "had become a southern college moved north."

The conservatives basically objected to two things about the dean. First, he had hired Keynesians. This was objectionable at Illinois while it certainly was not regarded as such elsewhere. Second, he brought in women, Jews, and foreigners, which was unacceptable. In particular, he had brought in Margaret Reed and Dorothy Brady as full professors, which was unheard of. He also brought in people like Leo Hurvicz and Franco Modigliani. Of course, he also hired several very bright, young, white American males who were also unacceptable because they were liberal. It was clear that I wasn't their type, and I wasn't offered anything until 1955.

What was magic about 1955? In the mid-1950s there was a serious teacher shortage and they were pretty hard up, so they offered me a job. As it happens, I had finally finished my dissertation. It had taken a long time to finish, in part because I had interruptions – two jobs in New York and then two children – but also because Gale Johnson thought nothing of taking a year to read a draft. Anyway, they offered me a job as a visiting lecturer and I was pleased to accept. I usually worked part-time. And they would always call me at the last minute. In fact, once or twice they didn't ask me to teach until after classes had started. That was embarrassing. How do you explain to your students why you missed the first class? Do you tell them that you weren't asked until they were desperate, or do you let them think that you were negligent? It put me in an awful position. But I was glad to have something. It was better than being unemployed.

I remained a visiting lecturer for fifteen years until 1971. As Bob said, it was an awfully long visit! I also did something extremely stupid during this time. I did no research whatsoever because I was fully occupied. Bob, who was an honest-to-God feminist in every other respect, hated and detested housework. He was not particularly interested in looking after young children either. So, I did all of that. I also taught three courses while everyone else taught two. And for a long time, I didn't even realize it. Bob never taught; he was a full-time researcher from the beginning. I was also the official pinch-hitter; I taught almost everything except econometrics and often had three different preparations as well as different courses every semester. So the work added up.

By the end of 1971, the department decided that it was awkward to ask for special dispensation every semester to hire me. They decided that it would be more convenient if I had a permanent job rather than a visiting position. After all, I was a great convenience to the department. I got good teaching evaluations and I was cheap. I was consistently paid as much as the incoming assistant professors, although I had a perfectly good PhD from Chicago. But I never complained or haggled about money, so they made me an assistant professor with tenure.

Coincidentally, at about the same time, a member of the economics department, who was also chair of the local chapter of the AAUP, asked if I might be interested in looking at the salary situation of women. This was about 1971. I thought it was kind of a neat idea and started looking around for someone to work with. I found a good statistician named Jane Loeb. She was a considerably younger woman in educational psychology. About this time, women, primarily in the humanities, were beginning to collect data on the number of women in academia and their average salaries. Not unexpectedly, they found that there were relatively fewer women than men, and women's salaries were lower. Jane suggested that we run regressions. As far as I'm aware we were the first to do that. Not long after we presented our results to the AAUP. We received a letter from Alice Rossi, an eminent sociologist and chair of Committee W (the women's subcommittee of AAUP). She asked us for permission to publish a chapter on our findings in *Academic Women on the Move*. When I tell this story I always say – the appetite came with the eating. From this project, we also published in *Industrial Relations* and in a journal in Jane's field. That was really the beginning of my career as a researcher. Interestingly, when Jane returned as a full-time faculty member after working for many years as an administrator, we collaborated again on *Academic Couples: Problems and Promises*, which was published in 1997.

I also did a research paper with Jane on lifetime patterns of publications. My pattern, I must say, was very unusual. The most common pattern is that people are either publishers or not. Regrettably, we also found a substantial minority who started out publishing and then petered out. The reverse is, however, very unusual.

Was the study focused on women? No, we focused on both men and women. In fact, it was essentially a study about men, because we didn't have enough women in the sample to reach any firm conclusions about them. We would have loved to have done similar work on minorities and women, but the samples were not large enough.

So you started your research at essentially the same time you were tenured? Yes, at about the same time. And once I began, it went rather well. I was promoted to associate in three or four years and then to full within another three or four years. And I am happy to say that I have not stopped publishing since. Everybody has a good ten years in them. Mine just came very late! But it has been a good bit longer now than ten years since I started publishing.

Marianne, did you ever feel at all discriminated against as a Jew in the United States? There was no question that there was discrimination against Jews in my college after the big fight that I alluded to before. But in my case, I don't know exactly which was the main problem – that I was a woman, a Jew, or a foreigner.

They didn't like any of these so any one of these would have disqualified me. Interestingly, around the time of my retirement, they made a big hoopla. I was interviewed here and there. You know I'm pretty candid and I quipped that they didn't like women or Jews or foreigners. This showed up in a university newspaper. One of these old codgers was outraged and wrote a nasty letter to the reporter. (Mind you, I'm 76 and I talk about old codgers! But in my view being an old codger is a state of mind and has very little to do with chronological age!) Anyway, he said, among other things, that only my abysmal ignorance of the history of the college could justify making a comment like that. He went on to say that during a period of about thirty or forty years the college did in fact have – now I may be off on these numbers by a magnitude of one in each case – two women, three foreigners, and three Jews. I wanted to write back and say, "I rest my case!" I should add that I was very curious so I tracked down the people he referred to, which wasn't that hard to do. One of the "foreigners" was a man who eventually became dean of the college and later president of the university. He was apparently from either Canada or the UK, which isn't very foreign as far as I'm concerned. Another man was double counted because he was both Jewish and from Russia! And one of the women was the daughter of the college dean.

Other departments also had reputations for not hiring Jews during this time. For instance, the chemistry department, a large department, and, I think, engineering for a long time had virtually no Jews. But that wasn't unique to the University of Illinois.

To illustrate my point further, some years after the blow-up with the controversial dean, they hired a guy named Fred Gottheil. I remember coming home from an evening seminar where I had met him for the first time. I told Bob, "I met someone tonight. Although I'm absolutely sure that the department would never hire a Jew, I could have sworn he was Jewish." It turned out the department head, who in addition to being incredibly bigoted, wasn't very bright, and had thought that Gottheil was a German name. He called him Fritz instead of Fred. I find it amusing that someone who insists on being anti-Semitic doesn't know a Jew when he sees one.

Eventually and mercifully, these people were unable to replace themselves so they ended up hiring young people who were somewhat different. The situation changed bit by bit, although it took a really long time.

So after fifteen years as a visiting professor, you became an assistant professor in 1971? Initially I was sometimes part-time, but I became a full-timer the last six to eight years.

When you entered the department how many women faculty were there? There were two women in the department.

Including you? No, three, including me. The other two were considerably older than I. One, I must say, was neither much of a scholar nor much of a teacher. She was the daughter of the former dean who I mentioned earlier. The other woman was a different case. She was a nice woman. She had done some research in her earlier years, and as far as I know was a competent teacher. However, she avoided all personal relationships with anyone. She was very friendly and said hello, but never accepted an invitation. She stayed totally by herself. My hunch is that she was treated so badly and so isolated that she gave up and eventually became unapproachable.

There is another story that is worth telling. As I noted earlier, the controversial dean hired a number of women. He not only hired Reed and Brady, he also hired a young woman named Harriet Hudson. I knew her somewhat from Chicago. She was in labor economics. She had been at the University of Illinois for two or three years when she was made an offer to become the dean of faculty by a women's liberal arts college. However, she was quite happy doing what she was doing and wasn't all that interested in moving into administration. But in those days, the senior man (and I do mean man) in the economics department "owned" the field of labor economics. He told her, and I quote exactly because I still remember it word for word, "We recently promoted a woman (the other woman had been promoted to associate) and the men are still smarting from this blow. I just don't think we will ever do it again so you might as well accept the offer." This left her no choice. She went to the liberal arts college and became an administrator.

When I received tenure, there were three women out of about forty faculty members. I was never the only woman. The older women retired, but, as I recall, they brought in Jane Leuthold before the second woman retired. She's still there. She did well, and she is now a full professor. Eventually they hired Fran Blau. She was a great addition to the department, but she has since become the Frances Perkins Professor at Cornell.

Marianne, how would you describe your evolution as an economist? For instance, has your theoretical perspective changed over time? I haven't had much of an evolution in the sense of changing my basic views. When the younger women started doing feminist theory, and I became familiar with their work, I felt like the little old man who suddenly found out he was talking prose all his life. I always had reservations about neoclassical theory. As far back as I can remember I was interested in trying to show what was wrong with the "establishment's" approach. My rather haphazard approach to research is that often I will read something that doesn't make sense, then I probe and try to see if I can show precisely what it is that is troublesome. Despite my Chicago background, I was never interested in developing or even trying to develop grandiose theories. I'd rather say, "Look, this theory you developed doesn't quite make sense. It should be modified, changed, or in extreme cases, done away with." For instance, although I think Gary Becker has been very innovative and deserved the Nobel prize, I disagree fundamentally with most of his views. At the most fundamental level, I don't think that people are rational maximizers. This is something that bothered me for a long time.

A lot of my work has been focused on providing an empirical basis for my reservations. This is somewhat ironic, because I can't do the statistical work myself. But happily, I have always found someone willing and able to do it. This is one reason why I have co-authors for virtually all my work. Typically, I have the original idea, and often do much of the writing, including the interpretation of the results.

Let me give you one example. When you estimate the value of women's non-market work on the basis of opportunity cost, it requires the minimal assumption that you have some idea of how much women can earn if they worked. Otherwise, the whole thing doesn't make sense. A few years ago, I wanted to estimate opportunity cost – that if women stayed home their work must be worth at least as much as it would be in the labor market. Well, Bob, who did consumer economics, was conducting a panel study with young couples which involved recurrent interviews. He let anyone who had a reasonable idea and could pay for the marginal cost of their additional questions piggyback on his panel study. I, as well as other colleagues, managed to get a bit of money from the University Research Board and took advantage of that. One of the questions we asked young women who were not in the labor market (this was in the 1970s so there was still a fair number of those) was how much they thought they could earn if they took a job. Many of the young women – even those who had not been out of the labor market long – said they didn't know. We had instructed the interviewers to probe and say, "Well, would you at least take a guess?" A fair number of respondents said they couldn't even do that. Now in view of these answers, how can one assume that the opportunity cost approach is sensible? Also, economists assume that when people make decisions, they weigh their alternatives. In fact, in those years, women rarely weighed the alternatives; they knew they were expected to become full-time homemakers and that was that. It had nothing or very little to do with how much they could earn in the labor market.

So the rationality assumption and the opportunity cost principle bothered you? Yeah, and there are other things that have increasingly bothered me, especially in recent years. Since Julie Nelson got me involved in feminist theory, I have become aware of some of the larger issues. For instance, much of traditional economics emphasizes measurement rather than what is really important. Now I admit that it's much easier to work with concepts you can measure, but it doesn't mean that this is what is really important.

For instance, it is relatively easy to measure how much income people have, and if their income increases we assume they're better off. That doesn't seem like an unreasonable assumption *per se*. But income is relative. It seems to me that how people feel about themselves depends as much on their relative income as on the absolute amount. This is the way I have often put the matter. Suppose you gave my colleagues, who are the sort of people I know best, the following two choices. First, one guy gets a 10 percent increase, but his colleagues get a 15 percent increase. Second, one guy gets no increase and his colleagues get a 10 percent cut. Then ask – which would make them feel better? I am deeply convinced that most of them would prefer the second alternative.

While a majority of people in our affluent country, let alone in the world, desperately need some actual income, when it comes to my colleagues (who have good earnings and nowadays often have a spouse who is working as well) they don't need the money that badly. I believe that even if both benefit, but one benefits more than the other, there is a low likelihood that both will feel good. But it's important that both feel good because what you want to maximize is well-being, not income.

Certainly I react that way. I actually brought a salary grievance once as late as the 1980s because I found out, inadvertently, that I was the second-lowest paid among a large number of full professors in the department. The person who was paid marginally less was a man. He had been promoted that year and did not have much of a research record. I was indignant, not because I needed or even wanted the money, but because I thought that it was an insult. I had certainly not set the world on fire; I never thought that I would. But I was publishing far more than the department average, and I was publishing in quite reputable journals, although at times they were in other disciplines. Most traditional economists flatly ignore the importance of this issue. They acknowledge that inequality has increased, but do not find this particularly disturbing and generally tend to ignore how important it is to people's morale.

I got into a long discussion one day with a colleague who spent his life working on national income accounts, with considerable success I might add. He asked me, "What is this feminist economics stuff about?" I searched for an example. I said that most feminists think we should put a value on housework. He responded, "But you can't measure that precisely." I argued that if you only included items in national income accounts that are measured precisely, we would all have to pack up and go home. His second line of defense was, "Well, there are many other items we don't include in the national accounts either." In other words, we can't spend our lives trying to improve the national income accounts. What kind of reasoning is that?

Now people have charged, and correctly, that feminist economics hasn't developed an alternative paradigm. Bob Solow says this in his comments in *Beyond Economic Man*. I've thought about this a bit and I am not sure that what we need is a new paradigm. What we need is the recognition that the world is far more complex than what can be encompassed by a rigid paradigm. I'm speaking from ignorance here, but I doubt that the other social sciences have such a paradigm. In my view, you look at the world and you try to interpret it as best you can, and give up the notion, mainly borrowed from the physical sciences, that the simplest explanation is always the best one. When it comes to the social sciences, this approach strikes me as patently absurd.

It usually took me quite a while to persuade students that there was not a single answer to any question. For instance, they would ask – are women paid less because of discrimination or is it because their performance is not as good as men's? Well it's not necessarily one or the other; it could quite possibly be some of both and there is clearly a feedback mechanism.

Marianne, you seem to claim in your book with Fran Blau that you are a neoclassical economist. How do you reconcile that with what you've just said? I don't believe it says we are neoclassical; I believe it says the book emphasizes neoclassical economics.

Then you agree that there are concepts in the neoclassical framework that you value? Well, you see, I am reasonably sure that some of my criticisms are justified, but I am by no means convinced that all of neoclassical theory should be scrapped. Rather, my idea is, and we do this in the book, to present the established theories, and then say, "Yes, but ...." However, it is also fair to say (and I'm sure that Fran Blau and Anne Winkler would say the same thing) that if I had written the book by myself, it would be less neoclassical. There would be less emphasis on theory and more on the critique. I also readily concede that it probably wouldn't have been as good of a book. We all believe that our talents and views are complementary. And in principle I really don't have any objection to the basic approach of the book. The way I often put it to students is that while I have serious doubts, for instance, about people being either rational or maximizers, I surely wouldn't want to assume that they are totally irrational or are indifferent to how much they get. In other words, as a first approximation, if you add enough "ifs" and "buts," the assumptions make a contribution. And I certainly wouldn't throw out all theories just because they are imperfect. After all, what economists do with their models is really what scientists (and I mean hard scientists) do in the lab. We eliminate a lot of the variables that exist in the real world, so that we can examine what happens when only one thing changes. Then we gradually add additional complications. That's a very legitimate approach. If you tried to look at the world in its whole complexity all at once, you'd throw up your hands. The problem is not the model *per se*, the problem is that many economists forget that it is not the real world, which is far more complex than our models. You can also see the problems this can cause when economists offer policy advice, which is by and large abominable. But basically there's some merit to the neoclassical approach. In other words, I would still teach demand and supply and most of the other fundamentals. But I would also make sure to point out that neither the assumptions nor the conclusions are realistic, and that we have to be careful in the way we use these tools.

Marianne, do you think that heterodox economics has anything to offer to the discipline? Well, heterodox takes in a broad range of views – everything that isn't orthodox – so I don't think that it is possible to generalize. Of the heterodox schools, the two that I know most about are Marxism and feminism. Marxism I know because I was interested in it and I taught comparative systems in the days when there were still different systems to compare. I have learned a good bit about feminist theory, although I've never regarded myself as a real feminist theorist. As I said, I'm not much of a theorist.

My view of Marxism is that it had quite a lot to contribute and in some respects it was also wrong, which is true of most ideologies. The problem with the usual approaches to Marx is that to an amazing extent people either totally dismiss him and think he had nothing worthwhile to say, which is ridiculous. Or they think that every word he uttered was the Holy Gospel, which is equally ridiculous. Clearly, his emphasis on class was a contribution. In fact, one thing that heterodox economists agree on is their critique of neoclassical theory's "economic man." Presumably, "economic man" is universal, encompassing everyone. But there are all kinds of potentially important distinctions. Apart from the obvious gender differences, there are clearly differences in race and ethnicity as well as class. Oscar Louis, a rather famous anthropologist on this campus, argued that people of the same class have more in common across nationalities than people of different classes within the same nation. There's a lot of truth to that. I can get together with academicians from almost anywhere in the world and have much in common with them. So clearly, class matters. Also, Marx's emphasis on conflict rather than the invisible hand is a contribution. I wish Marx had been wrong about this, but regrettably, he was not. There is a lot of conflict. As a rule, if you get more, I get less. Rarely is there a situation where everyone benefits. I also think Marx's under-consumption theory still makes a certain amount of sense. So I clearly think Marx made some significant contributions to economics.

As for institutionalism, I don't know that much about it because I have read very little of the literature, and frankly I did not understand much of it when I tried. I don't mean to put them down, it's probably a shortcoming of mine. I read some of Veblen, and I was able to understand him. He makes more sense than what is usually found in textbooks. His focus on conspicuous consumption seems obvious to me. I used to emphasize to my students that in affluent countries the majority of people spend a great deal of their income on things which they don't need or particularly enjoy.

Marianne, have you observed any significant changes in the economics profession over time? Obviously if you compare, say, Adam Smith with the prominent people of the current mainstream, the latter are far more narrow and less interesting. While Smith introduced the concept of the invisible hand, it is clear that he didn't believe that everyone's interests are harmonious. There is a famous quote that suggests that when you see businessmen together they're probably up to no good. Yes, I think as economists have developed their skills for mathematical modeling, they are more likely to do things that their techniques can handle rather than devote their time to things that are important in the real world. It seems to me that we would be far better off if economists were more willing to acknowledge what we still don't know rather than continuing to develop simplified models and then denying that the world is far more complex.

I would also argue, however, that this is not necessarily a long-term trend. Rather, it may be cyclical. I was intrigued at the ASSA January meetings in Boston (1994) because it was so different from the past. I was not the only one who thought so. There were many people talking about it, particularly among

feminist economists and other non-conformists. Of course, Amartya Sen organized the program that year. Unfortunately, the meetings have not been like
that since.

On the other hand, feminist economists have made some progress. I
remember for years after CSWEP was formed, it sponsored interesting sessions
on discrimination, occupational segregation, and so forth. The sessions were
well attended, but almost entirely by women. There were two or three guys
sitting in a back corner looking uncomfortable. However, the first time I participated in an IAFFE session, I had a big surprise – one of the biggest I've ever had
at an AEA meeting. It began when Julie Nelson called me. I had never met her
and didn't know anything about her. She asked if I would be willing to chair a
session at the AEA meetings. This was soon after IAFFE had been formed. I
told her that I didn't know anything about it, but she persuaded me that I didn't
have to know much of anything to chair a session. They wanted a senior person
who would at least not be unsympathetic. I agreed that I satisfied the criteria
and chaired the session. It was phenomenally well attended and there was a
large number of men in the audience! That was my surprise. Everyone was
surprised and tried to figure out what had happened. We conjectured that Don
McCloskey's participation was the explanation. However, I've been to any
number of these sessions since, and they have often been equally well attended
by men as well as women. This suggests that we are moving in the right direction, albeit slowly.

Marianne, why do you think more women are not attracted to economics? I
have always been interested in economic education, and believe that there are
problems with teaching economics at the undergraduate level. There are very
few women undergraduates in economics, far fewer than in most other sciences
and social sciences. There is even a substantially larger proportion of undergraduate math majors who are women. Few people seem to be aware of this. This
certainly refutes the common explanation that women can't handle the math.

One problem is that there are few women professors in economics. Several
studies have found that the number of women faculty does not influence
women's decision to major in economics. However, these studies do not
consider that when women students only see women faculty in primarily insecure positions, it is difficult for them to be inspired by the possibilities the
discipline has to offer. I used to think students didn't pay attention to that.
Perhaps some of them don't, but I found that many of them do. You wouldn't
believe how often when I was in my forties that students would ask me why I
wasn't a professor yet. It would be an interesting study to see what effect a larger
number of tenured women economists would have on the likelihood of women
students majoring in economics and going on to graduate work.

**Do you think there is anything to the argument that it is mainstream
economic theory itself that influences women's decision to major in economics?** I
have read and thought about this a fair amount lately. Some years ago I wrote a
chapter for a book by Saunders and Walstad on teaching the introductory

economics course. Recently they edited a new edition, and Robin Bartlett and I wrote a new chapter. We reached the conclusion that women are not as likely to accept the formalistic models that are widely taught. They are more likely to be alienated from much of the subject matter which is still more relevant to men than to women. For instance, you would think that by now introductory courses would pay some attention to the family, if only because of Becker's work. But this is not the case. In a typical introductory text, families are for all practical purposes non-existent. There is a lovely quote from a textbook which says that people act as individuals, but sometimes they band together in corporations, governments, and labor unions. I think there are other examples as well but, incredibly, the family is never mentioned. These are the same guys who also claim that the family is the backbone of the world. The fact that housework is not even considered work may also affect women's interest in economics. On the other hand, I've asked myself – why didn't this turn me off? Maybe because I never intended to do much housework! But that's only part of the explanation of why I was not bothered by the lack of attention to this issue.

I couldn't say with certainty how much of what has been called the "chilly classroom climate" still goes on. I do know that when I was director of undergraduate studies in the economics department in the 1970s and 1980s I would get complaints from students that indicated women were put down. One guy used to refer to "dumb blondes" in his examples. When I called him in to talk about it, there was no question that he meant dumb blonde women and not dumb blonde men. He argued that it was legitimate shorthand for expressing a certain type of person. But both the students and I agreed it was terribly offensive. Fortunately, not much of that sort of thing appears to go on now. However, many other factors may contribute to women not entering economics in larger numbers.

You obviously think that feminists have something to offer economics. Could you elaborate on that? As I have already said, I believe that questioning some of what has been done is useful. On my more optimistic days I think we are having a bit of an impact. For example, men are coming to many sessions on feminist theory and have indicated some interest in the issues. This is surely encouraging. I also think there is some progress in the recognition that the differences in the way men and women view things is not only biological. I don't think we have a way of telling at this point exactly how much is biological and how much is socially constructed. Children are treated differently from the time they wear pink and blue booties. As long as this is the case, men and women will have different responses in the same situation. For instance, the elasticity of supply of labor is different for men and women. Acknowledging these differences could lead to the broader recognition that variations along racial, class, and ethnic lines need to be accounted for.

There are some less auspicious developments as well. For instance, there is some dissension between African–American and white feminists. The more sensible ones in both camps recognize that they are natural allies against a model that is white and male. They also recognize that there are differences as well as commonalities between and within groups, and that each can learn from the other. Feminists also emphasize the value of looking at qualitative issues and of doing interdisciplinary work. It is not a coincidence that IAFFE makes a point of welcoming people working in other disciplines.

Now some people might ask, "Why do you call this feminist? There are also men who think and feel that way." My answer is, yes, happily this is true! Indeed, I wouldn't be that upset if we used a different term. It's just that this approach has come to be known as feminist, and I think it's harmless enough as long as we know what we are talking about. It certainly doesn't mean that only women can be feminists. After all it does not say female, it says fem-in-ist, which is quite a different thing. As Julie Nelson has pointed out, some of the feminist ideas date back to male economists. For example, Adam Smith talked about provisioning much more than about maximizing, which fits with feminist principles. However, by no reasonable standard was Adam Smith a feminist. So let's not quibble about words. The important point is that what is called feminist economics, along with other heterodox approaches, is certainly broadening, softening, and has the effect of opening up economics.

What do you think IAFFE has to do to make an impact in the profession?
Partly, of course, the problem is the numbers; neoclassical economists comprise the great bulk of the profession, particularly in the United States. As long as they don't accept the work of feminist economists, there's a problem. It is important to have a critical mass. According to Rosabeth Kantor, people who are tokens in the sense that there are so few of them stick out like a sore thumb. In the economics department at Illinois, for example, when there were two or three women, I became Marianne Ferber rather than "the woman." On the other hand, I served for some years on the executive committee of the Graduate College, a committee that was invariably dominated, as most things are at this university, by the physical sciences and engineering. For the first couple of years I was the only woman faculty on the committee and I was very conscious of the fact that when I opened my mouth they did not hear me, Marianne Ferber. What they heard was "the woman." In these circumstances you know very well that if I never said anything, which in my case would be somewhat unlikely, they would claim that women never speak up. But if we do, they claim that women talk too much. As I said, you become very self-conscious. As the numbers increase, however, this attitude changes significantly.

As you know, I have done some work on citations as a means of evaluating academics, and the results clearly show that men are more inclined to cite men and women are more inclined to cite women, even within narrow fields of specialization. One of my findings, which supported my claim, is that the difference between the number of citations of men and women was significantly smaller as the proportion of women in the field increased. In other words, as the proportion of women rises, they are more likely to be cited.

Marianne, do you think it is more difficult for women faculty to get tenure in economics today or is it easier? One of the problems has been that as women have begun to get somewhat of a break in academia, universities are falling apart. Tenure is much more difficult to get now than was the case earlier. It used to be that white guys got tenure for breathing for long periods of time. That's not much of an exaggeration. This has changed; getting tenure is becoming increasingly difficult. I have never looked at the distribution by rank among the members of IAFFE, but I suspect that the proportion of full professors must be small. When I die the percentage will go down significantly! [*Laughter*] Also, if a larger proportion of young women PhDs were at institutions where they had more of a chance to do research, things would be quite different. We have quite a few bright, capable, and ambitious young women who could be very successful, but they often have a teaching and service load which is ridiculous. And, of course, the representation of women in research institutions is still shamefully low, especially at the tenured ranks. Harvard for years had no tenure track women in the economics department. Then they had one for quite a long time. Many women who by any reasonable standard are at the top of their field are tenured, but not in economics. Irma Adelman at Berkeley is tenured in agricultural economics; Janice Madden at the University of Pennsylvania is tenured in the Department of Regional Science; Myra Strober at Stanford has been in the College of Education; Lourdes Benería at Cornell is in the Department of Planning; Mary Jean Bowman may have had some ties to the Economics Department at Chicago, but never had more than a joint appointment. This is an absurd situation! And of the few women who have appointments in economics, the majority are not feminists and, in some cases, are unsympathetic to feminism. For all these reasons our efforts at this time should be directed towards helping women who are already in the field to get stable and regular positions.

Do you think a woman could be hired and have her work accepted in a typical economics department today if she admits she is a feminist and if she does mostly unorthodox theoretical work? It would be more difficult. She had better plan to work very hard. But there are a number of ways successful women can help. Some, who are willing to "play the game" and who manage to be accepted by their male colleagues, can be a great help by writing recommendations, inviting younger women to participate in conferences, and getting them invitations to give seminars. And that's good. Other women economists are far more aggressive and do not win popularity contests, yet they do bring attention to existing problems, and make the rest of us look moderate [*laughter*], and that's useful too.

It is also important to remember that there's a great variety of views among feminist economists. I would not want to be a member of a group that must agree on everything. Of course, diversity can also be a bit of a problem. I certainly have grave doubts about the views of extreme feminists who argue that women are fundamentally better than men. I also disagree with feminists who think that all mathematical modeling is merely a male device to keep women out of the field. I believe there's merit to using these methods if they are used correctly and their limits are recognized. But disagreements are unavoidable. After all, neoclassical economists who are supposed to be basically in agreement on fundamentals also have substantial disagreements. Take, for example, someone like Rebecca Blank. She explicitly claims to be a neoclassical economist, but in fact agrees with many of the views and values of feminist economists. As feminists, what we have in common is far more important and significant than what separates us.

3

BARBARA BERMAN BERGMANN

The profession is remarkably similar to what it was when I was an undergraduate or graduate student. This so-called "science" has gone nowhere. ... There's been an explosion of knowledge in biology! ... Meanwhile, economists are still teaching – marginal cost equal marginal revenue. It's ridiculous!

(Barbara Bergmann, 1998)

Barbara knew she was a feminist from a very early age. She also knew she was not a Marxist, especially after a visit to the Russian pavilion at the New York World's Fair in 1938. This may explain why her work has focused on race and gender inequality, and not on class inequality. Nevertheless, it is difficult to deny the profound impact that Barbara's pioneering scholarship has had on the discipline in the areas of pay equity, affirmative action, occupational segregation, poverty, welfare, housework, and child care. Barbara's career as an economist began at the Bureau of Labor Statistics. She is also a former Senior Research Associate for the Harvard Economic Research Project; former Senior Staff Economist for the Council of Economic Advisors; former Senior Staff Member at the Brookings Institution; former Senior Economic Advisor with the Agency for International Development; former member of the Advisory Board to the Women's Law Project, the Board of Directors for the Public Interest Economics Center, the Congressional Budget Office Panel of Economic Advisors, the American Economic Association Advisory Committee to the Census Bureau, and the Price Advisory Committee for the US Council on Wage and Price Stability. She has held teaching positions at Harvard, Brandeis University, the University of Maryland, and American University. Currently she is a Distinguished Professor Emerita at American University and Professor Emerita at the University of Maryland. Barbara is also a former member of the Editorial Board of the *American Economic Review* and *Feminist Economics*; former President of the Eastern Economic Association, the Society for the Advancement of Socio-Economics, the Committee on the Status of Women in the Economics Profession, the American Association of University Professors, and the International Association for Feminist Economics; and former Vice-President of the American Economic Association. She received her BA from Cornell University (1948) and an MA and PhD from Harvard University (1959).

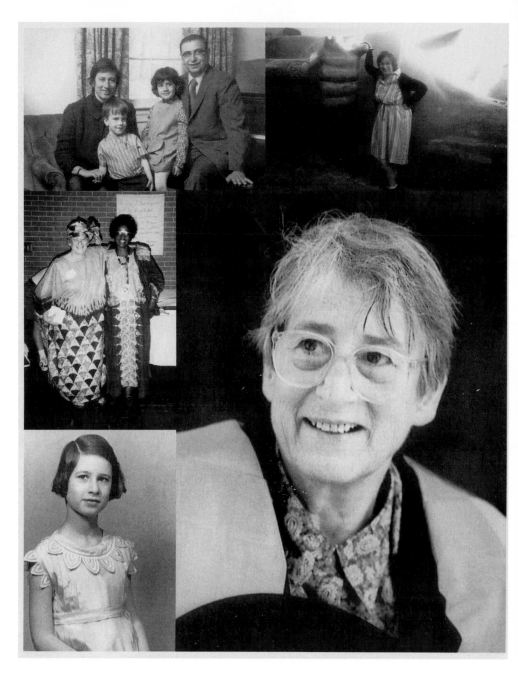

Plate 3   Counterclockwise from top left: Barbara Bergmann at age 43 with husband Fred and their children, Sarah and David; at IAFFE's 5th annual conference at American University, Washington, DC (1996); at age 9; main portrait (1999); at age 63 in Egypt with recumbent male giant.

Our conversation took place on a winter's night at Barbara's home in Washington, DC. She and her husband, Fred, had graciously invited us for dinner. For the record, Fred cooked, served, and did the dishes. After dinner, we remained at the dining room table and got down to business. In typical Barbara fashion, she expressed her reservations about our project and told us we were wasting our time. It's the candor we appreciate! We smiled, and began to ask our questions.

Barbara, let's begin with your family background. What can you tell us about your mother and father? My mother was born in Romania and came to the US as a baby. She claimed to be a relative of the Grand Rabbi of Bucharest, but that is doubtful. Her mother (and this didn't catch my attention until just recently) came over with five children and no husband. They pitched up on the slums of the lower East Side of Manhattan and the way they survived was to send their older children out to work. My aunt was sent into a trimmings factory. She sewed fancy cloak and suit trimmings by hand. She never went to school and never learned to read or write. She remained a simple person all of her life, although she founded a business, and I am still traveling on some of her money.

This is about what time period? They must have come around 1903. They may have been illegal, and they did not become citizens.

My father was born here, but his parents were immigrants. The really extraordinary thing is that none of my three grandparents (who had been in this country for at least thirty years by the time I knew them) spoke one word of English.

Were your father's parents Romanian also? No. They were from Poland; the Russian–Poland area. My father was a typographer, a typesetter. Luckily for us, he had a $50-a-week job throughout the Great Depression so we didn't really suffer. But living through the Depression and watching what was going on was an important experience for me. One of my earliest memories was in the Bronx, where I was brought up. Vendors would call up to the apartments and say, "I cash clothes" or "I sell vegetables," and so on. One day a man came around. He had a violin and a chair, and he sat down and played the violin. People threw down pennies. Afterwards he made an announcement – he would give the violin and the wooden, folding chair to anyone who would find him a job. You don't forget things like that. We, of course, grew up very big Democrats. I remember what a shock it was when President Roosevelt died. I felt like a father had disappeared.

Your dad was a skilled typographer? Yes. During World War II he separated from my mother. He was very bored with typesetting, so he became a merchant seaman. But it may have been too much for him because he had a heart attack around 45.

Did you have any siblings? No. My mother told me she had three abortions after she had me. When I asked for a cat or a dog, she said, "No, they are as much trouble as another child and I'm not having that."

When did she become a single mother? Not until I was in high school. She eventually went to work for my aunt during World War II.

Did she stay in the New York area? Always. I am basically a New Yorker.

Did she stay home with you before she went to work for your aunt? No. I don't recall that she stayed home at all.

She was always a working mother? Yes.

In the early years, do you recall any teacher who influenced your thinking? I went to elementary school in the Bronx during the 1930s. There was a very important influence there. In the sixth grade (I was 12) I had what was obviously a communist teacher. She would constantly introduce Russia into the lesson. For example, if we were studying geography, she would say, "Well, children, and where else are oats grown?" We knew the answer was always Russia.

Was your teacher of Russian heritage? No. She was Jewish like the rest of us. The Bronx at that time (our neighborhood, anyway) was 100 percent Jewish (all except for the janitors). When the World's Fair came to New York in 1938–9, we were taken there. She said, "We're going to the World's Fair and we are going to spend a lot of time in the Russian pavilion" [*laughter*]. This Russian pavilion was a huge building. In front of it was a huge statue of a man holding aloft a red star. (It was said that he was the only man in pants among all the sculptures at the World's Fair; all the rest had togas or little loin cloths!) Inside the building were huge rooms and in each room was an unbelievably large tractor or agricultural implement. The rest of the room was filled with the iconography of Stalin. There were bowls with Stalin's picture; teaspoons with Stalin on the handle; and, of course, pictures, sculptures, and plates with his image. I was repulsed by this. Although many of my friends have been Marxists, I have never had the slightest inclination in that direction. All the result of this one teacher.

Then we moved out to Queens, and I went to junior high where I had a very good teacher who sparked my interest in math. After that I attended Forest Hills High School. These were all public schools. Then I went off to college. I always knew I was going to college. My parents were very good about that. For some reason I only applied to MIT and Cornell University. I don't know why; maybe because one of my friends went to MIT and another went to Cornell.

None of your teachers encouraged you to attend college? No. I wasn't plugged into any career advice at all. For some reason I thought MIT only offered engineering, so when they asked my intentions, I told them I wanted to be an engineer. They asked me what kind. The only thing I could think of was civil engineer. They obviously couldn't picture that. The interviewer looked at me as though I was crazy. Although I had good math scores, I was rejected from MIT, but I was accepted at Cornell, so I went to Cornell.

You said that you always knew you would go to college, and your parents were very supportive of that. Were your parents educated? Oh, no. Neither of them had graduated from high school. My mother's first ambition for me was to play the piano at Carnegie Hall.

You took piano lessons? Oh, yes. My mother asked my teacher whether I had talent. The teacher thought I did, but I didn't practice enough.

Barbara, do you recall what percentage of your high school cohort attended college? Forest Hills High School drew kids from upper-middle-class Forest Hills and working-class Italian Corona. Although we were in the same school it was very segregated. I don't think any of the Corona kids went to college, but probably a higher proportion of the Forest Hills kids did. Recently, I witnessed a similar division at my children's school. We used to live in Bannockburn, a community bordered by McArthur Boulevard. It was a community of professionals with big aspirations for their children. The children had big aspirations too. On the other side of the Boulevard was a working-class community. The working-class kids were called red-necks. They didn't go to college; they dressed in a different way; they acted in a different way; and they had different aspirations. Anyway, both groups went to the same schools; elementary, junior high, and high school. They were all white. Yet, it was as though McArthur Boulevard divided these kids right down the middle. Nobody crossed over.

What about your children? They crossed the line a little bit. They weren't quite red-necks; they did go to college. But they were not the academic achievers that I would have liked.

At Cornell, did you attempt to major in engineering? No. I was admitted to the School of Arts and Sciences. Somehow I didn't connect Cornell and engineering. But the first day on campus, I saw young men surveying. I then realized there was an engineering school. But I was excluded from it anyway. I eventually majored in mathematics. Towards the end of my undergraduate experience I had a lot of extra time, so I took some courses in economics. That's how I became an economist.

Were there other women in mathematics or economics? I never even noticed.

In retrospect? No. Never noticed.

Did you have a mentor or role model? No. I didn't expect that. I sat in the class and took the exams.

So why did you take economics? Why do most people become economists? It's the enjoyment of the petty mathematical triumphs.

Did you get a major or minor in economics? It was a second major.

So you were attracted to economics because it provided problems to be solved? That's right. I didn't think I could become a real mathematician. In fact, the whole idea of graduate school was totally foreign to me.

But you wanted to be an engineer? Not exactly. Usually, you don't have to pick a major when you enter college unless you want to be an engineer. This is true at most schools. You enter as an engineer, otherwise you never get into engineering. That's one reason why women are often excluded from engineering. It's not like economics or mathematics where you can float into an elementary course and decide – oh, this is nice – I'll major in it. You cannot do that with engineering.

How did you decide to go for the PhD in economics? After I graduated from Cornell, I returned to New York to live with my mother. She asked me, "How come you're not married? What do you think I sent you to college for?" That started us off on what proved to be a bad patch for the rest of our lives (her life, anyway). She used to tell me that I acted too smart; that I should act dumber; that I'd never catch a man. Anyway, I tried to get a job. This was 1948, a recession year. I was unemployed for almost a year; I could not find any kind of job. I don't know whether it was because I was a woman, a Jew; who knows? After about a year, my mother said to me, "You're not doing yourself any good. Why don't you attend Teacher's College and become a teacher?" So I dutifully went to the Teacher's College at Columbia University to get a Master's degree. That was an experience; talk about a useless curriculum! It was ridiculous! One of the professors said (I will never forget this), "We have to prepare the children for collectivism because they are going to live under collectivism." You can imagine my reaction given my anti-Marxist impetus! There was absolutely nothing useful in that entire curriculum.

Thankfully, after a year I was rescued because my name came up on the civil service list. I had probably done very well on the civil service exam because I'm good at taking short-answer tests. I got a job in the information service at the Bureau of Labor Statistics (BLS). I essentially answered phones and told people what the CPI was. I did well and was promoted several times. I was a GS-9 after two years (I was hired as a GS-5) .

This was in New York? Yes, the New York regional office. Our boss was a very nice gentleman. Later, when he wrote my recommendation for graduate school, he said I was a young lady of culture and refinement [*laughter*]. I worked there about three years. One day an economist came into the office and asked me, "Do you have time to do your own work here?" I thought to myself – what work is he talking about? We had a conversation about research and he said, "You ought to go to graduate school." So, I did.

That was your first mentor? That's right. I applied to Harvard and Cornell. I got into both, but decided to go to Harvard.

With a scholarship? No. My mother had done well in the trimming business and I had saved money from my work at the BLS. It was not a hardship.

What year is this? About 1952.

Were you going for a PhD or a Master's? Well, I originally thought I would go for a Master's degree until I attended the first meeting of the new graduate students. The chair of the department gave a little talk. It turned out that everybody was there for the PhD. I got the message; it was ridiculous to go for a Master's. But I was not plugged in. I've never been adequately plugged in, and that's been the problem with my career. But there are also benefits. If I had been plugged in, I would have done what was expected of me. I would have been married with three children by that time. But I never noticed that I was a victim of discrimination (which I certainly was). Sometimes it's beneficial not to notice things.

How many women were in the program? There were about fifty people in the entering class. In terms of women, it was Alice Mitchell (later Rivlin) and I, and maybe one or two others. There were a few others ahead of us as well. This was also the first year that the Harvard Law School was opened to women.

Did the other women get through the program? Yes.

What was it like in graduate school? I was unusually good in mathematics, which is why they let me in. I got terrible grades as an undergraduate in everything, except in mathematics. At Cornell, they graded from 0 to 100, and I typically got 78 which is a C+. I did much better in mathematics.

Were you uninterested in other subjects? No, I guess I spent too much time playing bridge. When I got to Harvard I was really afraid I would not do well. But I found that they never gave anything less than a B to anybody, and they mostly gave out As.

How did you get into Harvard if you had bad grades? I think because I had a good math record. Or maybe it was a mistake, who knows? At that time, the admissions were administered by Radcliffe College. Anyway, in my second year I got a teaching assistantship in a statistics course offered by the sociology department. Fred Mosteller, a famous statistician, was the professor.

Who were your professors at Harvard? I took two courses in macro from Alvin Hansen and an introduction to theory from Edward Chamberlain (famous for his work on monopolistic competition). I took a course in business cycles from Gotfried Haberler, who I appreciated because his writing was very clear (I've always aspired to write clearly). Wassily Leontief, a Russian, was also there. Most people started off with Wassily's more advanced theory course. But I, not having much confidence in my undergraduate education, took Chamberlain's course. I'm pleased that I did because he had a view of economics that was more realistic than most. He was a very peculiar guy. He felt he had been cheated out of greatness and respect because Joan Robinson had written a similar book (not near as good) at about the same time. Very few people there respected him. In fact, the students laughed at him because he was so concerned with distinguishing his work from Robinson's. But I thought he was great, and still think so.

The first day of his class (my first class at Harvard), he handed out pieces of cardboard marked S for sellers and B for buyers, with prices on each of them. Those with S were supposed to sell above the price marked on the card. Those with B were suppose to buy below the price on the card. He told us to find the best bargain we could and he would write the transactions on the board. Some people got mixed up and bought above their buying price, and he reproved us. But in any case, we had a discussion about whether these prices averaged out to the equilibrium price. The answer was no. In fact, he told us that he had conducted this classroom experiment twenty times, and, on average, the price was lower than equilibrium. We then spent the rest of the hour trying to create hypotheses as to why that might be. No other experiment was ever done. In later years Vernon Smith (who had taken this class) invented experimental economics.

The next year I took Leontief's theory course and statistics from Guy Orcutt. He had invented a method of computer simulation which I later used. After the first year, I taught a course in econ math to graduate students. I taught many of the famous people who went through Harvard, such as Dale Jorgensen, Michael Piori, and so on. I also became a teaching assistant for Leontief and Modigliani.

Were you more successful as a graduate student in terms of your grades? I was very successful. But I wasn't very successful in identifying a thesis topic and writing a thesis. It took me a long time. It was not an outstanding thesis by any means.

With whom did you write your thesis? With a visiting professor named Ed Hoover. By that time I was an instructor.

What was the focus of your dissertation? It was sort of an input/output model of the New York Metropolitan Area. I can't say I'm too proud of it.

How did you choose the topic? There was money to do it. Anyway, I was there a long time because I was reluctant to go out into the real world. When I did, no one offered me a job.

When you graduated from Harvard did you want to get an academic job? What I was supposed to do after grad school was a mystery to me. I was just not tuned in. I remember when I was in my second or third year of graduate school, one of my friends told me he was publishing a paper. It had never occurred to me to do that.

Did any of the graduate students have mentors? I wasn't paying attention.

Did either Leontief or Modigliani serve as your intellectual mentor in any way? No.

Do you remember them mentoring anyone? I don't think Leontief mentored anybody. He was very egotistical. Most of them were.

Did you have any role models? What do you mean by role models? It didn't occur to me to associate myself with that caliber of faculty.

Do you feel that you had any constraints in graduate school? The lack of encouragement was probably a constraint. Who knows? Certainly, if somebody had offered me a better dissertation project, I would have done it, but nobody did. When I taught, I never allowed students to flounder around looking for a topic. I told them, "Here's a topic for you. It's something I'm interested in and I'd be willing to work with you. If you want to do it, fine; if not, go find someone else."

Did you join a study group in graduate school? Sometimes, yes. There were a few people. Men.

Did you party together at all? I didn't have much of a social life.

You were a serious student? Well, no, I just didn't. They probably had a better social life than I did.

When does Fred come into the picture? Much later, actually. They wouldn't give me an assistant professorship, so I had to find a job. Someone, probably Carl Kaysen, found me a job as staff member at the Council of Economic

Advisors. I did that for a couple of years and then I got a teaching job at Brandeis University, as an associate professor without tenure. I was denied tenure a few years later. Then I got a job at the Brookings Institution. On my way down to Washington, DC, I passed through New Haven to visit some friends. The economists were having a beach party. At the party I met Gus Ranis. Gus knew Fred, who had written to him that he was in Washington, DC, and had a miserable social life. Gus wrote back and gave Fred the names of two women from the party; mine was the first name on the list. Anyway, Fred called and we went out. He never called the other number [*laughter*].

You said you didn't get tenure at Brandeis. Were there any women who did? Not in economics. However, there was a man of no great accomplishment who entered at the same time I did, who did get tenure. In those days getting tenure was a lot easier for men.

You got a job at the Brookings Institution? Yes. I went to Bolivia and Peru to do a study as part of a Brookings' project. Then I did an unemployment study. Later I got a job at the University of Maryland as an associate professor without tenure. They promised I would get tenure after a year, and I did.

Were there other women working at Maryland? I was told that the previous dean had a "no women!" policy. I think the reason I got the job was because of Norton Dodge, who was on the faculty. I had known Norton as an undergraduate at Cornell. He, I, and Robert Fogel had taken a course in unorthodox economics at Cornell. (Fogel was a roaring communist; this was 1948, the Russians were taking over Czechoslovakia, and he defended it.) Anyway, Norton and I became friends. He was also at Harvard when I was there. In fact, the day I handed in my thesis, I saw his thesis on the secretary's desk, which he had just handed in. When I first came to Maryland, Norton was living in the meanest kind of student housing, a miserable little garden apartment. He and I married about the same time, but he acquired Cremona – a multi-million-dollar estate on the Potomac River with a swimming pool, field house, greenhouses, air strip, boat dock, rose garden, etc. The house was crammed with beautiful English antiques. He made his money in the stock market. Once Fred and I attended a Maryland faculty picnic there. After our visit, I told Fred about our parallel lives: Cornell, Harvard, Maryland, marriage in the same year; except Norton had Cremona. I asked Fred, "Well, how about it?" Fred responded, "Barbara, you've gone as far from the Bronx as a girl can go in one generation!"

What kind of experiences did you have at the University of Maryland? In the beginning, Maryland did not have a distinguished faculty. A much better faculty was assembled later on. I taught graduate macro, graduate micro, graduate econometrics, everything. Then, in the early 1970s, I founded a course on poverty and discrimination. This was one of the earliest courses taught on the subject. I also taught a wonderful course for undergraduates called computer methods in economics. In those days computers were "way out." There were no PCs. The only computers were mainframes, which you had to approach with a deck of key-punch cards. Maryland soon got demand processing and teletypes.

I started doing some computer simulations and taught it to my graduate students.

Did you ever hold an administrative position at Maryland? No. But once we needed a chair, and I administered a questionnaire asking the faculty who they thought would be a good chair. I counted the ballots. I came out next to last. But I was promoted to full professor. Promotion was much easier then.

Were you married to Fred by the time you went to Maryland? Yes.

How many children did you have? We have one biological child and an adopted child. I took a leave of absence from the University of Maryland to work with Gus Ranis at the Agency for International Development for a year. It was during that time that I had my child.

What was it like being a mother, full-time professor, and married to someone who worked full time? Well, I'm a great believer in commodification: hiring the help you need. So we did. My children weren't too badly damaged; they turned out to be Democrats.

Did you have a nanny for them? I had a housekeeper who did housewife duties: namely, cooking, cleaning, and child care.

Do you think it was easier then to find child care? I'm currently working on a book on child care policy. Looking back, there were no day-care centers that I was aware of. The day-care centers today are much better because they have programs for the kids and the personnel supervise each other. If I were advising people now, I would never advise them to get nannies or housekeepers.

Or babysitters? No, never. There is a very good book about nannies, called *Other People's Children*, and it's very damning. The problem with babysitters and nannies is that if you're working and they quit, or you are forced to fire them, you have to get somebody in there immediately. It's a panic. You can't possibly be too careful who you choose.

Barbara, at this point in your life, how serious were you about doing research? Well, I had been hired at Maryland under the mis-impression that I was a regional economist. The dean called me in and asked, "Why aren't you doing regional economics?" I told him I had no good ideas on the topic. He told me to have lunch with Werner Hirsh to get some ideas. I did, but none of his ideas were appealing. This was during the "war on poverty" programs. I got some research money and set up an institute at Maryland on the study of poverty and discrimination. I also testified in the landmark case against AT&T. Phyllis Wallace edited a book about the case, and I have a chapter in there.

What kind of institutional support did you have for your research? The best thing about Maryland was the free computer usage. I did a big computer simulation model of the US economy. It was a great piece of work, but unfortunately it fell into a black hole.

When you went into economics, it appears that math was the hook? Yes.

But you were not sure where that would lead? Yes, I think that's true. Which is not a good way to conduct a career, I may say. I wasn't plugged in. For example, if you look at my working papers, you'll see that I do not thank anyone.

It's a solo act? That's right. I also don't appear at seminars because I'm not invited. I'm invited to give talks on the books I write, but I'm never invited to participate in seminars in an economics department. Never.

Why do you think that is? People promote themselves. They have friends they call and say, "I have this paper and I want to give it." I'm not into doing that. I should be, but I'm not. I called Franco Modigliani once and told him I wanted to give a talk at MIT on my simulation model. I got an invitation, but grudgingly, and I've never done it again.

So you haven't had collaborators as a researcher in economics? Very few. I collaborated with Robert Bennett at Maryland on this big simulation model, for instance. Also, I've never been able to use students as research assistants. I've done it all myself. But I like computer work. I find it recreational.

In retrospect, if you had to do it over again, would you have chosen economics as a career or would you have done something different? I would have chosen economics as a career, but I would have been much braver about doing empirical work. For example, I do not believe that economics as currently practiced is an empirical science. It has almost nothing to do with real life. Most of what gets published in economic journals comes from someone sitting and thinking – how might a company act, or how might an individual act? That's totally different from finding out. Manipulating data generated by the Census Bureau does not constitute direct empirical work. I wasn't able to do empirical work partly because I wasn't good at finding collaborators. Maybe if I had been at a prestigious place and had the energy to form a group, I could have essentially done anthropological work in economic subjects.

Could you give us an example of why you don't think economics is empirical? Yes. Until about seven or eight years ago, all of the credit card companies charged the same, very high interest rate. It was a huge money bonanza for the companies that issued credit cards. Lawrence Ausubel at Northwestern (now at Maryland) published a paper in the *American Economic Review* (AER) in which he posited that the reason for the high interest rate was that there was no real competition. People, he argued, don't expect to run up their credit balances, so they are unconcerned about the interest rate. Moreover, he argued that there were too many credit card issuers for collusion to occur. Shortly after this paper was published, credit card firms started competing on interest rates. It would be an interesting project to investigate, in a detective-like way, what kept the interest rate up, and what caused the break? Of course, where would you publish something like that? There's no place, really. You would have to do what Vernon Smith did with experimental economics: start your own group, start your own journal, and make a lifetime career out of it. I'm sorry I didn't get to do that. That's a major regret. But I'm not talented at leadership. Sure, I've been the president of quite a few organizations, but in each case, they did the exact opposite of what I suggested. I'm sure the same thing will happen with IAFFE. But in every case, as it turns out, they would have done better if they had done what I had proposed.

Do you think it's easier for women to succeed in economics today than it was for your generation of women? No. It is much more difficult to get an academic job today, and it's infinitely harder to get tenure. You may have more female colleagues, but it's harder to get ahead. Maybe women, in general, are at less of a disadvantage *vis-à-vis* men. However, from the viewpoint of individual women, it's much, much harder.

Have you observed many changes in the profession over time? The profession is remarkably similar to what it was when I was an undergraduate or graduate student. This so-called "science" has gone nowhere. Fred is a biologist, and what has been discovered in biology in the last thirty years is amazing. There's been an explosion of knowledge in biology! The knowledge about genetics is all new. Meanwhile, economists are still teaching marginal cost equals marginal revenue. It's ridiculous!

Barbara, why do you think more women are not attracted to economics? I don't know. Their numbers have never been very high. Moreover, women have not had much success. Look at the *AER*; very few women published in there. I, myself, never publish in it.

Why do you think women in economics have not had much success? Maybe the problem is the exclusion of women from certain social networks that may give them clues about what to do. It may be more mysterious in economics than it is in, say, history or sociology.

Do you think it is institutional? I think it is. Recently, I received a letter from the editor of the *Journal of Economic Perspectives* asking me to write a short article on CSWEP's twenty-fifth anniversary. He assumed that because I had once been a chair of CSWEP, I would have some lovely anecdotes. I wrote back and told him that I'd be glad to write something, but it wasn't going to be something warm and fuzzy like he seemed to want. Instead, I told him I was going to compare the accomplishments of CSWEP with the accomplishment of similar organizations in history, sociology, and psychology. I didn't tell him that I thought the most CSWEP had accomplished was to publish a newsletter, primarily devoted to the biographies of committee members. By contrast, I've talked to historians and it's amazing what they've accomplished. When they began, only 50 percent of the sessions at the meetings of the American Historical Association had both sexes represented. Now it's 95 percent. We've never achieved 20 percent. Likewise, the sociologists send questionnaires to ASA candidates running for office and ask them what they have done for women lately.

You know, Barbara, some feminists have argued that, apart from the institutional problems of the profession, there is also something about the neoclassical paradigm itself that women do not identify with. Thus, women are not attracted to economics. I would reject that.

Why? Because I don't think it's true. I'm as capable of dealing with it as any man, and for years I thought it was the only way to conduct business myself. Why would economics turn women off more than men? I think it turns everybody off. Economics is no less realistic now than it was when we had plenty of majors. My theory about women is that it's their lack of knowledge about how to operate or network within the profession.

Like the connections you had to have to get the job at Maryland? That's right. I was hired by the chair, Dudley Dillard. He had a strategy for getting good faculty. He tried for many years to get a distinguished faculty and in the end he succeeded. He hired people he thought were smart, but had flaws that prevented them from being hired elsewhere. My flaw was that I was a woman; that's how I got the job. Of course, Norton also helped.

How long were you at Maryland? About twenty-five years.

How many other women were on the faculty? They eventually hired Katherine Abraham and Maureen Cropper. Myra Strober was an assistant professor there for a while; that's when we became friends.

When did you go to American University? In 1988. I took Emeritus status at Maryland and became a Distinguished Professor at American. Actually, I had my best student at American – Trudy Renwick. At Maryland, I was mostly shunned by the graduate students.

Why do you think you were shunned? I don't know. I'll give you an example. A very smart graduate student and I were walking on campus and she said to me, "You know, people take your course because it's a gut course."

What did that mean? I assume she meant that I was not a good role model for women economists, and that she resented that. A couple of years later, after she had gotten her degree, I gave a talk at the place where she taught. She changed her mind and became more friendly, because she saw that her colleagues respected me.

Do you think the students perceived you differently as compared to your male colleagues? Yes. After a while I wasn't teaching the standard courses: macro, micro, econometrics, industrial organization, international trade, and so on. They were not orthodox or mainstream subjects, and I suppose some viewed them with disrespect. Robin Maris, who was the chair for a number of years, actually told me my salary was low because of the fields I was working in.

Barbara, how would you describe your evolution as an economist? I've become a lot less respectful of the typical theorizing and econometric models that are published. Most of it is trash.

Why? Let me give you an example. Glenn Loury published a theoretical paper in the *AER* on affirmative action. There were several very complicated diagrams in it that purported to show that under certain assumptions, affirmative action could be harmful to its supposed beneficiaries. The main idea of the paper is this: if a black man is unable to get a job as a truck driver because he is discriminated against, he might become a lawyer instead. But if things changed and truck driving is opened to blacks, he wouldn't become a lawyer. So affirmative action prevents the acquisition of human capital. Loury ignores the possibility that the man turned away from trucking might be unemployed, or might take up a life of crime. Of course it is possible that affirmative action could do more harm than good for other reasons, but you would never know for sure using a complicated diagram. This is an empirical question. Affirmative action may be helpful in most cases, harmful in a few cases, or harmful in many cases; who knows? But it can't be proven by reference to a diagram. Or look at the dollar exchange rate for the yen. It fell for years and years. This is certainly not purchasing power parity. Purchasing power parity never seems to occur, but according to our theory it always occurs.

Barbara, do you consider yourself a feminist economist? Of course I'm a feminist. However, I don't know that everyone would agree that I'm an economist.

What do you mean? I work on social issues; maybe that's not economics. But I've been a feminist since I was perhaps 3 years old. I remember sitting on my stoop in the Bronx and thinking that you had to earn your own money or you were nobody.

Could you tell us a little more about why you're a feminist economist? Again, I'm an economist and I'm also a feminist. If feminist economics is postmodernist blathering, then I'm not a feminist economist. I have a very different idea of what feminist economics should be compared to what I see at the meetings of IAFFE, at the ASSA, and in the journal, *Feminist Economics*. There is a lot of social policy work that needs to be done. Many papers on social policy are written by antifeminist men and women, and they need to be challenged. For example, David Blau and Alison Hagy published a paper on child care in the *Journal of Political Economy* (JPE) in which they purport to show that if you subsidize child care, quality will go down rather than up. They argue that quality and quantity are substitutes. If you lower the price by means of a subsidy, parents will choose quantity over quality, so quality will go down. In other words, if I get a subsidy for child care, I will move my child to a lower-quality day-care center for a longer period of time. This is the equivalent of saying that when beef prices decline, people will switch from steak to hamburger, and consume more pounds than they used to. This type of paper is publicized and used by the right wing to counter efforts to help low-income families with child care expenses. Feminist economists should be publishing and demonstrating the flaws of these types of arguments. But most IAFFE members don't go near such topics. So I'm dissatisfied with so-called feminist economics.

Do you think that feminist economics has "anything" to offer to the profession? It would if we were doing social policy, confronting antifeminist research, and doing work that promotes equality. It really upsets me that the main practical interest of people on FEMECON (the feminist economist discussion list) is to include unpaid work in the GNP. With that and twenty-five cents, you can buy yourself a glass of seltzer; it's useless. It's not wrong, but it is of no practical importance. Yet that is what fires them up. Women need help with resources to raise their children.

In other words, feminist economists are on the wrong track? Yes. Except me, of course [*laughter*].

Can you talk about your basic approach to feminism or feminist theory? I'm somewhat allergic to the word "theory" in this context because too much attention has been given to the French trash, which is purposely murky.

Which French trash? Luce Irigaray, and that kind of stuff. Its content is mostly psychoanalytical and very abstract. I tend to distrust abstractions; they lead people astray. I want to talk about specific, concrete cases. For instance, it's more interesting to talk about sexual harassment in specific cases (like lawyers) than to talk about it in the abstract.

Barbara, could you discuss some of the main themes in your work? I'm obviously very interested in equality for women, so that's a big theme. I'm also interested in eradicating racial injustice; that's another theme. I would say those are the two major themes, except for the macro computer simulation model I did.

Did you integrate your interest in equality into your computer simulation work? No. I don't have a lot of sympathy with those who think of macroeconomics as a field for feminist economics. I don't understand the scope for it. Sure, the design of the unemployment insurance system has both gender and macro aspects to it, and everyone should have access to employment. But to tell you the truth, I've never seen much content to feminist macroeconomics. On the other hand, I can't pretend to have paid a lot of attention to it. When I see a session labeled "feminist macroeconomics," I tend to go in the other direction. I have been told many times that I am an intolerant person. I suppose it's true.

Why the aversion? I think it's going to be a lot of junk.

What advice would you give young women with an interest in economics? Publish in the *Journal of Political Economy.*

Can the kind of social policy work we've been talking about be published in the *JPE*? No, it can't. But there are other things you can publish in it. You can point out the anomalies in economic theory and try to understand them; that's valuable work. There are certainly worse things you can do. My idea of valuable work is definitely a minority view and it may not be correct.

Because you think policy work is important, would you ever advise women to take a policy job rather than an academic job, or maybe start their own policy institute like Heidi Hartmann? I think for Heidi, it is a hard life. I wouldn't recommend that to anyone. Being a professor is a lot easier. There's a lot of liberty. It has great potential for doing what you want, doing interesting things, and meeting interesting people. So I certainly think women ought to aspire to be professors. But to get a job, they must do what they have to do. The problem is, once they have a job, most get keyed into the usual research agenda and they keep on doing it. It becomes a bad habit.

In other words, it's difficult to switch from publishing in the *JPE* to doing work with some social relevance? Yes.

What are some of the policy issues economists should be working on, besides child care issues? I would say the support of single parenthood, divorce issues, child support issues, workplace issues, pay equity, and certainly health care issues. It is also important to work with lawyers on discrimination and other gender issues.

Are there any international comparisons we should be looking at? I published a book comparing the United States and France. It convinced me that we live in a very strange country. Can you imagine a country where millions of people have no access to health care? That's weird, isn't it? Clearly, there's more work to be done before we can change it.

How do we go about changing it? We must become more talented at public relations.

As economists? Anyone who works in the field of social policy. Suzie Helburn and I got foundation money for our book on child care policy. We built $15,000 into the grant to publicize the book. We'll hire a publicist to get on television, the radio, etc. That's what others do and it's not difficult to get this kind of backing. You just have to remember to do it when you're writing a grant.

Can you talk a little about this book? I had an idea for a book that would incorporate the results of Suzie's big study of cost, quality, and outcomes in child care. Our first idea was to provide parental advice. But then we changed to a policy focus.

Who is your audience? People interested in policy. People in the child care industry. I'm particularly hoping to reach the for-profit sector. We hope they will see fit to emulate the behavior of the defense industry which lobbies for appropriations; not for a cheesy version of the product, but for an expensive product. This is not what child care providers are currently doing. They lobby to be free of regulations, which is the opposite of what they should be doing. They should be lobbying for funding that will deliver a quality product. Note the Boeing Corporation; their planes are full of very expensive gadgets. They're not lobbying to produce cheap bombers, they're lobbying to produce expensive bombers.

Is the main focus of the book – how to finance child care? Yes. If you look at child care from birth to age 5, it's a major cost. For single parents who are making from $10,000 to $15,000 a year, high-quality child care (which is more likely to be found in an organized center) is an impossible expense. Helping people with child care is a major way to eliminate deprivation. The needs of poor families with children include the usual poverty budget plus child care. If we give a two-child family both child and health care, which adds up to approximately $14,000 a year, that's a huge financial lift. It's help that doesn't discourage paid work, but assists them to work. It doesn't deter them from marrying. It doesn't keep them home watching television, etc. They're considered useful members of society.

There's no stigma attached to it? Right, and none should be. Although welfare reform was engineered by people with nasty motives, it wouldn't be so bad if we could channel big bucks into government-supported child care.

A question that keeps coming up is – should we be helping stay-at-home moms? Susie and I have talked to the people at Children's Defense Fund who support paid parental leave. I do not. First, it's more expensive than paying for child care because caring for your own child is less efficient in terms of resources. For instance, suppose I'm making $30,000 a year. If I get $25,000 in paid parental leave, that's much more expensive than if I was given $6,000 dollars to put my child in an organized care center or to care for my child at home. But my main problem with parental leave is that it tends to perpetuate the gender caste system whereby women do the child care and men don't. And if women stay home, they are also responsible for all of the domestic work. There is probably no reason why they shouldn't. But it tends to perpetuate a system in which market activity depends on one's gender. Eliminating that system should be the goal of feminism, in my view.

Is there a strategy that you can envision that would make the child care industry less gendered or crowded with women? When you see women crowded in an industry, it's generally not the fault of that industry. It's the result of women's exclusion from other economic activities. It's certainly possible that there are women who enjoy child care, despite the lousy wages, because of the compensating pleasures they receive. If that's the case, then there's nothing to be done or even deplored. But we certainly have not done what we could to eliminate women's exclusion from other activities. Likewise, much of the work by sociologists is filled with stories about women in underdeveloped countries making clothing or athletic shoes, and how oppressed they are. They are oppressed in the sense that they are paid little and work under difficult conditions. But the real reason they are working under these conditions, in my view, is not that their particular employers are nasty. The real reason is that this is their only option, so they have to put up with it. It's the employers who won't hire them who are oppressing them, not the employers who do.

What else are you working on? I'm working on a cartoon book about social security.

You have a cartoonist? Yes.

How do you work with a cartoonist? I have not figured that out yet.

What is your vision for this book? About 100 pages with text and funny cartoons. Here's how it works. I ask him to illustrate something like the following. The advocates of privatized social security want to give retirees freedom to take their nest egg and do what they want with it. Imagine a woman who has been cleaning hotel rooms all her life. She retires and turns in her mop. Along comes her rascally nephew who says, "Auntie, I can double or triple your money for you." She gives him the money and, of course, she's left with nothing. Will we let her live in a cardboard box or bail her out? Either way, it's a social problem. I'll see what the cartoonist produces.

Do you think social security is in crisis? The argument that social security is in danger of bankruptcy, or that we have no chance of ever getting social security payments in the future, is a total misconception. Social security pensions are paid by current taxes. As long as we're willing to pay enough current taxes to cover the benefits, the system will pay benefits. The question is: how large should taxes and benefits be? The idea that the social security fund has been looted, broken into, or used for other purposes, is mistaken. There is also a problem with the idea that we have to start preparing for when the baby boomers retire (in about fifteen years). This argument has enabled the Republicans and the Democrats to raise the social security tax way beyond what is currently needed to pay pensions. Since the Social Security Administration doesn't need the extra money, it ships it to the US Treasury which uses it to finance the defense budget. In exchange, the social security system gets bonds – bonds which will never be redeemed, at least in my view. Politics will not allow it. This makes the tax system more regressive. Currently, a majority of government spending is financed through payroll taxes, but there is a maximum tax. We don't have to pay a payroll tax on earnings above something like $60,000 which is maximally regressive. It's a fake remedy to a problem that doesn't exist.

It's a shell game? Right. When Clinton says he's going to save the social security system, he's playing on the ignorance of people who think it's in danger, and he's pretending to do something when he's not, except maybe protecting the Treasury from pork-barrel spending.

But why is this myth so widely embraced? It's spread by people who have an interest in spreading it. The alleged remedy is to shift to a system of private accounts, which will profit the money managers on Wall Street. Many Democrats and Republicans have been pushing this crisis business. Pete Peterson is one, Senator Kerrey of Nebraska is another. What their motives are, I don't know. Maybe they misunderstand the situation, or maybe they are in the pay of Wall Street.

You are not denying that there is a problem? No, there is a problem: namely, the size of the baby boom generation of retirees. We can't avoid that burden because the bread retirees will eat must be baked. But it can't be baked thirty years ahead of time. When I retire my living expenses will come from selling my stocks or drawing money out of my savings account, but I will eat bread that is baked by the current generation of bakers. Part of the national product has to be assigned to retirees and diverted from currently employed workers no matter what the form of financing.

But the argument is that we need to invest today for retirees. What does investment do? It gives retirees a claim to the ownership of stocks, which they can sell when they retire and purchase freshly baked bread. This is replaced by the claim on the country's conscience, represented by social security. We can meet the latter claim by raising the social security tax when present taxes fail to provide enough to pay retirees a decent pension. Either way, it will mean a diversion of bread to people who are not working. The economists who favor prepaying and privatizing believe it will result in more investment, and that additional investment will enlarge the economy.

They, of course, assume that the economy will continue to grow. That's right. Currently, the rise in the social security tax has not increased investment because it's financing the defense budget. But if, for example, we started reducing the national debt and bought bonds from the general public, this might help social security in the future. It would reduce the tax burden by paying interest on the debt, lower interest rates, and maybe even improve investment. But there are macroeconomic management issues here. If we start paying off the debt, we might experience insufficient aggregate demand. This has happened in the past, and can happen again in the form of long recessions. There are certainly better ways to save social security. We can save some of the benefits, increase taxes, and make taxes less regressive. That's what we should be doing. Another interesting proposal is to reduce spousal benefits. But if we don't pay men higher salaries because they have spouses, why should we pay men with spouses higher pensions?

Can you talk a little bit about welfare reform? The incidence of single motherhood is up to 30 percent now, and the poverty rate among children is around 22 percent. Clearly, this is an intolerable situation which we haven't addressed. What does it say about a country if 22 percent or more of its citizens experience "nightmare childhoods?" Having a "nightmare childhood" certainly does not improve "character." We have to think about ways to support reproduction since the old-fashioned way to support it – marriage – is breaking down. It's a feminist concern because the burden of the breakdown has fallen on women. Women must either support families alone or collect welfare, both terrible options. Welfare is extremely demeaning and does not provide enough to live decently. The problem is that men have often escaped this burden by refusing to get married. One thing that has to be fixed is the child support system. We have to make absent parents pay child support.

In your view, what would a decent welfare system look like? I happen to think that everyone should have paid work. But obviously, there are exceptions: people with disabilities or people with disabled children. In such cases generous provisions should be made for them. However, any time you have generous provisions – waste, fraud, and abuse follow like the night, the day. Nevertheless, these people should receive assistance. Everyone else ought to have access to a paid job. Child care and elder care ought to be handled in the market with subsidies.

Could you share your ideas about the current debate over affirmative action? The opponents argue that it is unjust to pay attention to people's race and gender when making decisions. This is totally hypocritical. The critics of affirmative action have no objection at all when a dumb soccer player with a low SAT score is admitted to Yale ahead of more qualified people with higher scores. According to this reasoning, it's permissible to use soccer ability as an admittance criterion, but not race. Likewise, they do not object to special admissions criteria for children of alumni. Of course, there are reasons for all these exceptions to affirmative action. But the question is: which one is more justified – the one that improves the soccer team or the one that will give a black kid a chance at obtaining an elite job? My own view is that the Civil Rights Act represents an attempt to reverse racial discrimination and to

71

eliminate the advantages of white men who have benefited because of their race and sex. The intent was (and is) to make sure that a diverse group of people are hired and promoted. To do that, race and sex have to be recognized. Otherwise we will not eliminate racism and sexism; it's very persistent.

How do you counter the argument that affirmative action is a quota system? I'm one of the few people who does not deny it. Sometimes we need to do the right thing, and that may have disadvantages. But I would argue that the advantages of quotas outweigh the disadvantages.

One last question. Reflecting back on your career, what would you say is your major contribution to the profession? How would you like to be remembered? I think my best contribution is my book, *The Economic Emergence of Women*, which is now out of print.

Why that particular book? Because it touches on subjects that are close to my heart. St Martins Press wants to publish a new edition.

4

ALICE MITCHELL RIVLIN

The fact that more women are in public life – in Congress, in
positions of authority in various parts of government – has made a
dramatic difference. ... But it does surprise me that more women
are not in economics because it deals with an interesting set of
issues and it's a good perspective on public policy as well.

(Alice Rivlin, 1998)

At age 13, Alice watched as her mother testified before the Foreign Relations
Committee on Capitol Hill. Some thirty years later she became the Founding Director
of the Congressional Budget Office, and some fifty years later she became the Vice-
Chair of the Federal Reserve System. Her other accomplishments are no less
impressive. She is the former Assistant Secretary for Planning and Evaluation, US
Department of Health, Education, and Welfare; former Deputy Director and Director of
the White House Office of Management and Budget; former Director of Economic
Studies, Brookings Institution; and former President of the American Economic Assoc-
iation. She is the author of several books and numerous publications, the recipient of a
MacArthur Foundation Fellowship, and she has taught at the Kennedy School of
Government at Harvard University and at George Mason University as the Hirst
Professor of Public Policy. She is currently the Chair of the District of Columbia
Financial Management Assistance Authority and the Adeline M. and Alfred I. Johnson
Chair in Urban and Metropolitan Policy at the Brookings Institution. She received her
BA from Bryn Mawr College (1952), an MA (1955) and PhD (1958) from Radcliffe
College, Harvard University.

Alice was able to squeeze us into her incredibly busy schedule on two separate days
while she was serving as Vice-Chair of the Federal Reserve. We spoke in her office with
amazingly little interruption. After an hour of conversation, however, she noted that
she had to prepare a speech for that afternoon. We made plans to meet again two days
later. Again, we only had an hour, which explains why our conversation is a bit shorter
than the others in this collection. Nevertheless, the following narrative reflects the
quality of the time we shared together in February of 1998.

Plate 4 Counterclockwise from top left: Alice Rivlin with Vice-President Al Gore and President Clinton (1996); with granddaughter Laela Jones (2000); hiking in the Shenandoah Mountains (2000); marriage to Sidney Winter (1989); with children, Catherine and Allan (1962); in race (1984); main portrait as Director of the Congressional Budget Office (1975).

Let's begin with your family genealogy. What can you tell us about your background? My ancestors were mostly from England, especially Cornwall. I grew up in Bloomington, Indiana, where my father was a Professor of Physics at Indiana University. His father was a professor of astronomy at the University of Virginia. From that side of the family, I have a scientific, technical, and academic background. My mother's father was a lawyer. He died when she was quite young. Her grandfather was a banker. She grew up in Pasadena, California. My father did his graduate work at the California Institute of Technology (Caltech) in Pasadena, which is how my parents met. They were married in 1926 and went to Germany for a few years – that's what young scientists did in the 1920s. Then he got a postdoctoral fellowship at the Bartol Research Institute in Philadelphia. I was born that year. My parents were in Philadelphia for two years; then they moved to New York where my father was a professor at New York University. In 1938, we moved to Bloomington, Indiana. Recruiting my father was part of an effort by Indiana University to strengthen science by attracting a new generation of young scientists to the university. Indiana had a vigorous new president, Herman Wells, who was determined to put Indiana on the map in science. He recruited my father, who was in his 30s, to help build a modern physics department.

My mother was very active in public affairs and probably responsible for my interest in public policy. She didn't have a paid job, but she worked very actively in the League of Women Voters. She was a national officer in the League when I was a teenager. We were in Washington, DC, because my father's work during World War II brought us here. The first time I ever went to Capitol Hill was with my mother when she testified before the Foreign Relations Committee. I was about 13 then. She was supporting postwar aid for the reconstruction of Europe. Some isolationist senators gave her a hard time.

Did your mother attend college? No. She never went to college. Most women in her generation did not. She was a self-educated woman.

And your siblings? My sister was younger than I. She died about five years ago. She had, in some ways, a similar career. She was in the foreign service and then transferred to the Peace Corps, and then to the Agency for International Development. She worked as the mission director for AID in India and later in Bangladesh. She had a Master's degree in law and diplomacy from Tufts University.

In the early years of your education, do you recall anyone who might have influenced your thinking? I had some very good teachers. My high school career was affected by World War II. I started high school here in Washington, DC. I went to the Madeira School, which is a good private school for girls. It was a real shocker for a public school girl from a small town in Indiana, but it was intensive and challenging. I had a lot of excellent teachers at Madeira. After this very demanding private school, I went back to public school. I had a good experience there for a year, but I had taken everything that they offered so I had either to go on to college or go back to the private school. I did the latter –

went back to Madeira and graduated. That put me on the eastern track. That is, all my friends from high school went to eastern colleges.

Did you always know that you would go to college? Yes, I grew up in a university environment. My mother was especially supportive, perhaps because she didn't go to college. I think she thought she should have. I remember an episode when I was in graduate school which I thought was kind of cute. At Harvard, you received an automatic Master's degree on the way to a PhD, but in order to get the actual degree you had to pay a fee. I didn't want to bother with it. But my mother said, "Here's the $50. You make sure you have that degree." [*Laughter*]

I chose Bryn Mawr College. After my freshman year at Bryn Mawr, I spent the summer (1949) at home in Bloomington, Indiana. I couldn't find a job, so I decided to take a couple of courses in summer school. I had thought I was a history major, but as luck would have it, I happened into an economics course with a very excellent professor. He was terrific; he turned everybody on to economics. That is what got me interested in economics. So I switched my major when I went back to Bryn Mawr.

Do you recall his name? His name was Rubin Zubrow. He recently died. Later, he had a distinguished career at the University of Colorado, and we kept in touch over a long period of time. He was very proud of me.

That's wonderful!

So after the summer at Indiana, you went back to Bryn Mawr? Yes, and I majored in economics.

Did you have any mentors? It was a very small department. There were only three or four professors. The best-known professor was Mildred Northrop, who was chair of the department. She encouraged me to go to graduate school, although I didn't go immediately. I went to Europe for a year – sort of unexpectedly. I had worked here in Washington, DC, as an intern in the summer between my junior and senior years in college for an agency that ran the Marshall Plan. I enjoyed it a lot and they asked me to come back. This was the summer of 1952, when Eisenhower was running for president. It was the end of the Marshall Plan and Congress was downsizing the agency. Before I came back from Europe I got a letter from my boss in Washington saying that Congress had abolished my job. He suggested that I contact his colleague in the Paris office. I did, and they hired me. I then spent that year in France and the following summer in Germany. It was while I was there that I decided I needed to go to graduate school. I then came back to the United States in the fall of 1953.

Where did you work in Germany? I didn't work there. I just spent the summer there learning German and sightseeing. It was there that I met Lewis Rivlin. He was in the navy – stationed at Heidelberg. He stayed in Germany and came back later – after me. We didn't get married until 1955.

You came back for graduate school? What was that like? Harvard was a very intense place. There were very few women. I think I got a good education there, but I didn't particularly enjoy it. It was hard. It was strange being female in a basically male place. It was a very large department – forty or more students in the first-year PhD class.

Did you apply to other programs besides Harvard? Originally I had applied to the Graduate School of Public Administration (now the Kennedy School of Government) because I was already interested in public policy. However, they rejected my application on the grounds that a woman of marriageable age was a "poor risk." I then decided to apply to the economics department which was just beginning to allow women to obtain teaching fellowships and tutoring positions. I was accepted, and taught mixed classes. But I was assigned to tutor only women. One decided that she wanted to write an honors thesis on the Latin American labor movement – not my area of expertise – but the expertise of one of my male colleagues. He agreed to switch students. I would tutor a young man; he would advise my young woman. However, the senior tutor for the boys refused to agree to the switch on the grounds that being tutored by a woman would make a male student feel like a second-class citizen. Imagine, someone would actually say that!

In retrospect, I find it amazing that the women were not outraged. But I think we felt lucky to be there at all. Harvard was like a male game to outwit. For example, one of the university libraries did not allow women to check out books, not even through interlibrary loan. If I needed a book, I asked my male friend to get it for me. I don't remember getting that upset about it!

You mentioned a male friend. Did you have an intellectual or social life with the other graduate students? Oh, yes. The first year I wasn't married. Lewis was in Germany, so I dated other people.

When did you have your children? My daughter was born in March of 1957, when I was still in graduate school. I started in the fall of 1953. I took the comprehensives in the spring of 1955 and then we got married. I was a teaching assistant that year and the next. My husband was in law school. He finished in 1957 and we came to Washington, DC. I hadn't finished my dissertation yet, but I was working on it.

At this point in your career, was it difficult having a child to take care of? It was complicated, but I was very lucky. The spring semester, when my daughter was born, I didn't teach. I took that semester off. But when we found we were coming to Washington, I was panicked. I was leaving my thesis advisor, and I wanted to get a bunch of things finished before I left. So I took my baby to my mother's for a couple of weeks, came back, and worked very intensively. I finished the empirical work that I needed to get done. I was lucky to get a dissertation fellowship at the Brookings Institution. They actually paid me to finish my dissertation.

What was your dissertation topic? It was in demography. I was working with Professor Guy Orcutt on a big simulation model of the US economy. I did the demographic part of the model. It was part of a bigger project, so I had to finish on time. I had started another dissertation on the impact of social security on savings; later Marty Feldstein worked on that. I was kind of floundering on how to do it when Guy Orcutt asked me if I'd like to be part of this bigger project, and it seemed like a good idea.

Who were some of your other professors at Harvard? Carl Kaysen and Ed Mason. I was in Alvin Hansen's last class. He and John Williams taught a joint seminar on fiscal and monetary policy. John Kenneth Galbraith was teaching then. I didn't take his class, but he was a major presence in the department. So was Jim Duesenberry. Seymour Harris was chairman of the department.

Was there a particular course that greatly influenced your thinking? I liked the quantitative methods course that Guy Orcutt taught. I liked a whole lot of different things. Kaysen taught a very interesting course on industrial organization. The Hansen–Williams seminar was very good. Edward Chamberlain taught the introduction to theory. He was quite elderly by then, and not an especially good teacher. Wassily Leontief taught the second theory course and that was more lively. Alexander Gerschenkron taught economic history. I learned a lot from him.

And you had a dissertation fellowship at the Brookings Institution? Yes, that worked out very well. I finished the dissertation that year (1957–8), then they asked me to stay on the staff. That was unusual, because they didn't want to use the fellowships as a recruiting device. What happened was that Bob Calkins, who was the president of Brookings, was interested in working on the economics of higher education. The original idea was that I would work with him on a book. Then he got very busy, so I wrote the book. He wasn't involved at all. That was lucky, because I got two books out very quickly. The book on higher education was published in 1961. Simultaneously, the work I had done with Guy Orcutt and a couple of other people was also published. There were some articles published as well, so I got off to a good start. I stayed at Brookings for several years.

Did you have any particular mentors at Brookings? Yes, Joe Pechman. He took me under his wing and taught me how to do policy research. He also mentored many other young men and women. He considered it an important part of his job. But maybe because he had two daughters, I thought he was particularly good at mentoring young women scholars.

After you left Brookings, what did you do? Right after the higher education book came out, I took a leave for about a year and did two things at once. I worked at the Advisory Commission on Intergovernmental Relations and did a study on state taxes with Selma Muskin. That turned out to be a very good thing. We evolved "the representative tax system," which is a way of estimating the comparative tax capacity of states by applying an average tax system to their various tax bases. The methodology became a standard way of estimating comparative tax capacity. The study got me interested in state government issues, which became one theme of my later work. Working with Selma was a good experience. She was older than I, and a very intelligent and interesting person.

Simultaneously, I spent some time on Capitol Hill. I got a phone call one day (right after the book on higher education came out) from Adam Clayton

Powell – the legendary figure who was the chairman of the House Education and Labor Committee. He said that they were putting together a select committee on higher education and asked if I could help them out. So I worked on this part-time. That turned out to be very interesting and it gave me my first exposure to the Hill. Powell was engaged in a power contest with Edith Green, who was then chairman of the higher education subcommittee. He was essentially going around her to create this "select subcommittee." It was composed of junior congressmen – all in their second term – and the chair was John Brademas, an Indiana congressman who later was prominent in the Democratic leadership. One of the other Democrats was Bob Giaimo from Connecticut who was later chairman of the Budget Committee when I was at the Congressional Budget Office. One of the Republicans was Al Quie who later became the governor of Minnesota. It was a very talented group. I was just a consultant to the committee. We held some hearings and wrote a report.

I realized then that I really enjoyed working on the Hill. But I also realized that I couldn't do it right then. The hours were too long and too erratic. You had to work late into the evening. I had little kids then, and I couldn't do that.

How old were they? My daughter was born in 1957 and my older son in 1959. We didn't have another one until 1963. The Hill experience was 1961–2. They were toddlers (2 and 4 years of age), and I had to get home for dinner. At the time, I did think, "This is an awful lot of fun, and I would really like to work on the Hill again, but not with little children." So I filed that away and didn't get back to it for thirteen years.

Did you ever have an academic post? No. In those days, academia was essentially closed to women, except for women's colleges. In the early 1960s, I did think it would be interesting to be at a university, and also that it might fit better with my schedule (the kids were in school) because you can take the summer off. Or so I thought. I had a colleague at Brookings who was teaching at the University of Maryland. The economics department invited me to do a seminar, and it went very well. They told me there was an opening for an assistant professor, so I talked to the head of the economics department. He said, "It was a terrific seminar, you are the best qualified person that has come along for this job, and I wish we could hire you. However the Dean says we can't consider a woman for this job." It was that overt! He said how sorry he was. I said how sorry I was, and that was the end of it. The economics department was in the Business School, and the dean just said, "No women!" That was the early 1960s, so change was imminent. About two or three years later, the dean retired and they hired Peggy Richmond. That was the beginning of the end of gender discrimination. But in the early 1960s, there weren't many options for someone in academia.

So you never experienced the tenure process? No, Brookings was my academic link. I went back to Brookings after the year off and stayed there until I went to the Department of Health, Education, and Welfare. I was a visiting professor much later at the Kennedy School of Government in 1988. Then I taught at George Mason University for a year just before I went into the Clinton administration in 1993.

How would you compare your academic and non-academic positions? It depends on what you mean by non-academic. Brookings, where I worked for about half of my career, is very much like a university without students. The only students were the ones that, like myself, came on a dissertation fellowship. Brookings had an academic research atmosphere, but was more policy-oriented than a university. I was always interested in policy analysis so the Brookings Institution was a natural place for me.

Have you seen any changes in the economics profession over the years? I think the economics profession, certainly in its academic aspects, is much more theoretical, much more mathematical, and much less policy-oriented. The policy folks in academia now are less likely to be in an economics department. Instead, they are in public policy schools like the Kennedy School at Harvard. But those didn't exist in the 1950s and 1960s. There were schools of public administration, but public policy as a separate field didn't exist.

Compared to your experience, do you think it is easier or more difficult for women to succeed in economics today? I don't think it is that difficult today, certainly not in government or in academia. The mystery is why more women are not attracted to economics. Of course, there are a lot of options for women now that weren't there before. There's law, medicine, and all of the fields that were closed to women before. Many women who might be attracted to economics probably get an MBA now. But I still think it is a mystery why more women don't go into economics. Part of it may be the math-phobia thing. On the other hand, math and the sciences themselves are apparently attracting more women.

What do you think of the claim by feminists that it is due to the increasing irrelevancy of economics to women's lives; the failure to address social issues? This goes back to the fact that economics is not very policy-driven anymore. If you were interested in mathematical things, then why not be a mathematician?

Do you think it is important for women to become economists? Do you think they can make a difference in the discipline? I do think there are some differences between men and women in the way they approach problems and in the way they operate in interpersonal relationships. I've seen this on corporate boards, in the office, etc. Women are more likely to seek a solution or a compromise; they are less confrontational. Women can be quite constructive because they are less concerned about winning and more concerned about working together and getting the problem solved. I think that is a valid generalization, although there are plenty of exceptions. When there are few women in a situation, such as sitting on a corporate board, it will often be the women who move the ball forward. They cut off the debate and posturing and say, "Okay, what are we going to do here?" The fact that more women are in public life – in Congress, in positions of authority in various parts of the government – has made a dramatic difference. But it does surprise me that more women are not in economics because it deals with an interesting set of issues and it's a good perspective on public policy as well. Actually, I think, a PhD in economics is likely to give you a more disciplined and useful way of thinking about policy than a degree in public policy.

Are you familiar with the new journal *Feminist Economics*? Not really, but I have read some of the feminist literature in economics. I have some concerns that some talented women economists are devoting themselves to a fringe field. It is not where, I think, the main action is. I think the interesting things are the policy issues – what's happening to productivity, why is the economy working this way, what is happening to international trade – that's where I see the cutting edge in economics.

So what specifically should feminist economists be focused on? I guess I'm the wrong person to answer that question.

How would you describe yourself as an economist, specifically your theoretical perspective? I think I'm a middle-of-the-road, eclectic economist. I'm not associated with any defined school of thought.

Would you be comfortable being called a Keynesian? I don't really know what that means anymore. It isn't very useful. A lot of reporters want to put you in some niche. They generally think a "Keynesian" is someone who believes in big deficits or at least in using the budget as a countercyclical tool. Since I believe a budget surplus is the appropriate fiscal policy for the United States – because of the need to increase national saving as the population ages – and do not believe the budget is as useful as monetary policy to counteract the cycle, I don't fit the reporters' "Keynesian" stereotype very well.

In any case, I didn't start as a macro person. I started on microeconomic problems working on public policy problems like education, health, and welfare. That was my interest for a long time. I got into macroeconomic policy positions from the budget end. When I went to the Congressional Budget Office (CBO), I went as a "budgeteer" or program analyst. The budget was both a micro and macro problem. Some thought I was a curious choice for CBO director because I was not a macroeconomist.

Is there a major theme that runs throughout your work? As far as themes go, I think there are clearly strong ones. I've worked a lot on the relationship between federal and state governments, and I have some pretty strong views on that. I've also worked on social policy issues that intersect with the budget's role, such as health care financing, social security, and welfare reform.

Do you agree with the argument that social security constitutes a major problem in this country? Actually, I don't think social security is a major problem. The social security system works remarkably well. Looking forward, we will have a lot more retirees. Social security needs some adjustment right now, which can be done either by increasing the revenue or by lowering the benefits. We don't have to change it very much if we do it soon enough to put it back on a solvent track for the future Basically, what is often thought of as the social security problem – how are we going to fund the baby boom generation when they retire? – is not really a funding problem. It is a growth problem. We are headed for a society where you have more retirees relative to workers, hence the workers have to be a lot more productive in order to support the retirees and not have their standard of living fall. The question is: how do we increase productivity and how do we lengthen productive working lives? If people are going to live into their 90s, retiring at 65 or at 55 doesn't make a lot of sense. There are two pieces to this. One question is: how do we get more savings and investment to improve the productivity of the labor force (which means human investment – increasing skills)? The other question is: how do we design jobs or careers so that people can be productive longer? It doesn't necessarily mean that you stay in the same job – particularly, for blue-collar workers. You can't do the same kind of physical labor at 70 that you performed at 40. We are indeed seeing people, especially men, retiring earlier than they used to. That trend needs to be reversed. But it has to be reversed sensibly so that people are making a productive contribution in something they can do for a prolonged period.

What are your thoughts about current health care problems? I was at the Office of Management and Budget (OMB) at the time when the Clinton health care plan was developed. I was very much involved. The economic team preferred a more gradual approach to health care. In hindsight we were right. But I am afraid the window of opportunity – the opportunity to have a well-articulated approach to health care and change the whole national health care system at once – may have closed. The opportunity may not have been there even in 1993. We need to operate on the margins to improve the health care system incrementally. This may not be all that bad. We do have a large number of people who don't have health insurance and that number is still growing. So it's a serious problem. People who don't have health insurance are mostly young and many are children. At the other end, health care for older people is not a problem of insurance; medicare and other programs cover most people. It's a problem of cost; the cost of medical care at older ages. The cost will only get higher and higher, and that's not reversible. There are more and more remarkable things that can be done (such as my recent hip replacement surgery), but they are costly. We don't really have a national fix on how we are going to deal with the increasing costs of health care for older people. There are certainly reforms that can be made in medicare, but the basic problem is that caring for the elderly is going to get more and more expensive. To what extent do we want to ration health care? We don't have a serious answer to that.

Indeed, the US seems to be having trouble dealing with rising health care costs. Other advanced countries are having the same problem. Japan and Germany, for instance, face a worse demographic situation. They have a higher proportion of elderly people and similarly rising health costs.

How would you approach, for instance, the problem of child or elder care in this country? As you know, I wrote a book, *Caring for the Disabled Elderly*, with

Joshua Weiner on long-term care for the frail elderly. That's a major piece of what we were just talking about: health care for the elderly. Medicaid is taking up most of the cost of long-term care for people who are in the lower half of the income distribution. That seems to be working reasonably well for the interim. But a lot of older people are in dismal nursing homes. They are not really where you want to have your mother or want to be yourself. Yet, raising the standards to make them better nursing homes is very expensive. We have to figure out how to pay for it as well as how to keep people active longer.

Now I would like to talk about your more recent work. Can you tell me what it was like at the Congressional Budget Office? Oh, the CBO was terrific. That was a wonderful experience because hardly anybody gets to start a new public agency. The CBO was a brand new thing; we started it in 1975. Congress had passed the Budget Reform Act in 1974, but they didn't have a clear idea what they wanted the CBO to be. There is a short section in the law calling for the creation of a budget office; Congress wanted some kind of a counterpart to the Office of Management and Budget (OMB). They knew they wanted a group of analytical "budgeteers" on their side of the table to redress the balance with the administration, but they didn't have a clear idea of what they wanted these people to do. In fact, they had a couple of different ideas. The House had a rather technical view of what the CBO should do: that it should consist of number-cruncher types, and produce estimates and budget projections, and things like that. The Senate had a more analytical perspective. They wanted someone to do policy analysis; to figure out how to make programs work better. In fact they needed both. I was the candidate of the Senate. At the beginning, I had to deal with this serious tension between the House and the Senate. I was suspect on the House side because I had been the Senate's candidate and had a more analytical policy point of view than a number-crunching point of view. It was very interesting. In fact, somebody has done a Harvard case on the beginnings of the CBO.

It sounds exciting! Yeah, I'm very proud of that piece of my career. It was the longest job I've had; I was Director of CBO for more than eight years. I think we made the CBO into a very substantial and important institution on the Hill – a respected institution. That was not obvious to begin with. We recruited some very good people and we did good work. But we were under fire a lot, both from people who saw the CBO as a threat and from the various political forces on the Hill.

You, of course, also worked for the Clinton administration. What was that experience like? I liked the OMB a lot. I came in as deputy director under Leon Panetta and succeeded him as director after a little more than a year, when he went to the White House to become Chief of Staff. It was a period of very successful fiscal policy. After the election of 1992, the Clinton administration gave very high priority to getting the economy going and the budget deficit down. The economic team, of which I was a part, began meeting in Little Rock (Arkansas) before the President was inaugurated. The meetings focused on –

what should the Clinton budget plan be? This process of putting together the first Clinton budget was one of the most fascinating experiences I've ever had. It was really intense and interactive; we spent hours in meetings with the President. It was very much a team effort. There was a good deal of uncertainty about what we ought to do. The budget deficit at that moment was almost $300 billion. It was $290 billion in fiscal year 1992 and it was headed up. We had discussions about what was a reasonable goal. Could we cut it in half? We actually did decide that was a feasible goal: to get the deficit down to $145 billion in four years. There was no magic about that number, it just happened to be half of 290. Some thought that was too ambitious; that we might not make it. They thought we should cut the deficit in half as a percent of GDP, which would have been a little less ambitious. There were some on the political team (not on the economic team) who felt the emphasis on balancing the budget was a mistake. It was not obvious, yet, that the economy was fully recovered from the recession. At the end of 1992 and the beginning of 1993, people were worried about a "double-dip" recession – about the economy sliding back into recession again without fully recovering from the dip in 1990–1. Cutting the deficit by a substantial amount seemed risky. The economic team was balancing the positive potential of bringing interest rates down and jump-starting investment against the possibility that we might cut the deficit too much and retard growth in consumption. Essentially, the administration gambled and won. But at the beginning we were hedging our bets. We had the so-called "stimulus package." The idea was to bring forward into the summer of 1993 some of the spending increases that the budget had called for, such as investment in education and so forth. The point was to lower the risk of tanking the economy with overvigorous net fiscal reductions.

However, Congress didn't buy this stimulus package, and in retrospect they were right. We didn't need it. But that wasn't obvious at the time. The economy wasn't growing very fast, and there was a rationale for being a little more gradual on the expenditure cuts and tax increases. But the budget package worked. Remember, it only passed by one vote in each house. There were lots of predictions that the budget package would be a disaster; that it would throw the economy into recession. None of that happened.

The other tense moment, though, was after the Democrats lost control of Congress in the election of 1994. There was a lot of dissension within the Clinton administration about what to do next. Some felt that the 1994 election was in retaliation for the budget deficit reduction and that we should be cautious going forward. I did not agree with that. I thought we should vigorously pursue deficit reduction. The President was on the fence for quite a while. Indeed, we had a long, difficult set of negotiations with Congress in which the administration was reluctant to get committed to balancing the budget over five years as Congress wanted. Eventually, the President decided that was the right thing to do and it worked out better than either side had hoped.

Was it a natural progression for you to work at the Federal Reserve after that? Oh, no. It wasn't even my idea. It solved a problem for the President.

Alan Greenspan's term was expiring and Alan Blinder, who was Vice-Chair of the Fed's Board of Governors, didn't want to be reappointed. There was also another vacancy. The administration wanted to put together a slate of nominees so they could reappoint Greenspan and appoint two Democrats to the other two slots. I think my name was put forward because I had good relations with Greenspan and they thought I would be easily confirmed by the Senate. This was in 1996, which was an election year, and the relations between Congress and the administration weren't very good. The administration wanted to get this package up to Congress and passed quickly. They thought that I would strengthen the package and help get confirmation. It didn't work terribly well; there was still a long, bitter battle over confirmation. It wasn't really over me. Congress wanted to make some points about the budget, so the confirmation dragged out for quite a long time (from February to June).

How did you feel about it? It didn't matter much to me. I was working hard at the OMB at the time and was not terribly anxious to leave. But I was very pleasantly surprised at how much I enjoyed the Fed. I didn't really know what to expect. It was a leap!

What do you like most about working at the Fed? I enjoy learning new things. This is a whole new world. I haven't ever been involved with banking as such. I knew, of course, something about monetary policy from my other macroeconomic experience, but I really hadn't focused on the other things that the Federal Reserve does. For example, the Fed does bank regulation which we share with other agencies. Bank regulation currently involves a very interesting set of issues. The challenge involves adapting to the changes that are going on in the banking system itself, such as the consolidation of the banking industry and the disappearance of the boundaries between banking, securities, and insurance. The various financial services are becoming more and more intertwined and international. Bank regulators have to anticipate what the financial services sector, internationally and nationally, is going to look like in the next few years and what role regulators, including the Federal Reserve, will play.

Another Fed challenge is the payments system, which was something I had never focused on before coming here. The Federal Reserve plays a major role in the payments system including some fairly nitty-gritty things like clearing checks. We compete in the check-clearing market with other major banks and check-clearers. I just chaired a committee here that spent about a year looking at the role of the Federal Reserve in the payments system, particularly the retail payments system; that is, smaller dollar payments that go by check or wire transfer. We considered the possibility of the Federal Reserve getting out of this market and leaving retail payments processing to the private market. We decided that would not make sense. The Fed differentially serves small banks in remote locations. The committee spent some time moving around the country conducting payment-system forums, talking to a lot of different participants. We

decided that, in the interest of these smaller banks in the more remote locations, the Fed should stay in the check-clearing business and electronic
transfers. But we also found that there is a lot of uncertainty and anxiety about
the electronic payments methods of the future. The Federal Reserve will play a
more active role in working with the other participants in the payments system.
It can provide leadership in efforts to improve the payments system of the
future, but not necessarily have an operational role. It can facilitate and work
with the industry to make sure the payments system works, and to see when it is
necessary to set standards or to change the legal framework.

For example, it's quite clear when you write a check what your legal rights
are. If someone says you haven't paid the bill, you can produce the canceled
check. The evidence is not so clear with electronic transfers. So there are
certainly a lot of challenges ahead.

**Did your committee address international issues such as the increased
mobility of financial capital in the context of the current Asian crisis?** There is
clearly an enormous increase in the volume and rapidity of international capital
flows. We have always had bank crises and currency crises, but the fact that the
flows are so large means they can have more serious consequences. For instance,
the flows of international capital into Asia over a long period were very large.
When the flows reversed the impact was enormous. Certainly, the slowdown in
Asia affects our exports and the decline in Asian currency values makes it more
difficult for us to compete in certain markets. Therefore, the Asian crisis has
had a contractionary effect on the US economy. On the other hand, the US is
growing very strongly right now so we can absorb a considerable reduction in
our growth without sliding into recession. But it's a very uncertain situation at
the moment. It looks as though the worst is over in terms of the currency crisis,
except possibly for Indonesia, but the rebuilding of the Asian economies is
going to take a long time.

**How would you compare your job at the Fed with your job at the CBO? You
talked about what a wonderful experience it was to start the CBO. Is there something at the Fed that has peaked your interest as well?** I enjoy the fact that the
Federal Reserve is so regional. The regional banks play an important part in
the Federal Reserve System and are represented on the open market committee.
Interacting with the regional banks is part of the interest in the job. It gives me
a feeling of being in touch with the whole economy. When I was at the OMB
we used all the same economic statistics, but I didn't have the sense of being
connected to what's going on in Minneapolis or Dallas or San Francisco. The
boards of the regional banks consist of business, consumer, and agricultural
people from the region. There are also advisory committees to regional banks,
and to the board of governors as well. The governors interact with a very wide
range of people with different perspectives, and you get an illusion, at least, that
you're in touch with the economy all over the country.

Clearly, the Asian crisis is a concern at the San Francisco Fed? That's right,
they are more worried about the impact on their region.

What are your plans for the future? I'll be here a while. I'm 67, so I haven't thought about what to do next. I'm going to enjoy this job, do it well, and see what happens next.

Do you have grandchildren? Yes, I have three.

Are they all nearby? No. My daughter has two boys, but they live in California. My older son lives here, and he has a little girl. My younger son isn't married. He lives in Washington, DC, too.

And they all have careers? Yes, my daughter is a lawyer in San Francisco. She works for the Attorney-General of California. My older son is a public opinion expert. My younger son is in communications. He runs a public policy center for the Annenberg School of Communications at the University of Pennsylvania, which is where he got a Master's degree. The center is interested in public policy in communications: how the media covers health care and those kinds of questions.

And your husband? My husband is a professor at the Wharton School at the University of Pennsylvania. He is an economist as well (Sidney Winter). He has two sons from a previous marriage and one grandchild. That makes for quite a large family. I was divorced in 1977, and we got married in 1989.

We have time for one last question. What do you think are some of the crucial policy issues that economists should be focused on right now? From where I sit right now, I think the most interesting question is productivity. We don't really understand very much about what's going on with productivity and how best to increase it. Also the whole question of how to prevent and manage international crises.

From the perspective of a labor economist, what should be our focus? We don't really know a lot about how labor markets work. There has been a lot of speculation about why our tight labor markets haven't produced greater wage increases. One hypothesis is that workers are insecure, so they don't bargain as hard and they are less likely to be in unions than they used to be. Another hypothesis is that employers bargain harder because they are in a more competitive world environment so it is important to them to hold their costs down. But we don't seem to understand how employers or workers react to changes in the labor market very well.

One feature of the current good economy in the US is that regional disparities have declined. We don't have whole regions that are lagging behind as much as we used to. Are we getting more labor mobility or capital mobility? Does the knowledge industry mean that it's easier for people to work where they want to live or for companies to go where the workers are? There's not much evidence of that. There could be.

Plate 5 From top left, across: Suzanne Helburn in high school; at 3 years old (1933); the commune's twentieth reunion (1991). Down left side: in sixth grade at Ellis College (Suzanne is leftmost on the bottom step); with her daughter Sherry; at 11 with her mother; seated in front with her husband Nick at the commune's reunion (1991); main portrait (1995).

5

SUZANNE WIGGINS HELBURN

> I have been more interested in changing things than in impressing people in the economics profession. But I now think I should have been somewhat more concerned about my career. As a practical matter it is difficult to be influential without a reputation.
>
> (Suzanne Helburn, 1998)

As the principal investigator of Cost, Quality, and Child Outcomes in Child Care Centers, Suzie brought together a team of twelve nationally recognized researchers in four major universities to complete the most comprehensive study to date of US child care centers and their impact on children. She also participated in a parallel study, "The Economics of Family Child Care," and is currently collaborating with Barbara Bergmann on a book on child care policy. Her scholarship in the history of economic thought and the philosophy of Keynes is also noteworthy. She has also made important contributions in social studies education, particularly at the high school level. As part of the curriculum reform movement of the 1960s, she designed an innovative curriculum and co-authored "Economics and Society," a series of high school texts, teacher training manuals, and curricular materials. She has served on the Advisory Board of the National Science Foundation Education Directorate, and on the Board of Directors of the Social Science Education Consortium. She served on the economics faculty and as Department Chair and Dean of the Social Sciences Division at the University of Colorado at Denver since 1971. She is currently Professor Emerita. She received a BA (1951) from American University and an MA (1956) and PhD (1963) from Indiana University.

Our conversation began in 1996 at the IAFFE conference at American University in Washington, DC. We had a long conversation during a wonderful dinner, and another sitting under large shade trees at the university. Two years later, in February of 1998, we continued our conversation over dinner in a Washington, DC, restaurant. As we pieced together these two conversations, we began to recognize that it is sometimes difficult to capture the different dimensions of a story. In the case of Suzie, her incredible energy, intellectual acumen, and an insatiable enthusiasm for life are often lost in the translation to words. We hope the following does justice to her story.

Suzie, could you begin by telling us about your family, in particular about your class and ethnic background? I was born in Philadelphia in 1930. My mother came from a German family. Her father emigrated to the US when he was quite young. Her father and grandfather were tailors. The grandfather became a successful men's clothing designer. So I guess, they were lower-middle-class artisans. My mother and her sisters were skilled seamstresses.

My father's family trace their ancestry back to Roger Williams, the founder of Rhode Island. My grandfather was a traveling salesman. My father's family was a very loving, close-knit family. By contrast, my mother had a terrible father who ruled over his three handsome daughters with an iron hand.

My father was a drummer in a successful, small dance band. During the day he ran the dry-cleaning store that was owned by my mother's father. My mother had an eighth-grade education. She trained as a milliner, but worked as a stenographer, and devoted a lot of time to creating her own very stylish wardrobe. My father only completed the tenth grade because during World War I, he went to work in the Philadelphia shipyards. He became somewhat radicalized by the experience. He abandoned at least the Republican Party which was favored by the rest of his family, and voted for Norman Thomas and then Roosevelt.

When did your parents get married? They married in 1923. They were part of the flapper generation. I was an only child and very much wanted by my parents, because my mother had several miscarriages. I grew up in the same neighborhood in Philadelphia where my parents grew up, a mainly German enclave. My father died at 34 from a ruptured appendix. It devastated my mother. She died nine years later at 44.

How old were you? I was 5 when my father died. I remember him somewhat because he would come home at night after working and wake me up for a midnight snack. I remember waving goodbye to him at night. I remember being awakened to say goodbye to him when he went to the hospital and never came back. My mother died when I was 14. An important fact of my life is that I am both an orphan *and* an only child of doting parents and relatives.

What happened to you and your mother after your father's death? My mother had to go back to work. This was during the Depression. When I turned 10 years old, she sent me to a boarding school called Ellis College. It was a school for widows' daughters. The school was created by a Quaker philanthropist who decided to get promising young girls off the streets so their mothers could work. It was an early version of welfare for worthy mothers. I was there from the sixth through the twelfth grade and received a very good education. I was there when my mother died, beyond the reach of her father who had taken advantage of my mother in executing my father's will. My mother had put my small inheritance in a trust, so I could remain at the boarding school until I graduated and got a scholarship to go to college.

I became very independent as a result of this experience. Nevertheless, I had a lot of support from a pretty loving family. I don't remember or recall any of this history as tragic. Basically, I had a very happy childhood. What may be a possibly negative and permanent effect of my time at Ellis has been a feeling of inferiority around rich people. As part of my experience with the private school system (located on the main line of the railroad on the outskirts of Philadelphia), I was thrown into contact with rich kids through competitive sports, debating, etc., and I always felt insecure around them.

What did you do after leaving Ellis College? I went to American University in 1947 and worked my way through college.

What did you study? I started out as a chemistry major. I loved chemistry, science, and math in high school. But I didn't like the second-year physics course. I could not understand the notion of limits in calculus. I shifted to economics on the advice of a boyfriend who suggested that economics might satisfy my taste for scientific thinking. I also took a course in the history of economic thought. I really liked the course and the teacher. I was not, however, enthralled with the other courses in economics.

What did you do after you received your BA? I landed a great job in Washington, DC, as the assistant to the director of the collective bargaining section at the Printing Industry of America, a trade association. I had a wonderful boss who gave me a huge amount of responsibility analyzing contracts and federal price control directives, etc.

In the meantime, right after completing the BA, I got married. My husband was accepted at Indiana University for graduate work in the psychology depart-ment, so there I was heading for Indiana. But because I had this terrific job in DC, I wasn't willing to take just any job. When I couldn't find a job, however, I finally called the economics department at Indiana University to find out whether I could apply for graduate school. I got a research assistantship. This is why I went to graduate school [*laughter*].

Could you talk about your experience in graduate school? Well, it was a strange and wonderful experience. I was both learning and growing up. My husband was in a very prestigious department with many female graduate students, and I was in a mediocre department which already had a bad experi-ence with a female graduate student. The only reason I got the research assistantship was because somebody had dropped out at the last minute. Every year after that I had trouble getting money, although I always ultimately got it.

But the prejudice worked both ways for me. I was pretty, so they were intrigued with me. Any time I said anything half-way sensible they thought I was brilliant. I never really knew how good I was because I wasn't sure whether my straight As were measuring my competence level. I was the most accom-plished kid in both my high school class of twenty-one students and my college class of 400 students. I had never attended a school that provided much compe-tition. Similarly in graduate school, I could never quite gauge my worth. I never knew if I was really doing well or if they were just impressed with my looks. I was interested in math so I got a math minor. In those days we took an outside minor in graduate school. I took fifteen hours of math as a graduate student:

advanced calculus, linear algebra, and probability theory. I also did an econometric dissertation. I taught myself econometrics. The department offered no courses in econometrics in 1953. I used the first edition of a textbook by Lawrence Klein, and went through it on my own as an independent study course.

Did you have a mentor in graduate school? No, I didn't. Partly it was my own fault because I was somewhat ambivalent about economics as a career. I had a baby at the end of my third year in graduate school. I took my labor field exam and had the baby the next day. My marriage was not very good either. So it took me seven years to finish my dissertation. My husband's first job was at the University of Rochester. The following year, he got an appointment at Stanford. Despite a deteriorating marriage, we agreed to go together to California, partly because I didn't want to be stuck in Rochester. Luckily for me, the economics department at San Jose State had a position open and I got an appointment without a doctorate.

After about a year and a half in California, we got a divorce. It was amicable. My daughter and I lived with another divorced woman and her two boys for about four years in a house I was able to buy with the last $2,000 left over from my mother's estate. Eventually I realized that, as a single mom, I needed to finish my dissertation and get serious. I called Indiana and found out I had six months to finish. By that time, my advisor had left the university.

What was your dissertation about? It followed the work of Meyer and Kuh on investment demand in two-digit industries. Using time series data I estimated investment demand functions for each industry. Then I did a series of non-parametric tests of the hypotheses on the differential effects of the determinants of investment depending on the structure of the industry. It came out beautifully. It was a very nice dissertation which I never published. No one on the faculty knew anything about the subject. I did it totally on my own. The department was impressed and submitted it for an award for the best dissertation of the year. When I failed to get the award, I didn't submit it for publication. I was on to a new project.

How would you characterize your experience as a graduate student? I was discriminated against both positively and negatively. I always had a difficult time getting financial support. At the same time, the faculty considered me a very good student. Maybe I really deserved those grades but I never quite knew.

How many other women students were in your graduate program at Indiana University? None.

You were the only one? There was one other woman in the program before me, but she never finished her dissertation.

How did it feel being the only woman? Was it an issue for you at the time? Sure, it would have been nice to have had other women around.

Were there women faculty members? There was one. She was an older woman who was very nice and supportive of me, but she didn't teach graduate courses. So she didn't really influence me.

In what way was she supportive of you? Oh, by just being around. I don't think I was supportive enough of her; that was the problem.

Are you in touch with anyone of the people you went to graduate school with? No. There were no more than ten people in our class. Some of them have gone on to be fairly well-known economists. One of them ended up on my dissertation committee. He joined the faculty at Indiana after his first job.

One thing about me (and something that I have noticed about some of my women students) is that I was not very creative.

What do you mean? Women make a lot of points by earning good grades but, somehow or another, we are not often expected to make major contributions to the creative development of the discipline. By and large, we don't. I remember daydreaming as a graduate student about making some really terrific breakthrough. I think I had these fantasies because I thought that there was something in me. I don't know why I had these dreams. It might have been my adoring parents. I had a lot of love and support as a child.

Do you think they helped you to develop your self-confidence? Yes, but I am still quite shy under certain circumstances. For instance, I am very shy around IAFFE women whom I do not know. But if I feel comfortable I will come forward, take risks, and exert my leadership. So I have some faith in my inner resources but not enough confidence to draw on them all the time. I don't know whether this is common among women or not.

But you did in fact finish your dissertation? Yes, I finished in six months.

What year did you finish? In 1963. I was in graduate school at Indiana from 1952 to 1956, but I didn't decide to become an economist until after I left grad school in 1956. Adlai Stevenson, the only presidential candidate I've ever been enthusiastic about, was running for president. We were living in conservative upstate New York and I was staying home with my toddler. I joined the League of Women Voters and I was doing research for them on things that I knew nothing about. We conducted a poll of the ordinary person in the street: what they knew and thought about. I was absolutely horrified about the ignorance of our electorate. I spent a huge amount of time working for the League, but I wasn't using my expertise. This is when I decided to be an economist rather than donating my services to projects where I had no expertise. Economics was never something I was very driven to do. Although I share with neoclassical economists the love for the aesthetics and the elegance of economic theory, I am more interested in social and political issues than in most of the fields in economics.

When did your politics get formed? We arrived at Indiana University in 1952, mid-way through the McCarthy scare. The McCarthy hearings got me into politics. When I was a freshman at American University in 1947, I became interested in Henry Wallace's presidential campaign, but I was not active. I was not political, except for some pro-labor convictions.

Where did your sympathy for labor come from? I simply objected to the injustice that I saw. But during the McCarthy era, when we were in

Bloomington, Indiana, a woman on the state board of education tried to get *Robin Hood* removed from the state textbook list. We formed the Green Feather Campaign to picket and demonstrate; that experience got me started. Of course, in graduate school you don't have a lot of time, so these were isolated instances. But the McCarthy era was so horrible that we watched it on television as much as we could.

When you think back to the development of your politics, who influenced you intellectually? In 1957, I got a job at San Jose State. With the 1960s came the civil rights movement, the free speech movement, and Vietnam. A fellow faculty member at San Jose State, James O'Connor, a brilliant Marxist theorist, influenced me. I became involved in the politics of the 1960s. I was an active union member in the American Federation of Teachers which was attempting to organize faculty. The union and the progressive members of the faculty learned that the state college presidents and the system chancellor had secretly agreed to prevent southern black activists from enrolling in the state college system. We exposed this in an article in *Dissent* and caused the resignation of the president of San Jose State. We then became involved in organizing the state college system.

Then in 1968 the Supreme Court ruled that US citizens could not be prevented from going to Cuba. Saul Landau had made a movie on Fidel Castro and was going back to make another one. He organized a series of trips to Cuba for academics and journalists to provide a cadre of people to inform Americans what Cuba was all about. I went on one of those trips. We were the guests of the Cuban government and Saul was there to open doors and make introductions. We met intellectuals and film-makers. Highly committed young people were running the boarding schools, farms, and research stations in this poverty-stricken country. I was particularly interested in the new research Cubans were undertaking to try to solve their unique problems. They were experimenting with uses of sugar cane and cattle breeding. When I returned to Berkeley where I was living at the time, it was in a state of siege. While I was in Cuba there was literally bloody warfare going on in Berkeley over the free speech movement. This is how I got radicalized.

You described the development of your politics. How would you describe your evolution as an economist? You started with an interest in math and economet-rics. Where did you go from there? I also started with an interest in labor economics and in problems of inequality. But I was not particularly interested in women's issues because this was the early 1950s, and my consciousness had not been raised. The six-month *tour de force* finishing my dissertation had rekindled my interest in Keynes and macroeconomics.

My interest in economics intensified through involvement in a curriculum project. In the early 1960s the Joint Council on Economic Education and the Committee for Economic Development published a series of national reports publicizing how ignorant most students graduating from high school and college were about economics. The reports also argued that the implementation of

Keynesian policy depended on greater public understanding of economics. John Sperling (a colleague and economic historian) and I read these reports and decided we should write an economics textbook for high school students. We made arrangements to visit and teach some high school classes, wrote a book outline and a chapter, and got a contract. All of this was happening while I was finishing my dissertation, teaching full time, and performing other duties as a single mother. After we got the contract, we put the project aside so I could finish my dissertation. The next year our contract was rescinded. We success-fully sued the publisher. We reasoned that they had probably acquired a better product than ours. Therefore, we were determined to turn our book into a smashing success. This was the post-Sputnik era of curriculum reform when the National Science Foundation invested in math and science curricula that were designed by teams and headed by scientists and mathematicians. NSF and the Department of Education also financed The New Social Studies Projects. We wrote a proposal to develop a teaching system for high school economics.

In 1964, John and I got a sizable grant from the US Department of Education to develop a high school economics curriculum. I got a three-year leave of absence from San Jose State. I moved from Palo Alto to Berkeley to develop the materials in Contra Costa County, where we were working with teachers in the classroom. The model involved a kind of action research strategy requiring continual formative evaluation and revision. Out of this we developed individual lessons and modules to work with students. Hilda Taba, a major figure in curriculum reform, was developing an inquiry-oriented, elemen-tary school curriculum at a national level. I worked jointly on our project and on hers, adapting many of her teaching strategies for use in economics with older youngsters. We read all the literature in education that we could get our hands on, and worked with and learned from Hilda, who was a really powerful woman.

The experience was hard on me, but it was an important experience. She would not accept any excuses, and was not interested in why I had created something she did not like. She simply sent me away to start over again. I learned about curriculum, and I had finally found a mother figure and mentor who didn't seem to like me very much [laughter].

Creating ECON12 was a great experience. I had to ask myself what is economics? What is important about economics for high school students? It took us from 1964 to 1974 to publish Economics and Society by Addison-Wesley; a ten-year project. It included six books, along with a teachers' guide, and training materials as well as audio-visuals. One book, on economic justice, never got published because the subject had gone out of vogue [laughter]. The teaching strategy was based on the notion of organizing all student learning around the basic structure of the discipline which includes both organizing concepts and theories as well as methods of inquiry. We introduced basic knowledge of the organizers through programmed instruction modules and then created a series of student-centered learning activities that engaged students in applying the material. The purpose was to encourage them to accommodate these new ideas and assimilate them into their own cognitive structures.

We had great success in getting kids actively involved in economic controversies. But the experience working in the public schools made us increasingly aware of the function of education in maintaining the status quo. To a large extent, schools are not intended to teach critical thinking or to encourage higher-order learning. Schools provide a socializing and babysitting function. Children learn their place in society and how to conform. These lessons are pretty stultifying. It is no wonder that many students rebel in various ways. What society wants is effective schools for elites. Only they should be allowed to think on their own.

One of the effects of the project on me was a growing awareness that the structure of the discipline acted as a control mechanism. It imposed one way of looking at economic questions. I became more and more interested in alternative theoretical perspectives. By the time we finished the project I had begun to reject the disciplinary structure of economics. I have always had a love–hate relationship with the discipline. This is despite a strong belief in the importance of understanding economic structures and the process of society, and that neoclassical economics is sometimes useful in understanding certain kinds of behavior.

What economics influenced you the most intellectually? Marx and Keynes have had a big influence on me. I spent about ten years studying Marx. One of the six books we wrote for the curriculum project was on communist economies, which required me to learn more about Marx. The book was organized around three case studies: Cuba, China, and the Soviet Union. This involved historical research. I had to identify appropriate primary sources for student readings. I read Marx, Mao, Lenin, Castro, among others. In 1978, I took a sabbatical in London where I devoted the year to reading Marx. It was a wonderful year. I finally felt confident about my understanding of Marx. I spent years teaching and helping students to comprehend the three volumes of *Capital*.

The influence of Marx on my thinking has been muted and transformed by my work on Keynes. Aspects of Marx's thinking are still part of my world view: for instance, the labor theory of value, his description of the course and nature of capitalist development, and change as a dialectical process. It is clear to me that value is created by human labor. Business students in my class on Marx invariably took it for granted that the whole objective of systems of management control was to increase the amount of work performed by workers. Neoclassical economists focus on the inadequacies of the labor theory of value as a price theory and dismiss the most important dimension of the labor theory of value as a theory of exploitation. By contrast, Marx used the theory to show that the price system transfers value from those who produce (even capitalists involved in labor-intensive production) to the highly capital-intensive sectors of the economy.

Dialectical processes figured in my curriculum reform work as well.

Obviously, the process of change is dialectical, both in society and in one's own thinking and actions. In educating students we try to help them undergo intellectual growth and transformation. This introduces new, possibly conflicting, organizers into their cognitive structure by encouraging a process of accommodation and assimilation. The discovery and application of dialectics helped me understand how people change and grow. It also helped me understand the process of social change as praxis. Keynes, though totally disdainful of Marx, recognized change as a dialectical process based on continual adaptation of theory to practice.

How did you get interested in Keynes? I got interested in Keynes through a funny coincidence. I met Mark Blaug during my 1978 sabbatical. I was reading Marx and I couldn't find anybody to talk to. The Marxists at the Institute of Education had no time for me. I finally made an appointment with Mark Blaug who was on the faculty at the Institute. As an ex-Marxist, he provided a powerful critique. He introduced me to the Kuhn–Popper–Lakatos debate and the notion of scientific paradigms or research programs. As the 1983 centennial of Keynes and Schumpeter's birth and Marx's death approached, I decided to organize a conference on Marx, Schumpeter, and Keynes. Mark agreed to give a paper. Because of Blaug's participation, Robert Heilbronner agreed to give the keynote address. We had a highly successful three-day conference at the University of Colorado at Denver, and published a book including my four chapters introducing the philosophy of science debate and each of the three main characters.

The need to write the introduction on Keynes and to understand the nature of Keynes's liberal politics sparked my interest in him as the quintessential twentieth-century liberal. The first volume of Robert Skidelsky's biography of Keynes had just been published. Skidelsky referred to Keynes's early unpublished papers on philosophy which were housed in the King's College archives. After finishing the book, I began studying the documents at King's College. Of particular interest to me was Keynes's admiration of Edmund Burke, the arch conservative, as well as his other papers on ethics. Although a new cottage industry was growing up to interpret Keynes's early papers, most scholars focused on his methodology. However, the philosophical underpinning of Keynes's methodology was his ethical position. Most scholars were interpreting this as utilitarian. It is very hard to classify Keynes because he doesn't really fit into categories. However, there is a strong Aristotelian influence on Keynes, as there was on Marx. He questioned how one makes ethical personal decisions and public policy under conditions of limited knowledge. In two or three papers I argued that Keynes basically took an Aristotelian position, emphasizing the importance of an ethics of virtue in which leaders must acquire sound judgment over a lifetime of experience. This is an elitist position, but I actually agree with him.

What is the connection between twentieth-century liberal politics and the influence of Edmund Burke on Keynes? Burke lived in the era in which civic virtue was extolled and Keynes, of course, practiced it. Burke made a distinction between utilitarianism as an appropriate ethic for public policy decision making and a personal ethic. These fit together for Keynes through an ethics of virtue. When appropriate, one can use utilitarian, consequentialist reasoning. Most of the time we have limited information and, given the specific circumstances, we must make the best judgment possible. In the curriculum project, for example, even though we solved the technical problems by developing an effective teaching strategy, the institutional circumstances limited its use. Keynes was helpful to me in making judgments based on the "art of the possible." He devoted his life to reform. Persuasion and persistence were extremely important to him. He was a great educator, opening up people's minds to the possible, and preparing the groundwork for change.

Can you tie your intellectual life during this time to your personal life? I was a divorcee in California for about nine years. I moved to Berkeley in 1965 because of the curriculum project. I went on sabbatical leave in 1967 to participate in the Experienced Teachers Program at the University of Colorado. This was an NSF-financed MA program to train teachers to teach economics. I directed the teaching practicum. A friend of mine introduced me to Nick Helburn, who was the Director of the High School Geography Project. We really hit it off and ultimately got married in 1969. That caused me to leave San Jose State. Nick got a job at Western Michigan University in Kalamazoo and I got a job in the business school as their token woman and token Marxist. They thought it was amusing to have me on the faculty; I was totally marginalized.

The next year Nick got a job in Colorado as the Director of the ERIC Clearing House on Social Science and Social Studies, and we moved back. I was 40 years old and could not find a job. So I decided to go back to San Jose State where I still had an appointment. I commuted. I left on Monday nights and came home on Thursday nights. In San Jose I stayed with a friend whose daughter was deeply involved in trying to free George Jackson of the Solidad Brothers from prison. He had been imprisoned for a minor crime and kept for over ten years in the Solidad prison. Her house was the organizational hub. Young activists came and went. The phone was tapped, and the police hung around. One weekend while I was in Colorado, someone drove by the house and shot up my bedroom. During the weekends I went home to be with Nick and our two teens (his and mine). We were trying to get the family back in order. Then I would go back to San Jose to the house in the middle of a war zone. One leader was murdered in the back yard. By the end of the semester I was a wreck and resigned from San Jose State. The next year I got an appointment at the University of Colorado's Denver campus.

You finally settled in Colorado? Yes. When we moved back to Colorado in 1970 we were still involved in the educational reform movement. We had concluded that fundamental change in public education was unlikely for the reason I already discussed. The new curriculum materials were not widely adopted. Most teachers and text committees thought they were too difficult for students and teachers, and they were skeptical about encouraging student inquiry. As a result, we became interested in experimenting with changes in the institutional structure of schools.

In the meantime, we attended a Quaker meeting in Boulder along with Elise and Kenneth Boulding. One rainy Sunday we all went back to the Bouldings' house to discuss problems of educational reform. We mentioned to Elise our interest in experimenting with a model where teenagers would live in an intentional community. They would learn life skills and develop a sense of responsibility, but they would attend public schools for formal education. She said she had been thinking about that, and convened a group of interested people. We met for about four months under Elise's leadership.

She introduced us to a man who had organized a successful research commune in Switzerland. Elise had to eventually drop out because Kenneth was not at all interested in communal living. Individuals in the group had the training and experience needed to operate a youth collective. There were teachers, a psychologist, curriculum developers, and a psychiatric social worker. After discussions for four or five months, we decided to take the plunge and began looking for property. We bought a run-down 118-acre [48-ha] farm outside of Boulder. Nick and I were the main financial backers; two other members eventually contributed money. We bought the farm because there were potentially five buildings to house people. We had to convert the large chicken coop and two garages into houses. We had to dig a new well and put in a sewage system.

So you started an intentional community. How long did it last? It lasted for five years. The first few years were devoted to converting farm buildings into houses, and learning how to farm and to cooperate. After three years it became clear that we were not going be able to start the youth collective without a large infusion of money. The building codes did not permit us to construct low-cost housing for use as a school. So many in the initial group left and were replaced by people interested in starting a goat farm and a cooperative construction company.

The community learned to use group process effectively. From our experience designing curricula, Nick and I already knew a lot of the techniques for team building, quick decision making, and consensus building. Collective living requires many meetings. We all learned to run them successfully. We were reasonably task-oriented.

How many people lived in this commune? It varied. At first there were twenty-five; about fifteen to seventeen adults. Houses were shared, and we had very little private space.

How was it organized? One house, the converted chicken coop, became the community center where we prepared and ate evening meals together. Nick and I lived in the coop with my daughter until she went to college. A larger family joined the community and needed the space. All the other houses were smaller and shared. We moved into a tiny house of 700 square feet [65 square meters] with two bedrooms, a small kitchen, and a bathroom, and a basement which we used for an office. We converted the hayloft of the barn into community space.

Did you know much about construction when you began this project? No. My husband had some carpentry experience. One of the other men had done some framing and that was it. Work was complicated because of our devotion to reducing the gender division of labor.

Nick and I were holding down full-time jobs. We were the main financial providers for the community. For the first two years, everyone tithed two-thirds of their income to the community. This financial arrangement finally broke down. The unequal financial position of the group was deadly because it gave us (Nick and I) too much potential control. Although we did not exert this control, we could. So we moved to another arrangement where each person paid the same amount per month and this worked quite well.

How would you evaluate collective living in retrospect? We learned and gained a lot from collective living. Nick and I were finally exhausted and dissatisfied with the new direction of the community. It was difficult operating a poorly organized cooperative business. In one exercise to compare individual labor contributions, Nick and I figured we had devoted 104 hours of work per week. We could not keep this up, and did not want to under the circumstances. We wrote a paper analyzing the problems that we saw in the community. Everybody essentially agreed with our analysis, but most didn't want to change. We moved off the farm to give the community time to decide whether or not to buy the farm from us at the original purchase price. The group decided against it. We eventually went through the equivalent of a property settlement.

We moved back and rented out the houses. We tried to retain a collective spirit, but even the low rents were not enough. The landlord–tenant relationship worked against us. However, we were able to continue some collective activities. We participated in group gardening. We had bees, chickens, and an orchard. We organized trips to the mountains to cut trees for firewood in order to heat the houses. I can't actually imagine how we had the energy to do it all.

What years were these? The intentional community lasted from 1971 to 1976, and the rental period lasted from 1976 to about 1982. Then my daughter married a contractor. He immediately realized that all this was way too much work for us. He suggested that we subdivide the property, sell off the houses, and get permission to build two more houses, one for us and one for them. Everyone would own their own place, and share community space, and there might be a better chance of successful cooperative living. So that is what we did. It works quite well. The amount of cooperative effort depends on people's interests and private lives. We share and maintain some common grounds and outbuildings. We have two barns, a big long shed, a new chicken house, and a pump or wash house. We raise chickens, ducks, and turkeys, the favorites of the children [*laughter*]. We still have bees and the orchard, and a little pond so the kids can go fishing. We have a big park with a trampoline, playground equipment, an

Olympic-size sand volleyball court, a half-size basketball court, and room to play baseball and soccer. One of the barns is a community building with carpentry shop, a pottery studio, and a meeting room. It was built in a "barn raising" over two weekends. We are good at organizing. I think it is chapter 13 in volume I of *Capital* that Marx talks about the efficiency of collective work. It's true. If you get a bunch of people together for a short period of time and get them organized, they can do a huge amount of work.

How large is the community now? There are seven households, five of which have children. It is an absolutely wonderful place for the kids. It's wonderful for me as well. I live next to my daughter and her family. I've been able to participate in raising my grandchildren. This is more than most grandparents. I have also learned to not intrude too much so I could have a close relationship with my daughter.

Do you think the fact that everyone has their own private property has contributed to the stability of the place? Oh, yes. There are mixed attitudes about the degree of interdependence, but everyone *loves* the place. The collective has been in existence now for seventeen years and only one house has turned over. During the commune phase, there was a constant flux. Nick called it a people's farm for young people to get their act together and then leave [*laughter*].

Did this experience make you evaluate some of what Marx had said, or at least some of the ways his work had been interpreted? Yes. We learned a lot about building community in the United States. In order to keep the collective together, some of the members must be totally devoted to it. Also, it is important to have rather modest goals. We started the commune with the intention of making it a place to live, to work, and to practice our politics. This is difficult to pull off without a guru. Our current arrangement is similar to co-housing where several households come together and create a living situation that supports the private needs of families. This involves some cooperation. Even co-housing cooperatives require some people in the group who bring the rest together. We have lots of rituals: a Christmas party, a Halloween party, a Memorial Day camp-out, and an Easter party for the children. These events are important for everybody. Community is especially important for the children. They have complete run of the place. Our farmstead is about 10 acres [4 ha] with about a 110-acre [45-ha] out-lot. The children can go anywhere and into any house. We do not use babysitters very often. The community is a substitute for the extended family. It will be an interesting test case when Nick and I get old enough to need help, to see if the community will provide it. This is our experiment and we are quite proud of it.

Well, this is quite a story because it continues. In 2001, it will be our thirtieth anniversary.

Can you talk about your career before you retired? One of the sad things about academic life today is the tendency to marginalize older faculty at the end of their careers. Some people in my generation cannot compete in a publish-orperish environment because they started their academic careers mainly as teachers with limited expectations about publishing. Although I have had an active and productive career, I do not have a lot of peer-reviewed articles on my vita. Older faculty often experience salary compression which finances the salary increases for the younger, more "productive" faculty. There is a general disregard for older people.

About ten years ago, when I started experiencing this kind of marginalization, I decided to go on administrative strike in order to use my time and tenure to do what I wanted to do. This is when I started the child care research project. It allowed me to end my career on a wonderful successful note. However, my department chair thought that I should be writing peer-reviewed articles. He discounted my life's work and considered the child care project just one more of my worthless projects. The fact that the chancellor thought I walked on water and the vice-chancellor and the dean were very pleased with my work made it even worse. But the chair reflects the narrow values of the profession which disregards community work and research with *real* public policy implications. Improving the department's reputation means writing peer-reviewed articles. Well, a 60 year old, who is not accustomed to writing articles for the *American Economic Review*, can't do it [*laughter*]. Sadly, this kind of experience happens more often than not at the end of a person's career.

An interesting side note about my relation with this chair was that I was extremely supportive of him. But for some reason or other he did not perceive this. In fact, he discontinued an education practicum I had introduced to train teaching assistants. It was a fabulous program. Many of them have turned into great teachers. One of them is now vice-president of a national union and uses these techniques all the time in his union organizing. The department has reverted back to the standard model of good teaching which includes lecture, entertainment, and good student evaluations. Brilliant!

If you could go back in your career and do things differently, what do you think you would do? I wouldn't be an economist. When I was in graduate school, Keynes and the new economics were the paradigm and I was in tune with the profession. Maybe I still would have decided to be an economist then, but I certainly wouldn't choose to be one now. I don't advise my students to go into economics unless they have conservative tendencies or love mathematics and econometrics.

So you're sending all the conservatives into economics? [*Laughter*] Well, not all, but anyone who decides to become an economist needs to understand what the profession is all about, particularly young women.

Are you happy with the development of your career? Given that you did become an economist, do you think you should have done some things differently? I am a bit torn by it. I just finished my transition year from a full-time faculty to a retired person. I was never a careerist. I have done a couple of really big projects: the ten-year curriculum development project and the ten-year child care project. I also spent quite a bit of time working on Keynes; published a few articles. Then I devoted a few years to cost-of-living studies and welfare reform. I think I did pretty good work. I have been more interested in changing things than in impressing people in the economics profession. But I now think I should have been somewhat more concerned about my career. As a practical matter, it is difficult to be influential without a reputation. I don't know how to answer your question. I actually am pleased with my life, and economics has been a big part of it.

Do you think that economics is more insular and more inward-looking as a social science? I think so.

Why do you think that is? In Kuhn's terminology, economics is a mature science. It's not necessarily good science, but it is mature in establishing a dominant paradigm so that our training is narrowly focused on the neoclassical paradigm. The notion of rational economic behavior developed fairly early, at least since Ricardo, and laid the basis for mathematical modeling. There is nothing comparable in the other social sciences. Heterodox economists haven't had much of an impact on the profession except at the margins. Neoclassical theory is so mathematically elegant, even beautiful, that it is hard for economists to give it up. Furthermore, students are so busy learning the math that they don't have the time or inclination to study alternatives.

Some people have argued that economics has become more narrow over time. Do you agree? Sure. I think it is partly due to the ideological function of neoclassical teaching. With capitalist development and the increasing emphasis on financial capital accumulation, economists have become increasingly more conservative and devoted to neoclassicism.

Why do you think more women are not attracted to economics? I have never taught in a PhD-granting institution, but the study published in the *Journal of Economic Literature* several years ago may provide a clue. The authors reported that fewer undergraduates were attracted to economics. The field may not attract students interested in studying social problems. It is quite easy, however, for students with a feel for mathematics.

Let's talk a little bit about feminism. Do you consider yourself a feminist? I don't know whether I am a feminist or not. I call myself a feminist. I have experienced being marginalized as a woman. The experience of being a woman in a man's field has been demeaning. So my sense of injustice for the disadvantages women face, coupled with my own personal experiences, have made me whatever kind of feminist I am. However, with a few exceptions, I haven't been very active in feminist organizations. I was on the board of a small foundation in Colorado devoted to providing grants to women's groups and service agencies. I also serve on the board of the local YWCA, and I'm a member of IAFFE.

Even though I am sympathetic to feminism, there are other injustices in the world, some that in my opinion are much more serious. I don't think sexism is the number one oppression in this world; it is one of many. On the other hand, economics as a discipline and a profession is male-dominated so that clearly the issues of great importance to women, to all of us, are ignored or misunderstood. So I think teaching feminist economics, teaching courses related to women, and incorporating a feminist perspective in the economics curriculum are all essential. I taught a course on women in the economy for years and tried, quite unsuccessfully, to introduce graduate students to feminist theory in my seminar on critical evaluation of economic theory.

What kind of impact, positive or negative, do you think feminist economics can have on the profession? I have read a lot of literature on the feminist critiques of economics. I liked Heidi Hartmann's work, for instance, on the historical development of women's condition. I think that kind of work is very important. But we need to be more pro-active in identifying and doing research related to women's issues. Young feminists in economics need to protect their careers without succumbing to the predominant fashions set by neoclassical economists. Women need to become both cunning and courageous in order to push forward a feminist agenda in economics. There is a great need, particularly for applied research. Women academics need to play politics but maintain their integrity. They must develop a strategy for getting tenure and promoted while creating a research or scholarship program that addresses women's concerns. Building a feminist economics should eventually lead to its legitimization.

I would like to see more emphasis on empirical policy research addressing feminist concerns. Feminist theory should develop out of our research efforts. We should be doing solid empirical and historical research to promote progressive feminist causes so kids don't go hungry and women don't continue to be victimized. We have to work with a spectrum of people who have different politics and are at different points in their lives. We need to be careful not to just talk to each other.

Suzie, can you talk about the child care project you directed? The child care project grew out of my sabbatical work in 1985. In the beginning of the Reagan era we organized a weekly seminar to discuss research collaboration that might counteract the conservative takeover of the family issue. After a year I realized the seminars were not productive because the individuals involved were engaged in their own research agendas which they were unwilling to give up. I was at a stage in my career where I wanted to start a project. I had been working on Keynes, but it didn't seem to have any real social significance. I decided to use my sabbatical year to redirect my research towards the study of the economics of child care. When I returned to Denver, an advocate of child care asked me to estimate the cost of living for low-income women. With a colleague, we estimated poverty budgets for Denver. Then the City of Boulder asked us to replicate the study. This work was very influential. Next, the Department of Social Services contracted with us to evaluate the adequacy of Colorado's standard of need, which served as the basis for AFDC eligibility requirements. This study also included a survey of how welfare recipients were spending their money.

This research highlighted the crucial role of child care costs for poor single mothers. We teamed up with a local early childhood professional (a person I had met at the University of North Carolina on my sabbatical) to design a study of the cost and quality of child care. We raised about $20,000 from the community and another $15,000 from the Ford Foundation for a pilot study to test the feasibility of collecting the data. We were not sure that centers and family child care providers would cooperate to provide financial information and permit evaluations of their programs. But we did get cooperation. We wrote three or four articles and developed a decent reputation among the child care community that allowed us to approach the foundations for a big grant. Luckily, the program director at the Carnegie Foundation was very interested in the project and helped us get the money. It took us four years to do the research. Early childhood researchers from North Carolina, Yale, and UCLA joined us. This is how we put together the project on Cost, Quality, and Child Outcomes in Child Care Centers, which I directed.

It must have been quite a challenge managing such a diverse group of scholars. It was a difficult project to manage because of the interdisciplinary nature of the research team. We brought together child development experts and economists. Statistical procedures and traditions differ between the disciplines. We had a running battle between the statistician-trained psychologist and the econometrician. They just couldn't listen to each other. My training in econometrics was out of date so I had a difficult time mediating the disputes.

We studied both the cost and quality of services in 400 child care centers in four states. This was the biggest study ever done. We also collected data on the staff that permitted further labor market research. We collected data on parent evaluations of the quality of care. We collected data on the cognitive functioning and social competence of 800 children. These children were followed over time by the early childhood team members, creating longitudinal child outcomes data through the second grade.

What were the major findings of the study? Our results document the mediocre quality of child care in this country, its high cost, and the effectiveness of good-quality child care on children's social competence and cognitive functioning. We also discovered some interesting facts about the economics of the industry. We hired the Communications Consortium, a Washington-based public relations agency, to help us manage the release of the study's findings. The results were well publicized, and have had an important impact on national public policy formation and in the four states where the data were collected. Our results have also been published in academic journals.

Is this study also related to the work you are doing now? Yes. Barbara Bergmann and I met in 1985 when I was back east interviewing people about child care. Barbara reviewed our proposal. She was very appreciative of the project because in her work she had advocated increased public subsidy of child care as an appropriate strategy for reducing poverty among single mothers and their children. Barbara and I are now collaborating on a book on child care that makes use of the project findings, justifying a major expansion of child care vouchers to make good-quality child care accessible to all families. We hope the book will contribute to a national discussion of the child care dilemma and a major change in public willingness to expand public financing.

I have also just edited an issue of the *Annals of the American Academy of Political and Social Science* on child care. Together with John Morris (also involved in the Cost and Quality Study), I am completing a research project financed by the Aspen Institute, which compares the quality of services provided by profit and non-profit centers. Most studies show that for-profit centers provide significantly lower quality than non-profit child care centers, which is not unexpected. If parents are relatively uninformed about quality, profit-oriented centers are expected to provide parents with what they want. What they want is what they see when they drop off and pick up their children. The lower quality of non-profit centers is associated with characteristics that are difficult for parents to observe or monitor. We have also found pockets of lower quality among non-profit centers owned by community agencies and churches, suggesting a need for more study of these sectors.

6

ANNE MAYHEW

[W]e naively went marching out of the University of Texas not knowing that it had been a special place. We marched out when the whole discipline of economics was in a transitional stage. Before this transition, [the profession] had more tolerance of and appreciation for … heterodox economics. But, neoclassical formalism was becoming dominant and intolerant in the mid 60s.

(Anne Mayhew, 1997)

Raised in rural Texas, Anne felt like an outsider and always knew she would leave as soon as she could. Today, as a noted scholar in institutionalism, she remains an outsider within a discipline that marginalizes institutionalist thought. But once more, she has found an escape route. She is the Acting Vice-Provost in the College of Arts and Sciences at the University of Tennessee and, although she still holds the title of Professor of Economics, the History Department proudly claims her as their own. At the University of Tennessee, Anne has also served as Associate Dean for Academic Programs, Chair of the Economics Department, President of the Faculty Senate, and Chapter President of the American Association of University Professors. She is a recipient of the Veblen–Commons Award; former Editor of the *Journal of Economic Issues*; former Honorary Research Fellow at the University of Exeter, UK; former President of both the Association for Institutional Economics and the Association for Evolutionary Economics; and former Vice-President of the Western Social Science Association. Currently, she is writing two books on Clarence Ayres and on the monetary theory of the firm. She did graduate work in anthropology at the University of Chicago (1958–9), taught at the University of Illinois, and received a BA with honors (1958) and a PhD (1966) from the University of Texas at Austin.

Our conversation began during lunch in early December, 1997, when she was Associate Dean at the University of Tennessee. We returned to her office and talked for another hour, but her story was far from complete. So the next day we met periodically, in between her previously scheduled appointments. By the time we finished, it was late afternoon. Anne, after all, is a historian. Therefore, it is fitting that she had much to recount about her life and work.

Plate 6   Clockwise from top left: Anne Mayhew as a schoolgirl (1948); traveling in Crete with husband, Walter C. Neale (1988); in Scotland (1997); in Austin, Texas (1968).

Could you begin, Anne, by describing your family genealogy? Sure. I grew up in rural Texas. I was born in the lower Rio Grande Valley of Texas, along the Mexican border. My father was a farmer and my mother was a housewife. Both of them had grown up in large, farm families in rural, central Texas. My grandparents at various times during the nineteenth century came to Texas from Mississippi, South Carolina, and Arkansas. They raised cotton, wheat, and did mixed farming in central Texas.

So both of your parents migrated to southern Texas? Well, my father went south because the lower Rio Grande Valley was an interesting place in the 1920s. There were people who had big plans to turn it into a kind of Florida. They have similar climates; it's right on the Gulf Coast and it rarely freezes. People had set up big citrus orchards. So my father went down and started farming for other people. I guess, about the time I was born, he had bought the first of his citrus orchards. He also did truck farming. He and his brother grew tomatoes and eggplants and stuff like that and hauled it up to San Antonio, which was the nearest big farmers' market. This was the rural existence that I first lived.

The interesting thing about this area – one of the things that made it different – was that it had two markedly different cultures. Most of the people spoke Spanish as their native language. Then there were Anglos (that's what we were called) who spoke English. It was a pretty segregated society.

Our farm was pretty isolated, quite far from town. The population was really scattered out.

Did you take a bus to school? Oh, yeah, about 20 miles [32 km]. And this was one of the nice things that happened to me in this peculiar life. It was a very big school district, but they consolidated it to create one large and good school. I was in an accelerated first and second grade. The bad thing was that the schools were really segregated. The Chicano children went to one school and the Anglo children went to another. I wish we had gone to school together and had used both languages. It was a terribly cruel system. Spanish-speaking children were not allowed to speak Spanish, and got into great trouble if they did. Not surprisingly, not many of them stayed in school for very long. Also, a lot of the families (not all of them, but a lot) went off to pick fruit in the north in the spring and summer. The harvest season for all crops in the Valley pretty much ended in the late spring because it's very hot there. Many kids were part of these migrant families, so they left. Consequently, not many Mexican kids finished school in those days as a result.

But most of the white students continued school? Oh, yeah, absolutely. And the school that I went to – a Hidalgo County School – was a very, very good school.

Did your family remain in the lower Rio Grande area? No, my father and uncle realized that the war would end pretty soon, and correctly foresaw that San Antonio was going to be a booming area. You see, back in the late 1930s, as part of the public works programs, they had built a dam on the Medina River –

which was just west and south of San Antonio – so much of that area would be irrigated. My uncle and father did more irrigated truck farming than citrus farming (they still grew ruby red grapefruit), so they decided to sell their farms in the Valley and move to San Antonio. In 1944, we moved. We lived for half a year in San Antonio itself. But my mother, who had never really lived in the city and was having a lot of trouble coping with four kids and the city, decided that we should move back out nearer the farm.

Where did you move to? A little town called Lytle. That's where I completed my schooling, including high school. Lytle had, in those days, a population of maybe 1,000 at best. It was probably about 30 miles [48 km] southwest of San Antonio, and although that doesn't seem very far today, it was a long way. We were not a suburb of San Antonio by any means. Throughout my school years in Lytle, I had a good time, and participated in all sorts of things. For instance, I was editor of the school newspaper in high school. There was always for me, however, a sense that I was a little bit of a misfit – an outsider. There was never this deep sense of belonging, and I always knew that I'd leave as soon as I could [*laughter*].

What kind of education did your mother and father have? My father had a high school diploma. He had gone, maybe not quite a full year, to Southwest Texas State, a teachers' college, which is now Southwest Texas University in San Marcos. He taught briefly in the late 1920s. In those days you could teach without a college degree. My mother's family was fairly remarkable in that all nine children went to college. My mother was one of the youngest. She graduated from Baylor in 1933. Then she taught briefly. It was very hard to get teaching jobs. In fact, it was very hard getting any type of job during the 1930s. She and my father were married in 1934. She left teaching and moved to the Rio Grande Valley. She later went back to teaching.

So your parents expected you to attend college? Certainly. The expectation for me was that I would go to Baylor. But somewhere, I suppose about halfway through high school, I began to have serious doubts about this plan for my life. However, I don't think I had any other plan either.

Do you recall anyone who influenced your thinking in those early years? One of the terribly important things that happened to me was this little town of Lytle was a poor town and it couldn't hire proper teachers. So, I had two high school teachers without proper teaching credentials who had attended the University of Texas and graduated with Bachelor degrees (one in economics; the other in sociology). They couldn't get jobs in the bigger school districts because they didn't have teaching certificates (which they earned later). But they really affected my thinking, in part, by getting me to read all sorts of books and to talk about ideas. I've often thought that if I had gone to a school where people had proper teaching credentials, they wouldn't have been as interested in the ideas that were important to me.

Do you recall some of the books you read? Yes, things like Schlesinger's, *The Age of Jackson*, which I remember to be a really difficult book to read as a sophomore in high school. These two teachers used to take me to Austin, and I also had an uncle who lived in Austin and who I would visit, so I knew about the University of Texas. The teachers told me all about the people who taught economics, sociology, and political science at the University, so that's where I increasingly wanted to go to college. But, my parents did not want me to go there, and the University of Texas was then (and still is in parts of rural Texas) thought of as a "godless place," which is one of the really nice things about it.

What made it possible for you to attend? Somewhere in 1948–9, it stopped raining in south Texas. It just quit. Although my father was no longer farming (he had sold his farmland to my uncle), he had set up a general store in Lytle. Most of the income came from selling feed and seed. But there was a terrible drought and Medina Lake eventually went dry, and he couldn't sell much feed and seed. By the time I graduated from high school in 1954, my father had to sell his store. We moved to Corpus Christi just as I got out of school. The drought was a financial disaster for them. But it was good because I was able to attend the University of Texas, which was very cheap. Baylor was not expensive in those days, but it certainly was more expensive than Texas.

Did your siblings attend college? Oh, yeah. My brother went to the University of Texas and got his Master's degree in biology. He works for the Chemical Manufacturers' Association in Washington, DC, doing environmental work. One sister became a school teacher in Texas. The other sister has a PhD in German. She teaches English as a second language for Houston Community College.

Were you raised a Baptist? Oh yeah, absolutely. But by the time we moved to Corpus Christi, I had pretty much become an atheist. Although, certainly, I wasn't prepared to tell my parents. I never did tell my parents, though they knew it. My parents attributed my atheism largely to the two high school teachers, plus the fact that I went to the University of Texas. I think it would have happened in any event, but who knows?

What was your experience like at the University of Texas? They had a wonderful program with a very unexciting name called Plan II [*laughter*]. Plan I was the standard curriculum. Plan II was created back in the 1930s by a number of good people; Clarence Ayres, Walter Prescott Webb, and others. The idea was to create a kind of honors program that would integrate learning.

Was it interdisciplinary? Yeah; so instead of taking some sociology, some psychology, or some economics courses, they created a year-long course called Social Science 610 and a western history course which was taught by a man named Archibald Lewis, who was a well-known historian. They also created special English courses. It was a selective program which admitted 100 students each fall. And because this was a populist state and a populist university, people who graduated at the top of their high school class got a crack at the Plan II program. Well, I went to a very small high school, and I was not the valedictorian because I got into trouble with home economics, which I did not want to take [*laughter*].

I'd like to hear about this. All the boys took farming and learned about hogs and chickens. All the girls took home economics. Actually, looking back, it probably wasn't a totally bad thing. It's interesting because it was obviously a course that involved a certain amount of social change. You learned what nutritional meals were; that's good. You learned about vitamins. You learned a little bit about interior decorating; about taste. Obviously it was a way to improve taste in rural America.

Was etiquette included? Actually, there wasn't much etiquette; that's kind of curious. You learned about modern appliances. They had these home economics books (I don't know if you've ever seen them) that told you about washing machines, dryers, etc. The courses were designed to spread the idea of how to run a modern American household. In the pre-television era, and particularly in rural areas which were undergoing rapid change, these courses had their place. But I decided in my senior year I would not take the fourth unit in home economics, so I didn't sign up. The principal asked me why and I replied, "Because I don't need it to graduate." They instead offered me a special geometry course. I loved geometry, so I did that. It was a very limited little school; we didn't have foreign languages or much in the way of sciences, so it was exciting to have this special geometry course. But they also insisted that I take home economics. I did a very polite and subversive sit-down strike; I made a B. I decided I would not make less than that, but I wouldn't try for an A either. Of course, I don't know if I could, even if I had tried [*laughter*].

Did you qualify for Plan II? I didn't automatically get into Plan II, but I did pass the screening at the beginning of the year and got in. It was wonderful because there were approximately 100 of us. The first year was good, but the second year was really exciting. I took Social Sciences 610 taught by Clarence Ayres. I also took my first anthropology course, and a philosophy course taught by John Silber who later became famous as the conservative and hard-nosed president of Boston University. He was a brand-new assistant professor in philosophy. He was difficult, and worked very hard to make students think. I don't think he was nearly the reactionary he later became, or if he was, I was unaware of it. I was only aware that he was in conflict with the ideas I was learning in anthropology and in the Ayres course. John Silber was a Platonist; there was "a beauty," "a truth," and we must find that "truth." He was decidedly non-relativistic. That was, for me, a very exciting and informative year. I was involved with ideas. Although I eventually gave up Plan II and majored in anthropology because I needed to work full time, I have always thought myself very fortunate to have been part of Plan II for two years.

You said that you quit Plan II to work full time. Could you explain? What happened was, in the summer of 1955, Gilbert McAllister asked if I wanted to work as a grader for him. I was delighted. I had been working in the library, but grading was a much better job. Also about that time – half-way through my undergraduate career – my family's financial problems worsened. The store that my father had bought in Corpus Christi near the Naval Air Station began to fail. It was a common story then: a chain came in and built a supermarket nearby and the little mom and pop stores began to disappear. However, my mother was teaching school in Corpus Christi and was reasonably happy. By then, my younger siblings were attending school in Corpus Christi.

Was there anyone in anthropology that influenced your thinking? Well, there was one, McAllister. I took a course from McAllister who was widely known among undergraduates as a rather flamboyant teacher. It was very clear to me, even from the beginning, that he wasn't nearly the intellectual heavyweight that Ayres or some of the other faculty were. However, he was important to me in the sense that he helped me to formulate ideas that still run through twentieth-century social science. Otherwise, there wasn't anyone else in anthropology who was my intellectual guru. Although it was a good faculty.

Do you remember any female professors as an undergraduate? Yes, one, Ruth Allen in economics. I rather accidentally took her course. I don't remember now why exactly, but I thought that maybe one of the things I might want to do was economics. I had three options I could major in. I considered majoring in English, economics, and anthropology. Someone told me that if I wanted to major in economics that I probably ought to take one of the two introductory courses. (You see, if you took Social Science 610 you were exempted from all introductory social science courses.) I thought, OK, I'll take this micro course. I was told it would not be covered in Social Science 610. Micro was taught by Ruth Allen. She was a remarkable woman.

How so? She received her PhD in economics from Chicago in the 1920s, and did some remarkably good work. She published a book on the east Texas lumber workers, a very interesting group. She also did fieldwork on farm workers' families in the South during the 1930s. She was basically a labor economist. She was a very interesting woman, and an institutionalist in the best sense; she thought the study of economies was about studying the way people were organized for production and distribution, etc. Interestingly, I have often been asked whether she and other professors at Texas were institutionalists. What I explain is that I don't remember anyone, including Clarence Ayres, identifying themselves as such. They were simply economists, and so that's what economics was. Indeed, in 1954–5, when I took Ruth Allen's course, that was still pretty much what economics was.

Do you recall anything about her course, in particular? Ruth Allen was a very dry wit and sardonic woman. In some sense, she was not a very friendly woman. But I particularly remember two things about the course that influenced me. One is that, when she taught the basic supply and demand curves and all that, she taught them always with a sardonic twist so that you knew that you weren't supposed to take it too terribly seriously. She didn't attack it. But it was also not taught as a matter of faith; it was one way of analyzing things. The other thing she did, which was very amusing to me, was that she picked on, in a most vicious way, the young, male students who were by and large very conservative. Her class was part of the business school curriculum. The economics department at Texas was definitely not part of the business school. They refused to be, and were very hostile to the business school. But, freshman economics was required by the business school. Many of the faculty in the economics department, then and later on, took it as part of their task to challenge the status quo among business school students. Miss Allen (I call her Miss Allen because that was what she was called; it now seems wrong to substitute Ms for the emphatic and proudly worn "Miss") was an absolute master at this.

Were there other women in your classes? No, not many; I think practically none. I just don't remember. I certainly felt like an outsider. In those days, you see, many of the women who were at the University of Texas were either in the College of Education or in the College of Home Economics. But there were also a fair number of women in Plan II.

Why did you choose anthropology as your major? Frankly – partly because of Clarence Ayres. He made anthropology seem central.

Was he your mentor at Texas? Yeah, in an informal way. He was a wonderful undergraduate teacher if you didn't want anything that was very structured. If you wanted structure, that was not what he offered. In Social Science 610, he'd come in and simply start talking and asking questions. He would engage in dialogue with students, but it wasn't lecturing in any kind of organized way. I found it absolutely wonderful. Many students did not like it at all. Many found him extremely radical, and certainly he would provoke students about economics. The very first day of class he gave us a quiz. We were supposed to say whether the means of production (which he somehow defined for us) should be privately owned or state owned. We had to choose and write a sentence or two. Then he bellowed at us for the next hour about the stupidity of the choice he had given, and that one could not answer the question without additional information. But what got to most of the students was not his economic radicalism (which was clearly there), but his religious and philosophical radicalism. Most of us were from pretty conservative Texas backgrounds. And one of Ayres's big points (which was essentially the anthropological perspective) is that what you know and what you believe, etc., is cultural, and that not only does this change with time, but it can be changed by people taking deliberate action. Most of the people in that class were smart enough to realize that this included religion.

I remember a tall, good-looking man who eventually got his PhD in philosophy, a very self-certain person who could hold forth loudly on some aspect of something like Dostoevski. Many of us, who didn't know who Dostoevski was, were absolutely overwhelmed by his knowledge. But he got really upset with Ayres in Social Science 610. I remember this wonderful exchange where he rose from his chair and shouted to Ayres (who was also a very tall man), "Are you saying that it makes no difference if I kill my mother?" And Ayres said, "I'm saying that it makes a lot of difference to you and your mother, but to the universe, no Mr X, it does not." [*Laughter*] Of course, everybody was horrified, except for a few who thought it funny.

Did you have other courses or contact with Ayres? I took a small seminar with him on current issues and got to know him better. He would stop you if he saw you on campus and talk about novels. He would lend you novels. He loved music, and in those days you could go to the university Coop and listen to records in booths before you bought them. He used to go there. If he saw you listening to records, he would talk about why Bartok was a person you ought to appreciate. He'd give a whole lecture on Bartok while we stood there. In that sense, but only in that sense, he was kind of a mentor.

You also said that he influenced your decision to major in anthropology? Yes, and the first steps towards a graduate career. I went to see him about a major. He was strongly supportive of my leaning toward anthropology. So, I wound up doing it. You see, one of the things you have to understand about me is that I never decided that I was just going to be an economist or a historian or an anthropologist. I guess it was the Social Science 610.

Because your education was interdisciplinary? Yeah. The people in anthropology talked about what the people in economics were talking about.

There was a dialogue? Yeah, there was a dialogue. The other thing was that economic development was a brand new sub-field. There was a lot of excitement associated with thinking about the changes in traditional economies etc. So the overlap between anthropology and economics made a lot of sense, and I continued to take courses in both.

By your senior year, did you know what you were going to do after you graduated? Women didn't have to know what they were going to do. It wasn't that I was planning to get married. Although all of us thought we would. But we weren't career-oriented. I mean there were all sorts of possibilities out there, so I wasn't worried. This may be one of the peculiar things about the 1950s. We thought that there would be jobs and money. Our parents were terribly worried about things, but I thought things would be OK, although I didn't know what I was going to do.

How did you decide to go to graduate school then? Re-enter Ruth Allen into my life. She was a fairly ardent feminist. Of course, in those days there were lots of things that women couldn't apply for. But she asked if women could be nominated for the Woodrow Wilson Fellowship. They said yes, and so she nominated me. I had to decide. I talked to a number of people in anthropology and, of course, Ayres. I asked them what I should do and where I should go. The Woodrow Wilson Fellowship was wonderful; I could go anywhere. But the general agreement was that the University of Chicago was the best place in anthropology.

In the meantime, however, I decided to get married to my first husband, who was also an anthropology student. He had graduated and was working on a Master's degree in anthropology. He was very, very bright, but he didn't have a very strong work ethic. Anyway, things got complicated because I had decided to get married in spring of 1958, but I had also received this fellowship which I didn't expect. Jack said, no problem; he would be quite happy to go to Chicago and work for a while.

So your husband's name was? Jack Brown.

Is Mayhew your family name? Yeah. In my first marriage, I did not use my maiden name. But, in my second marriage, I insisted.

When did you go to Chicago? In the fall of 1958. I did a solid year of graduate work in anthropology. It was great fun in a sense. But in another sense it was kind of a disaster because the faculty fell apart on us. One reason I wanted to go to Chicago was to study with Robert Redfield, a big name in anthropology. He did what could be considered development work. Redfield died the month before we got there. In addition, the University of California system started expanding and hired a good part of the Chicago faculty away. At the end of the first year of graduate work, all of us with Woodrow Wilson Fellowships left. I stayed around, worked, and took some course work. But the following year, after my first child was born, I decided against anthropology. I was disenchanted with it. Some of the work I did in Chicago was no more sophisticated than the work that I had done as an undergraduate. I lost any sense of where things were going. It didn't make any great intellectual sense to me.

You said you worked in Chicago? I worked as a researcher for some psychologists. The most interesting job I had was on a project directed by W. Lloyd Warner and James Abegglan who did studies of business executives and of federal bureaucrats. I coded their questionnaires, which was great fun. I liked the team of people I worked with. But Jack and I decided to go back to Austin and he would finish his Master's degree. I think, truth be told, we were both terribly homesick for Austin. I wasn't terribly fond of living on the south side of Chicago either; it was difficult living. Moreover, almost everybody who has lived in Austin has loved Austin. It has great charms. So we went back there and, although now it seems very strange to me, I thought I was going to settle into the life of a housewife.

Well, you had a child? Yeah, and that was what you did. This was all perfectly normal. Then, I had a second child. All my friends (people I had gone to college with) were doing the same thing.

What was your experience as a housewife? I couldn't stand staying at home all the time. I was terribly bored. There was nothing fun about it. I mean I liked my kids, and I liked doing a certain amount of cooking, but beyond that I was going stir crazy. I think, in a sense, there's been a change. My daughter is staying at home now with her three children, but she leads a very active life of organizing school events and doing all sorts of things. She has a productive life in addition to what she does at home. There wasn't that same kind of activity available, or if there was, I wasn't aware of it and able to take advantage of it.

So being a housewife wasn't working out for you? I was miserable. Looking back on it, I probably went through a period of what today would be called clinical depression. But, in those days, nobody did those kinds of diagnoses. We also had enormous money problems. Jack was a very, very bright man and, in many ways, a very nice man. He had intellectual goals, but was unable to complete projects or papers.

Did he ever finish his Master's? No, no, he did not. And he was a misfit in the local job market. There wasn't anything that he could do very well. He had several jobs that weren't bad jobs, but he didn't like them. He was either not successful or would quit. When my youngest child, Doug, was about 9 months old or so, it became clear to me that I needed to go back to work, both for the sake of my mental health and also because we desperately needed money. So I started looking for a job in Austin and discovered that I also was a misfit.

Where did you look for a job? Austin was much smaller than it is now (about a quarter million). It was dominated by the state government and the university. But here I was, a very peculiar person, having done a year of graduate work in anthropology and had not concentrated on practical courses as an undergraduate. My only real skills were secretarial. I went to work as a research assistant/secretary to Ben Higgins, the development economist in the economics department. He was more of a traditional economist than the people with whom I had studied, but he was interested in interdisciplinary matters. He had worked in Indonesia with Clifford Geertz and other anthropologists, and I was interested in this stuff, so I went to work for him.

Did you continue to take course work at the university? Right away Ben suggested that I register for his development course. So, I did. In that way, without ever consciously deciding, I started taking graduate courses in economics. Then it occurred to me that this was a very good thing. I had two small children and a husband who was not successful in finding work and who, by the way, was developing a drinking problem. (I knew this, but I don't think at the time I was fully aware of how serious the problem was. I was naive. I knew that, in some ways, the whole Chicago experience had been stressful and difficult, but I didn't know how serious the drinking problem was going to become.) Anyway, it occurred to me that a Master's degree in economics might be a good thing. I didn't think I would be able to teach in a local high school or junior college with a Master's in anthropology, but I could in economics. I took courses in economics for about a year. I also continued to work in the department, which involved a wide variety of things, including secretarial duties, research assistance, etc. Several of the faculty members had received a grant from *Resources for the Future* to do a study of the Southwest. In the beginning, part of what they did was to figure out how to define the Southwest. Should they include Louisiana, Arkansas, Texas, Oklahoma, and New Mexico? Should it start with Texas and Oklahoma? How far east did you go? How far west? There were all sorts of issues; I worked on those, and took course work.

Who took care of your children? I had them in child care.

At the university? No, but there were private child care centers around the University of Texas. There were many women who worked in clerical positions while their husbands were attending graduate school. This was a common pattern in the 1950s and 1960s. By the time I returned to school, in the spring of 1962, child care wasn't bad. First, my children went to the home of an older couple. But I became somewhat alarmed. They were nice enough, but they didn't provide much activity for them. Then, I put them in a place they both still remember fondly. I don't remember the cost. It was pretty cheap. But, on the other hand, I wasn't getting paid much, so it used up most of my salary. They went all day, until about 5 p.m. I tried to study after they had gone to bed, but it was pretty difficult. It wasn't a bad life, however. I had an ideal job. Ben did a lot of traveling on various sorts of UN things. I was left to mind the mail and that sort of thing, so I had time to study.

How did you end up getting a PhD in economics? At some point (maybe 1963), I went to see the graduate advisor, Forest Hill, to talk about signing up for a Master's thesis. He pointed out, somewhat to my surprise, that if I did another year of course work, I would have satisfied all of the requirements for a PhD, partly because they would accept my year of work in anthropology as a collateral field. That would never happen in economics today! It seemed like a very exciting possibility. I said, "Well, why not?" I could continue to live in extreme poverty for another year. We were exceedingly poor. I switched jobs and became a teaching assistant. I taught principles of micro and macro for a year. I enjoyed it, but found it pretty scary. I also finished my course work.

Did you take any graduate courses with Ayres? He had retired, but he was still teaching one course here and there in the graduate program. I never did take another course with him; this was partly at the recommendation of Forest Hill. He suggested that, because I had done several courses with Ayres as an undergraduate, there were other things that I needed more. I agreed. So I took other courses. The micro sequence was taught by H. H. Liebhafsky, who had an enormous impact on all of us who went through Texas in those days. He was the department's price theorist. He terrified everyone because he made you go to the board and solve problems. He never forced me to go to the board, maybe because he knew I was terrified – really terrified.

In retrospect, what was graduate school like? I have to say, even though my home life was falling apart, even though I was awfully poor, and even though I was frequently stressed out by working too hard, in some ways, those were really great years. There was a coffee room where bunches of us hung out for many hours, probably to the disgust of some faculty, although faculty also participated. We had wild discussions. I think that I probably learned as much in there as I did in any course.

Were you the only woman in your graduate program? There were a couple of other women in the graduate program. One woman came from Oregon State where she had done graduate work (I think). But I was usually the only woman in the coffee room. The coffee room group did a lot of partying together. They were generally radical in one way or another. It was a time of political radicalism. This is the early 1960s. There was also a lot of social radicalism. That poor woman was much more conventional. I don't think that she ever felt very comfortable. She got married not too long after she came and went to work for the Dallas Fed. Another woman in the statistics program took course work in economics. She and I worked together and got along, but she was also never part of our group. There was also a woman, somewhat older than I, who had a child with mental problems of some sort. She spent most of her time worrying and dealing with that. Another woman, Ann Lower, was a closer friend. But she left and had a successful career as a political consultant and consumer advocate. Sadly, she died very recently.

Were all your professors male? Yeah. There was one woman who came as a visiting professor. But this was after I had finished my course work, while I worked on my dissertation. I didn't have a female role model. I wasn't particularly aware of the need for any, which isn't to say that I was superior. In a sense, my role models were those two high school teachers. They were role models, not in the sense that I wanted to do what they had done. (I'm sad to say, I eventually lost touch with them.) They were my role models in a more important way – in my thinking. Certainly, Ayres was also an important role model in my thinking. His courses reformed the way I have continued to think. It's curious to me that it wasn't until much later, when I became more aware of the problems facing women, that Miss Allen became a role model. I had really enjoyed her, but I don't think I ever thought, "Aha, I want to be like Miss Allen!" I'm sorry to say, she was not intellectually important to me at the time. I wish she had been. I wish I knew then what I know now; I could have learned a lot from her. Just a footnote here. When I thanked her for nominating me for the Woodrow Wilson Fellowship, she said, very brusquely, something like, "Don't thank me; you did it!" Then she walked away.

Were you inspired by any of your graduate professors, in particular? I took course work with Wendell Gordon who was important to me. He had a dry wit and was an awfully good teacher in international economics. I took development and economic history courses with Walter C. (Terry) Neale, who was there as a young faculty member. He later became my second husband. I had also taken American economic history with Forest Hill, who was the first editor of the *Journal of Economic Issues* (*JEI*). Forest was a disorganized teacher, but he was wonderful to talk to outside of the classroom and very helpful. I also took Steve McDonald who was an interesting man. He had received his PhD at Texas, gone to Louisiana State University, and then they brought him back. His specialty was petroleum economics, which was a big deal in Texas. He also taught an excellent graduate macro course, one of the great courses. He was a good teacher, an organized teacher. I really liked macro. I had gotten a good deal of Keynesian economics from Ayres in Social Science 610 (without knowing that's what it was). So it all clicked for me; I understood Keynes. My official examination fields were economic history, labor, and development. I should add that I took course work in labor economics with Ray Marshall and learned a lot (though I didn't know it at the time). Everybody had to do the history of thought in those days, besides micro and macro theory.

Can you tell us something about your dissertation? Well, my dissertation is a disaster story. As I approached the dissertation stage I had no idea what to do. I thought I wanted to write something about anthropology or development. It was suggested that I apply for a *Resources for the Future* dissertation fellowship and do it on some aspect of the Southwest project. I was reluctant. But I talked to various people, including Terry. And by the way, at this point, Terry and I had absolutely no thought whatsoever of being married. There was nothing ever between us then.

Was he part of that coffee room group you've described? Yeah, he was very much part of the coffee room group. But he was also a proper young, married man with three kids.

Did he attend your parties? He partied on occasion. But mostly, the parties didn't involve the econ faculty. It was mostly students from chemistry, economics, and a lot from local political groups, including people who played guitars and sang the songs of the 1960s.

One story that summarizes my memory of the period has to do with my children. They grew up without a religious upbringing because I had completely rebelled against that Baptist stuff. The song *Joe Hill* was a standard part of the parties. As it turned out, my daughter thought that Joe Hill and Jesus were the same person because "I never died, said he" is the punch line of the song, *Joe Hill* [*laughter*]. We were involved in various protests and political activities during the 1960s, but this best summarizes my memories of the time.

Did you apply for the fellowship? The idea of applying for the *Resources for the Future* (RFF) fellowship had a certain appeal because it would be a fast project, and I would get paid. I really needed money. I talked to various people, including Terry, and he suggested that I apply for the fellowship because I had a responsibility to buy the kids shoes and that sort of thing. So I did a dissertation on east Texas, a depressed part of the state. This was during the mid-1960s, when there was money for regional development. The Appalachian Regional Council had been set up. Similar funds were available elsewhere. East Texas was designated as one of these areas. The purpose of the dissertation was to figure out why this area qualified; what had given rise to the economic characteristics that qualified them to be a depressed area. It was a very pedestrian dissertation. I did read some interesting stuff, including Miss Allen's work on the east Texas lumber workers.

Who was your major advisor? Steve McDonald, because he was involved in the RFF project. I collected lots of statistics and finished it, and that was that. A great disadvantage to me was that it didn't provide the basis for further work.

Did you enter the job market after you finished your dissertation? No, I was not finished. I went to the University of Illinois in Champaign-Urbana for my first job in 1965, and I didn't finish the dissertation until the spring of 1966. It was essentially done, but there were a lot of little things to do. I hated it so much that it took me a long time to get it done. But it was an easy time to go on the job market because the baby boomers were starting college. They needed lots of teachers and it wasn't essential that you were finished. Although there were plenty of jobs, the job market was not nearly so well organized as it is today. You learned about jobs mainly through personal contacts and applied.

But I was awfully naive about what kind of job I wanted or what I could do. So I made some serious and stupid mistakes by not pursuing jobs that might have been more interesting. I also learned a few interesting things. One was that they might not be interested in me because I was a woman. Honest to goodness, it had not occurred to me before that this would be a problem. The faculty in the economics department at Texas had been so supportive that I just assumed that was the way the world would be. Another problem, which was more subtle, were questions like, "What do you intend to do?" I replied by telling them about future research projects and what I would like to teach. I answered naively, thinking that this was what they were asking. Of course, what they were really asking (and I only learned this when I interviewed at Illinois because a couple of people were more explicitly male chauvinist) was – didn't I really intend to quit, have more children, and be a housewife? It was only late in the interview process that I realized what was going on.

Another problem I noticed when I interviewed at a northeastern school, was the question, "Isn't it true that the faculty at Texas are way out in left field?" I was stunned by this. This had never occurred to me. I had done no comparative shopping on where to go to graduate school after I went back to Austin. The Texas faculty had connections all over the country and in those days, there was no stigma attached to being an institutionalist. This is something I have tried to explain to younger institutionalists who feel so embattled and wonder what the elders did to survive. I don't think that they felt "different." I certainly didn't think of the faculty at Texas as being particularly odd; I thought of them as "economists." So I was kind of stunned. But then I realized, it was a problem. What happened to me and my friends was that we naively went marching out of the University of Texas not knowing that it had been a special place. We marched out when the whole discipline of economics was in a transitional stage. Before this transition, places like Illinois had more tolerance of and appreciation for what we would, today, call heterodox economics. But, neoclassical formalism was becoming dominant and intolerant in the mid-1960s.

How did you get the job at the University of Illinois? Some historical context, first. Economists had begun to jump on the "education" bandwagon as a major source of economic growth and development. Many things were written about the contributions of education and social overhead capital. This was brand new. Denison and Abramowitz had both published articles on "the residual." The idea was if you used something like the Cobb–Douglas production function, it did not explain total growth in the US economy from sometime in the mid-1900s (when the first reliable numbers were available) to the 1960s. Growth had been much more rapid, and so how do you explain it? Denison did a study in which he parceled out the residual. He concluded that some of it was due to increases in health, and some of it was due to increases in education (something like 16.19 or 28.23 percent). I don't remember the exact numbers, but I do remember that it was carried out to some ridiculously precise figure. This was in 1964–5, when Johnson's Great Society was cranking up.

And Gary Becker had just written his dissertation on human capital. Yeah, exactly; the emphasis on human capital had begun. It was also when colleges of education were receiving money from the Kennedy and Johnson administrations, particularly during the Johnson years. One of the arguments was that education produced economic growth. We've all become so accustomed to that argument that we no longer think of it as having a beginning. But, it comes from the mid-1960s.

What was your job like at the University of Illinois? The Bureau of Education Research in the College of Education was interested in an economist who would do research and write in this area. They arranged a twelve-month, joint appointment with the economics department, paying $12,500. I shall never forget that; it was an enormous sum of money. It was more money than I ever thought I would make in my entire life.

Were you still married to Jack? Yes, Jack was enthused about the job. He had grown up in a suburb of Chicago, so the idea of returning to Illinois, in some ways, appealed to him. Since he never got along with his parents, I don't know why he wanted to return. Anyway, for a variety of reasons, I took the job, and boy, was that ever a mistake.

How so? While I was interested in the process of economic growth and economic change, I could not, or would not, do what they wanted me to do, which was to produce a Denison-type statistic. It became clear during a conference my first year. One contributor gave a paper in which he refined Denison's statistics to show the truer contribution of education. I foolishly said that it seemed to me that the assumptions required to get these numbers – that the wage is equal to the value of the marginal product, that markets were all perfectly competitive, etc. – made the numbers suspect. In other words, I was very critical of the paper. Needless to say, this did not go over well with my bosses who wanted these nice numbers. Afterwards, I was uncertain about what to do. What I wanted to do was not what they wanted. Unfortunately, one of the consequences was that I didn't do much research. Instead, I spent more time on teaching. I did an honors principles course, which was fun. I also taught American economic history. I spent most of my time reading US economic history in preparation for class. Well, this didn't make the Bureau very happy, and quite rightfully. In retrospect, I don't know why they didn't fire me. In the end I quit. I was also unhappy in the economics department.

Why didn't you like the economics department? Illinois had a huge economics department. There were some good people, but I didn't get a sense of any great intellectual excitement. I was also on the periphery of the department because I had a job in educational research. Split-appointment jobs are, by and large, a bad idea for new faculty because you don't really belong to any one place. That probably added to my unhappiness there. But, even more so was the fact that my marriage was in deep trouble. Jack had worked for a while. He had a pretty good job as a production editor (copy editor) for a journal. But he was having a difficult time as the second wage earner in the household. I think it's too bad. We've made progress in this country helping men accept different kinds of roles. But, at that time, it was still pretty tough. His drinking problem got worse, his unhappiness got worse, my unhappiness got worse, and our marriage was clearly falling apart.

How did you get together with Terry? The way I got hooked up with Terry was that a group of graduate students from Austin (plus Terry and a few others) had several meetings of something called the Conference on Problems of Economic Change [COPEC]. Terry had organized this as a way to bring together a group of us who had been in Austin, plus others in economic anthropology, like George Dalton and Harry Pearson. Anyway, it was a small gathering. We met maybe once or twice a year in either northern Illinois, Bloomington, Indiana, Chicago, or Washington. This was enormously valuable because all of us who had left Austin felt a terrible loss of people to talk to. It wasn't that the people in the economics department at Illinois were hostile or inhospitable. It was just that one felt completely cut off from any kind of conversation that we had previously been a part of. Electronic mail is so important because it helps people continue discussion. But in those days, the only recourse was snail mail. It was difficult, and so many of us felt completely isolated. Many of us were members of AFEE. But I don't remember attending an AFEE meeting or being particularly aware that there were AFEE meetings. I find that curious. I certainly got the *JEI*. If we attended the ASSA meetings, it was for the purpose of job searching. This was well before AFIT was organized. So, COPEC was, for many of us, an early form of association for institutionalists.

You and Terry got together then? At one of those meetings Terry and I began a different kind of relationship. In 1966, the year after I moved to Champaign–Urbana, Jack and I got a divorce. He went off to the University of North Carolina and did graduate work for a while. But he didn't succeed, and eventually went back to Austin. Later he went to Mexico and taught English. He died there about two or three years ago in a gas-leaking accident. Anyway, Terry was still on the faculty at Texas and in 1967, we got married. I was still on the faculty at Illinois, so for almost a year while he was on leave he commuted. We began looking elsewhere for jobs to be closer together. In some instances, they would hire me, but not him, and vice versa. Finally, we found out about the University of Tennessee. Our contact was Bill Cole who had been a student at Texas. In fact, he, John Adams, and I had taken all of our comprehensive exams together. Also Hans Jensen had been at Tennessee for a number of years before they hired Bill (in 1965). The university was growing pretty rapidly, and the economics department was expanding. They offered both Terry and myself a job, which was wonderful.

What was your experience as an untenured faculty at the University of Tennessee? Well, it wasn't bad. There were certainly faculty members in the economics department, and more so in the College of Business, who gave me the role of faculty wife. But it wasn't too bad because I used my own name, and I always had a fairly independent existence. There were people who were bothered by this, but they didn't say much of anything. Yeah, I felt included in the economics department.

How large was the department then? Probably about fifteen people.

Were you the only woman? At first. Then Karen Vaughn, who is now at George Mason, was hired. She and her husband came, but they didn't stay. In those days, we had different sets of money problems. I certainly had more money than before, but Terry had three children who were in college, and I had two kids. So he and I both applied for summer school, and so did Karen and her husband. The dean would not let Karen and I teach summer school because our spouses were teaching. We marched into his office and protested. He was very taken aback, and we got summer teaching.

Were you untenured for very long? No. Curiously, where I ran into trouble was in the promotion process to full professor. For a while, I didn't publish much. It was a time of turmoil. My kids were in their early teen years, and in some ways this was a more difficult time than when they were younger. I was also doing a lot of teaching and other stuff. But after I started publishing again, I began to think that there was a real problem about my promotion to full. I wasn't quite sure what I ought to do. Unbeknownst to me, Terry went to the dean and said, "Look, I don't know, I think Anne is thinking about this, but I'm going to recommend that she accuse you of sexual discrimination if you don't consider her for full professorship." As it turned out, a new department head came in and asked if I was ready to go for promotion. I said, "Sure." What I learned later, and has always colored my view of a few members of the department (who were my age and hadn't published as much as me, by any means), was that they were against my promotion; I hadn't done proper economic theory. I was really resented for that.

Today, one of the big issues for women is course load. Do you recall what your course load was like? I had a heavier course load than other faculty. There were many cushy arrangements made. People who taught graduate courses didn't teach as much, and I didn't do much graduate teaching. In retrospect, I should have been more outspoken and complained more. My publication record was probably the second or third best in the department. There was no other reason to keep me from teaching graduate courses than the simple perception that I wasn't doing "proper economics." Indeed, what I did was always marginalized by the department.

Didn't you eventually become chair of the economics department? Yes, in 1986. That, I suppose, was a controversial choice by the dean. Well, not entirely. For the first couple of years, I had strong support from practically all the faculty. We started working on the graduate program. I had always been deeply involved with the undergraduate program, with undergraduate advising, etc. I was a very energetic department head. I certainly spent a lot of time on graduate student recruitment. The year before I became department head, we had hired Paul Davidson as the Chair of Excellence. What I did was to advertise broadly that we had strengths in both post-Keynesian and institutional economics. We attracted a lot of really good students because of that and before it all ended we were placing our PhDs in very good schools; we had one of the best placement records in the university and one that many programs envied. The program was growing. As department head, I wanted to build on the post-Keynesian and institutional strengths. We had good people in both areas, but we were kind of thin. Terry was getting close to retirement and Hans had been retired for some time, so I wanted to bolster this strength. We went through a couple of unpleasant years of searching. We tried to find someone who could fit the niche but would also be satisfactory to everyone. We had a couple of good candidates for a micro position; they were very adept at the modern mathematical language of microeconomics, and also questioned it from a more or less orthodox perspective, but also had a post-Keynesian under-standing. They were not acceptable to the faculty, who had grown concerned about the role that institutionalism and post-Keynesianism were playing in the department. There was increasing concern about the graduate students that we attracted; they were excellent but they were also critical when presented with orthodoxy as faith. That began to send up all sorts of red flags. So things grew more hostile.

In other words, they wanted a mainstream department? Strictly neoclassical. They also wanted to isolate Paul Davidson and get him out of the graduate program. The dean of the College of Business also made it clear that he wanted to put all of his efforts into an MBA program. I lost support as department head and was forced out. I decided that I didn't want to be part of the transformation of what had been a strong program into a mediocre conventional department that primarily served the business school. Eventually, and after considerable difficulty, I moved to become a professor of history. But before I had settled into that role, a new opportunity arose.

Can you tell us about that? Well, the newly appointed dean of the College of Arts and Sciences was a long-time friend. She asked if I would be interested in taking over the job she had been doing as associate dean. I was enormously happy to do it because it involves stuff that I had been working on for years: curriculum issues, management of our interdisciplinary programs, and related issues. I no longer have any ties to the economics department, which is a great feeling of relief. I feel so much better not having to think about economics all the time. I realized how economics, over my lifetime, has become a more and more miserable intellectual endeavor to be involved in. I still very much enjoy editing the *JEI* and I like most of the history of economic thought (not all of it), and some of the economic history that is being done. I just don't want to think about the other issues that dominate economics. When I was in the economics department, I always thought that I ought to attend my colleagues' presenta-tions, read their papers, read the journals, and pay attention to where these debates were going. Being released from that is just an incredibly good feeling! I have just felt … [*sigh*].

Are you teaching now? Not this term. I will teach an undergraduate US economic history course in the spring.

And after this appointment? I might go back to history. I would like to offer a course in financial history again and a course on the history of the modern US firm. I might also decide that I want to retire. I don't know.

Upon reflection, how would you describe the development of your career? Well, like I told you, I never made any decisions about anything. It seems to me that this latest move is quite consistent with everything else that has happened to me. It's kind of serendipitous. If you look at my publication record, you see the same thing. In some ways it's a weird publication record because there's no apparent consistency to it.

Is it eclectic? Yeah, that's right. Although, I do see some absolutely stable themes that run through my work. Going back to my sophomore year, there is a kind of Ayresian understanding of economies as cultural systems, and how that overlaps with anthropology with the addition of Polanyi's understanding to it all. I found Polanyi's work enormously powerful because it tied a lot of stuff together. During my year as a graduate student in anthropology, what was particularly frustrating was the inability to talk sensibly about "economic" anthropology, particularly about the work of Melville Herskovits and his exchange with Frank Knight, and the other pieces of literature that existed. It seemed such a confused mess. I couldn't sort it out. When I encountered Polanyi's work in Terry's course (around 1963), it all came together. It made sense within this kind of Ayresian–Polanyian perspective. That has been the core of my work. The first article I published on education and earnings by occupation stands out as a real aberration in my mind; a consequence of the work I did at the Bureau of Educational Research in Illinois. It was an effort on my part to try and make sense of the research charge that I had. But beyond that, my article on the agricultural protest is straight Polanyi (although, I don't know if I used Polanyi's name). It was an application of many of Polanyi's ideas which occurred to me while I was teaching US economic history. It's also a common theme that runs through my publications.

Can you elaborate on Polanyi's influence on your work? Polanyi's book, *The Great Transformation*, allowed me to see classical and neoclassical economic theory as developing out of the process of cultural transformation. This transformation emerged from the fact that the Industrial Revolution took place in the commercialized economy of England during the early nineteenth century. Ayres and Veblen provided the big picture of cultural change; Polanyi provided the specific history to understand nineteenth-century economic history and the history of economic thought. When I applied Polanyi's understanding to my teaching I began to see how the US economy was transformed from a largely self-sufficient, though commercialized, system into the kind of self-regulating market system that became the ideal of nineteenth-century liberals, and remains today the ideal of free-marketeers. This perspective also allows you to see the reaction of the populists and progressives, and to see the New Deal as "protective reaction" (Polanyi's term). By this he meant protective of human society; a human society that is something other than an extension of a self-regulating market system in which all is commercial and everything is for sale. Polanyi's argument is powerful, though frequently misunderstood by friend and foe alike. It has been a theme in all of my work and remains today a fundamental basis for my ongoing research.

You have mentored many women at the University of Tennessee. What kind of advice do you give to them when they go on the job market or go up for tenure? To listen very carefully. They will probably get questions, even if they are not illegal, they are still illegal in intent. That is to say, people will ask questions that are none of their business. The best thing to do, usually, is to ignore it and to pretend that they are people of good faith. But if you feel that there is hostile intent, then deal with it very directly. Ask: "Are you asking me – do I plan to get married and quit, or am I serious about this? If the latter, then yes, I'm serious." I've been frustrated talking to young women in the last several years. Many of them don't understand the extent to which there is likely to be bias against them. I didn't understand it, and that was bad. Today, there is less of a reason to fail to understand it because there has been a lot more discussion about it. They need to know that this attitude is still there. I have been relatively impatient with all of the other advice given to women; about how to dress, etc. I tend to regard that as being less relevant than how women come across intellectually. My advice, generally, is to play up their best strengths; to be themselves. I also strongly advise against students applying for jobs in big research universities where they are expected to publish articles in orthodox journals. They are likely to fail or be unhappy, so why bother?

Why do you think more women are not attracted to economics? Well, I think the reason for that is obvious. What we teach in economics is so antithetical to anything that makes sense to them. There is no good reason for them to major in economics. Recently I went to a conference where one of the issues discussed was the declining number of economics majors. There were two views expressed. One was that we need to worry about how we present the material; it was a pedagogical problem. Others argued that it is the substance of what is taught; you can't make irrelevancies interesting because they have nothing to do with the world in which people live, and it has nothing to do with a better world that they might want to create. I think that's the problem.

Would you recommend a PhD in economics to someone? Until fairly recently, because it was selfishly convenient for me to do so, I held the view that people should get PhDs in economics. They could always get jobs at liberal arts colleges. That is where most of my PhD students have gone. I believed they could do some good there; they could succeed; this was worthwhile. More recently, when I talk to bright undergraduates who come to me, I suggest that they avoid economics in graduate school. This is one reason why I had to leave the economics department. This is not a happy position to be in. If students came to me, either because they were interested in coming here as graduate students (we kept getting people who thought Tennessee was a good place to come) or because they were asking advice, I had to say,

> Are you sure this is what you want to do? Find a good program in public policy. There are other things you can do, and I'll help you find ways to do that. Take some work in economics, the history of thought, or economic history, even if you want to do something else.

I say this because I am convinced that the economics profession has tipped too far over to be brought back as "economics." We should try to preserve the good economic ideas in both institutional and neoclassical economics. Indeed, I've always thought there is a rough-and-ready truth to "orthodox economics," but that it has become buried under ideological free-marketeerism and pseudo-scientific formalism.

Would you like to elaborate on that? OK, let's take the simple use of supply and demand analysis and think about the incidence of taxation and the effectiveness of various forms of taxation. When one talks about these issues, plotting out supply and demand curves, or basic stuff like that, makes a lot of sense. This is a perfectly good way of thinking about it and may be quite useful. I have no problems whatsoever with that. But when you think of it as something other than a tool, you lose all perspective. I've spent lots of time over the past couple of years reading American economics from the turn of the twentieth century and early twentieth century. There is a strong sense of this rough-and-ready truth of economic analysis as opposed to a refined and precise truth.

What do you mean by rough-and-ready truth? I spoke earlier about the early statistical estimates of the contribution of education to US economic growth, down to two decimal places. This is an example of the really stupid kind of economics that economists have come to do. It's one thing to say education is important for economic growth. That's fine; it's true. But when you say, I'm going to measure its precise contribution, then you have lost a sense of what you are saying. It's the whole misconception of the nature of human society, reducing it to commercial activity and making it seem necessarily true by false precision. This is the strong part of the feminist critique. It also has to do with the whole set of issues in the debate over postmodernism and modernism, the idea that there is a "truth" out there (which is a very strong part of neoclassical economics).

How do we preserve the "good" ideas? That's my real concern. How do we preserve the knowledge of economics, even though the academic discipline of economics is likely to fade away? This is a matter of concern because historians, sociologists, anthropologists, and others in the social sciences are largely afraid of economics and economic analysis. They either don't incorporate it, or incorporate it in a non-useful way. Again, an example. It seems to me that economists know a good deal about how banking systems work and how they are incorporated into economic systems. Most historians tend to be afraid of understanding banks and make various kinds of foolish remarks. I recently served on a doctoral dissertation committee in the history department. The student argued that part of the problem was that there were no banks in a particular area. Another problem was that people were paying with paper; that paper was chasing paper. Several other remarks like these were inconsistent. I pursued this and asked, "Are you sure there were no banks? What was the paper that was used?"

Who was issuing it? Yes. For whom were these pieces of paper liabilities? Things that you and I would know to ask because, as economists, we've learned something about how banks work. Neither the candidate nor the other committee members, who were all historians (political and social historians), knew how to think this through. We are in danger of losing that. I feel this very keenly. Sometimes even my institutionalist colleagues do not understand the changes in the American banking structure over the course of US history, and therefore make bad mistakes in understanding various debates in the past. I'm afraid we'll lose that. That becomes the challenge. As I said in my talk that I gave at Franklin–Marshall (and elsewhere), economics departments are going to disappear. They'll shrink and become converted into business economics departments. They may survive as small, very specialized decision science. They may call themselves economics departments, but I don't see them as major players in the reconfiguration of universities.

Switching focus a bit, do you consider yourself a feminist economist? Oh yeah. Oh yeah. For years, I was a little leery of what we thought of as feminist economics, because I essentially associated it with neoclassical work that made arguments about women's pay. While I was certainly convinced that women were underpaid, I wasn't comfortable with neoclassical approaches to this. I came to understand after IAFEE was formed that there were other approaches to feminist economics, which are more consistent with my approach to economics. Yes, I became an enthusiastic feminist economist. I'm a member of IAFFE, but not particularly active, partly because of too many other commitments.

Is there anything feminist economists in general, and IAFFE in particular, can learn from the experiences of institutionalists? Yeah. But I'm not sure that it's a very happy one. In so far as AFEE and AFIT have articulated their disagreements with neoclassical economists, and in so far as they have articulated their disagreements with Marxist economists, and in so far as they have articulated their cohesive and coherent points of view, they have tended to set themselves apart. That's the purpose. As you do that, you do two things. One is that you run a real risk of developing a serious case of bunker mentality. This is a terrible problem in AFEE and AFIT; you feel under siege all the time. One thing this does is to draw the group ever tighter and tighter together; these are your friends; these are your colleagues in the foxhole; these are the people you will die for no matter what. That's lovely as a set of human emotions, but it's not good for intellectual dialogue. It means that you can't argue, because it is interpreted as turning on your friends and colleagues. The bunker mentality in AFEE and AFIT has reduced the quality of intellectual dialogue. This is a danger among feminist economists: not wanting to criticize fellow feminists. Intellectual dialogue is about criticizing. It doesn't have to be done brutally; it doesn't have to be done in an arrogant way that often happens in economics, but it does have to happen. That is one lesson for feminists. On the other hand, you must differentiate yourself. If you make feminist economics simply economics "about women" or "for women," then it is difficult to articulate common intellectual goals. I see this playing out on FEMECON all the time. People who are neoclassical seem horrified with the positions that are not. This seems to be a major tension. One lesson is that you have to be careful and avoid the bunker mentality. It also makes it difficult to attract new people. If you're suspicious of outsiders and if you're suspicious of anything that's not said the right way, you cut yourself off from the world. This is the real danger.

One thing that keeps IAFFE from becoming a pure support group is its international component. For instance, at the conference in Mexico, there was a much different group than what one would expect at the upcoming conference in Amsterdam, with some overlap among the US contingent. Yeah, plus, it's also new enough that there's still a lack of definition. It won't face that problem immediately. What will probably happen is that feminist economists will define themselves as methodologically different from neoclassical economists. Institutionalist feminists have already done so; maybe the Marxist feminists will do so. There seems to be movement in that direction. Hopefully, those groups will be able to join with other social scientists to preserve some of the good ideas from economics and create a more viable and intellectually alive social science. All of the social sciences are in trouble right now because nothing exciting is happening. They were created in the early part of this century.

And now students see college as the training ground for jobs, so we respond by focusing on vocational training. Indeed, that is what I am most passionate about right now. I'm trying to preserve the idea of higher education as something other than vocational training. That is what I would like to devote the rest of my working life to.

Do you see a future for feminist economics? I have been cheered by feminist economics, and I have argued with various people in AFEE that I thought feminist economics was the best thing that has happened in a very long time in economics. But we have a number of people in AFEE who are deeply suspicious of it. There is a deep suspicion of people who do not say things the same way that the institutionalists do, although many of the ideas are the same. There is also the view that, if we are saying the same thing, why don't they join us? But there are many encouraging signs. I'm less pessimistic about social science over a somewhat longer period of time. However, I am very pessimistic about economics departments.

Is there anything else you would like to talk about? Yes, I thought of this last night. I remembered an experience in graduate school. It struck me forcefully that I had an advantage over my male friends. Many of them were scared to death about passing their comprehensives and what would happen to them after that. I wasn't very scared, partly because one of my talents in life was taking tests. I always know more on tests than I do at any other time. This has been the secret of my academic success from the time I started the first grade. So I wasn't particularly panicked. The other advantage was that I could drop out of the program at any time and nobody would have said, you failed. There were no serious expectations that women should necessarily do this. There has been an enormous amount of progress for women since those days. For one thing, no one seriously talked about the possibility of different careers. I often thought that I should have been a lawyer. But that was not something that was discussed as a possibility. I knew some women who went to law school, but that was different. They had fathers who were lawyers.

Do you think it is easier for women today? It is much harder for women today, in the sense that there is an expectation that, yes, you should do it all. That puts pressure on you.

If you could start all over again, what would you have done? I have absolutely no idea. Terry and I have often talked about that. I suspect I would be a lawyer. What appeals to me is that lawyers are actively involved in both thinking about and in remaking the rules by which we live.

In setting policy? Yeah. But I'm not sure that I could do that. I don't know if I have the patience to get through or if I want to do it enough. Sometimes I think I would be a biologist because obviously biology is the exciting part of science right now. But, no, I would have been a social scientist; that interests me the most; human beings and their social interactions. But the social sciences strike me as so dull right now that I can't imagine … .

What is it about the social sciences that makes them so appealing to you? From the 1880s and 1890s to the 1950s and 1960s, the idea that was exciting and that propelled everything was the idea of culture. It might sound trite, but it was this idea that people have social habits which we share as part of a common culture. One could describe them and they could be remade. That's where the idea of progressivity comes in. The idea of social science was simply the idea that this could be discovered and determined, and different groups could be identified by their different patterns. This was such an exciting idea. Then, in the 1950s and 1960s, there was a move away from this idea, in part, for some very good reasons. What replaced it was the idea of the individual as the unit of analysis; the individual as the chooser. This is one reason why microeconomic theory has flourished; why it has had imperialistic success. You can see why the individual became important in this era. In this world, where there is so much mobility and so much cultural overlap of people, the early twentieth-century idea of culture won't work. We've now gone as far as one can go with the idea of the individual chooser and the individual as the important unit. We haven't, in any productive way, been able to put these two ideas back together again. There are ways to do so, which can be rediscovered from the literature in the early part of the twentieth century. But this task has barely begun. For this reason, there will be a resurgence of social science, but it's going to take a while.

What is your next project? Well, I'm writing a book on Ayres and it's almost finished. As soon as that project is done, then I have a book project with two colleagues in which we will incorporate ideas about the business firm into a monetary theory of production. The idea is to reorganize Chandlerian ideas in terms of the firm from the standpoint of monetary theory of production rather than from the cost and output theory of production (on which neoclassical economics is based). I want to also return to the early twentieth century, both from the standpoint of economic history and the history of thought. I have a paper that will be coming out shortly on the ideas about the firm in the early twentieth century. Eventually, I would like to do a history of the social sciences between 1910 and 1940, with an emphasis on how institutional economics wasn't something separable, but part of the social sciences development at the time. That's what I would like to do.

Well, thank you so much for your time. I hope I've told a reasonably accurate story. One is always aware, in thinking back over longer periods of time, that you are telling only one version. It's kind of scary to think of how biased or different the story I told today might be compared to a story I might have told ten years ago or might tell ten years hence. Indeed, the view of my life changes as I go along.

7

MYRA HOFFENBERG STROBER

I finally got my courage up and went to see the chair of the economics department to ask him why I was a lecturer and why two of my former classmates were hired as assistant professors. He told me it was because I lived in Palo Alto. ... I was stunned by his answer and didn't know what to say. ... I always say I became a feminist on the Bay Bridge ... because it was only as I drove home that I realized how ridiculous it was. I wasn't an assistant professor because I lived in Palo Alto!

(Myra Strober, 1998)

Despite her enormous accomplishments as a labor economist, Myra demonstrates a refreshingly light-hearted humility when she reflects on her experiences. Her four books and over fifty articles stand as testimony to her many accomplishments. Her work has primarily focused on gender issues in a variety of work settings, economic education, child care, and the economics of combining work and family. Unwilling to "sell her soul," Myra defected to the School of Education at Stanford University, where she currently holds the position of professor. At Stanford, she was the Founding Director of the Center for Research on Women, Director of Stanford Education Policy Institute, Dean of Stanford Alumni College, and Chair of the Faculty Senate and Provost's Committee on Recruitment and Retention of Women Faculty, among other things. Beyond Stanford, her contributions on behalf of women have also been varied and substantive. She is the former President of the International Association for Feminist Economics, and former Board Member of the Now Legal Defense and Education Fund, the National Council for Research on Women, the National Center for the Workplace, Sage Annual Review of Women and Work. She has also served on the editorial boards of several journals and as faculty advisor to the Rutger's Women's Leadership Program. She has also taught at the University of Maryland and the University of California, Berkeley. She received a BS from Cornell University, School of Industrial and Labor Relations (1962), a Master's from Tufts University (1965), and a PhD from the Massachusetts Institute of Technology (1969).

Our conversations began at Myra's hotel in Amsterdam and at a sidewalk café during the IAFFE conference in June 1998. We spoke again in December that same year when she visited Alverno College. Her forthrightness and sense of humor added both a light-heartedness and a sense of purpose and seriousness to our conversations.

Plate 7   Top left: Myra Strober's marriage to Jay Jackman (couple on the far left) with stepson Rashi Jackman, stepdaughter Tenaya Jackman, son Jason Strober, and daughter Liz Strober. Top right: Myra in 1973. Second row from left: Myra in 1946, 1983, 1992. Third row from left: Myra in 1963; father Julius Hoffenberg and mother Regina Hoffenberg (1970); sister Alice Amsden, mother Regina, and Myra (1985). Bottom left: Myra with husband Jay (1994). Bottom right: Myra at sweet 16 birthday party with great aunt Anna Rubinson, mother Regina, and maternal grandmother Bessie Scharer (1957).

Myra, let's begin with your family background. What would you like to tell us about that? All of my grandparents came to the United States from Europe. My father's mother came from Russia and the other three came from what was then the Austro-Hungarian Empire.

My mother was the oldest of eight children and my father was the oldest of three. Both of my parents were born in New York City. I was also born in New York City and was the oldest grandchild on both sides of the family. There was a lot of fuss over me when I was a young child. Sometimes it was great, but I often longed to be left alone. Reading was terrific because it gave me a wonderful excuse to be by myself, uninterrupted.

My mother was an elementary school secretary and my father was in the garment business. He was a middleman. He sold woven cloth to people who would cut and sew it into men's clothing. My father never went to college but my mother did. She went to City College at night and was very proud of the fact that she had a degree in business.

Did your mother go to college before or after she was married? Partly before and partly after, but before I was born. My parents were married seven years before I was born. My sister was born about two years later.

Are there just the two of you? Yes.

Your sister is also an economist, isn't she? Yes. We were recently talking about how both of us became economists. I think the reason I became an economist is that my father – whom I absolutely adored – was always afraid of losing his job. The men's clothing industry was very volatile. Firms went out of business all the time. He worked for his cousin. But he knew that if business turned bad, his cousin would have to let him go. He was afraid of that prospect, especially because he had lived through the Depression and clearly remembered what it was like for friends and relatives who were out of work.

My mother always worked. She took a short maternity leave when I was born and a slightly longer one when my sister was born. But she always worked – in part because my parents were concerned about the stability of my father's job, in part because they wanted a higher standard of living than my father's job provided, and in part because my mother was less than enthralled with being a housewife.

Did your father ever in fact lose his job? We were fortunate. In fact, my father never did lose his job, but that fear colored my childhood. I was fascinated with "the economy" – this mysterious thing that my parents said could "do in" our family. I think the origins of my concern with equity also stem from that experience. It always seemed so unfair that somebody who worked hard and wanted to continue working hard might face the dismal prospect of not finding work. At a deeper level, perhaps I became interested in economics because somehow it would help me to help my father.

But that was only part of it. My family's most interesting dinner conversations often had something to do with economics. My parents were both very impressed with FDR and saw him as the country's savior and hero. They were in favor of unions and what unions had been able to accomplish for working people. We talked all the time about the Depression. My parents were very interested in making sure we understood what the Depression had been like. Interestingly, they were more concerned about having us understand the Depression than World War II.

Give us some dates so we can have some historical context for when your family was having these conversations. My mother was born in 1905 and my father was born in 1908. They were married in 1934 and I was born in 1941. Our conversations took place in the late 1940s and early to mid-1950s. I graduated from high school in 1958 and started college that fall. By the time I went off to Cornell, the Depression had been over for almost twenty years. Still, it remained the defining experience of my parents' lives. As I said earlier, in retrospect it is very interesting to me that they had been much more fearful of the Depression than of the war. And despite the fact that we are Jewish, there was almost no discussion of the Holocaust. From what I have read, my family was not unusual. It took many years before Jews talked openly about the Holocaust and taught their children about it.

You said your father never actually lost his job, but he must have done well to afford to send you to Cornell? I went to a tuition-free college at Cornell – the School of Industrial and Labor Relations. But my parents were able to pay for my room and board. And I worked all through college, not only in the summers, but also during the term. I had also worked after school all through my last two years of high school.

My mother was very adamant that my sister and I be able to support ourselves and not be dependent on somebody else economically. She never called herself a feminist, even after the women's movement was reborn, but she was certainly a feminist. When I was in high school, she insisted that I take shorthand and typing "just in case" [*laughter*]. As far as I could tell, I was the only girl in my high school who was in an academic program and also taking shorthand.

What do you mean by an academic program in high school? Was there another program as well? Yes, there was a commercial track and an academic track. I was on the academic track, but I never took chemistry or physics because I was busy taking shorthand and typing [*laughter*]. Actually those courses stood me in good stead because I was able to get secretarial jobs all through high school and college.

Before we move on, please talk a bit more about your high school. I went to a huge public high school in Brooklyn called Midwood High School. In my class alone there were 1,000 students. It was exceedingly crowded and we had double sessions. But it was an absolutely first-rate school. Woody Allen went there [*laughter*]. At that time, some of the New York City public high schools were really first rate, and Midwood was one of them. I had excellent teachers, particularly in social studies. I always did well, but I never knew *how* well until fall of my senior year when we all received an envelope telling us our class ranking. I was number eighteen. That ranking turned out to be unbelievably significant because Midwood had a quite unusual way of dealing with the massive number of students who went on to college. I'm sure the Antitrust Division of the Justice Department, had it known about the arrangement, would have viewed it with considerable suspicion.

I don't know the proportion of students who went to college, but a huge number applied. The way it worked was that we could apply to only three schools. For top academic students, the guidance counselors seemed to have some sort of agreement with the elite colleges. For example, only the top-ranked man could apply to Harvard and everyone knew he would be accepted. Only the second-ranked man could apply to Yale, etc. The same thing happened for women. Only the top-ranked woman applied to Radcliffe and so on. In any case, my class ranking dictated that I apply to Vasser. I was accepted and offered a full tuition scholarship. But I turned it down. I was accepted at Cornell, and decided I preferred to go there. The college counselor was extremely angry with me – I'd messed up her system. But for the things I cared about, I couldn't see attending an all-girls school. (We called them girls and boys, although today we call college-age students, women and men.) I wanted boys in my classes. I wanted to know how boys thought about unions, unemployment, and jobs, not just how girls thought about them. Also I liked having boys around on a regular basis. Having to wait until the weekends to see them just didn't seem like much fun.

What was your experience like at Cornell? I absolutely loved Cornell. I loved the program, the university, and being out of New York City. The first year I had the single most valuable course I ever took. We called it Bus Riding 101. Every Wednesday all sixty first-year students got on the buses, went to a nearby factory, and spent the day. First, we would take a plant tour. Then we met with the union and management, listened to their talks, asked questions, talked to workers, etc. Our weekly assignment was to write a paper about the major issues in the industry, plant, industrial relations, etc. We went to a coal mine in Pennsylvania, a steel mill in Syracuse, an IBM factory, a pajama factory, and Corning Glass Works. This class was the most amazing experience. We saw what industrial production was all about. It gave me grounding in the real world of work that has stood me in good stead all my professional life. When I see the diagrams of firms in economics, I don't just see abstract "companies." I remember those plants; their smells and their feel. I remember the workers; how they looked and what they cared about.

You were in the School of Industrial and Labor Relations as an undergraduate, and not in economics? Yes. I took economics classes in both Industrial and Labor Relations (ILR) and in the economics department. But I was in an interdisciplinary program. I had a wide variety of courses, including human resource management, sociology, and anthropology.

Were there any women professors? The only woman professor I ever had was Alice Cook. But if you could have only one, she was the one to have. She was an incredible woman who remained a friend until she died. She lived until her mid-90s and continued writing until a few months before her death. She had been a union organizer, and taught us about the inner workings of trade unions. One of the class highlights was the day she brought in Frances Perkins as a guest speaker. Perkins had been the Secretary of Labor under FDR. She was the only woman in the Cabinet and a visiting professor at Cornell for several years. I remember she only wore black and a hat all the time. This outstanding and accomplished woman talked with us about her experiences in the Roosevelt administration. It was most inspiring.

Were you preparing to get your Bachelor's degree and to immediately work? Yes, I was preparing to be a high school teacher in social studies. Just as my mom had insisted that I take stenography and typewriting in high school, she also insisted that I take education courses in college so that when I graduated I could teach right away. I was taking courses in social studies, history, economics, and education to become a high school social studies teacher. Then two things happened in my senior year to change things.

First, the day the high school teaching exam was given in New York City, I was sick and couldn't take the exam. So I took another exam the following week. This one was for teaching social studies in junior high school or middle school. I passed, and graduated early in January of 1962. I was interested in graduating early because I knew that college was a financial strain for my parents, especially because my sister was also in college.

I returned to New York City and tried to get a job as a junior high social studies teacher, but there were no jobs to be had. Believe it or not, although I had not taken science courses at Cornell, I was offered a job teaching science in a junior high school. I turned it down because I was absolutely unqualified. But it turned out that, by passing the junior high exam, I was qualified to teach fifth and sixth grade. So I got a job teaching fifth grade, which I loved. I had to learn how to teach long division [*laughter*]. That was challenging! But I primarily taught social studies and had a terrific time with the fifth graders.

The second major event during my senior year was that the dean called to tell me that I had been recommended by several faculty for the Woodrow Wilson Fellowship. He asked me if I wanted to go to graduate school. I said no. I told him I was going to be a high school social studies teacher. He said fine, and we probably both figured that was the end of the whole idea [*laughter*]. But, then I related our conversation to my husband-to-be, Sam Strober. Sam and I had met between my sophomore and junior years, while we were working at a hotel in the Catskills. I was a secretary and he was a bellhop. He asked me why I wouldn't consider going to graduate school. I replied that if we were to marry, I needed to work while he attended medical school [*laughter*]. He didn't like that idea at all. He said if both of us had fellowships, we could both go to graduate school.

Why did you think you needed to work while your husband went to graduate school? My number one goal was to get married, no doubt about it.

Is that right? [*Laughter*] Absolutely. But when I realized that he was OK with it, and we could still get married, I thought graduate school was something to pursue. I also talked to my parents and asked them what they thought. They asked what Sam thought, and I told them. They said that as long as this new plan didn't interfere with getting married, it was OK with them too [*laughter*]. We were all fixated on this getting married business.

What did you do next? I went back to the dean, rather sheepishly, and told him that I had thought more about his proposal and I was interested. He asked me what subject I wanted to study. I, of course, hadn't thought about that one [*laughter*]. He told me to think about it. I can't believe that I only took about three or four days to think about it. Only two subjects were possible, economics or history, because I had taken a fair amount of both. I decided to go into economics because I talked to an economics professor I had, and he was very encouraging. I can't believe I never talked to a single historian [*laughter*]. Not one!

Why didn't you talk to a historian? Truth be told, the reason I didn't go into history was that I thought that while I was smart, I wasn't *that* smart. I thought that historians had to know about everything for all time. It never occurred to me that people specialized in a period or a subject! [*Laughter*] If I had bothered to ask around, I might have become a historian. But I never did. I tell you this story to emphasize how important it is to ask what the world is really like. I took lots of history, but never talked to anyone about what historians do. The economist that advised me was M. Gardner Clark who was a Soviet economist specializing in the steel industry. I knew that as an economist I could specialize. I wanted to be a labor economist and specialize in issues of unemployment and labor unions, issues I found exciting. Probably, if I had become a historian, I would have become a labor historian.

How did you decide which graduate school to apply to? Sam was already a medical student at Harvard, so we expected to live in the Boston area. I consequently applied to Harvard, MIT, and Tufts University. Tufts only had a Master's program in economics. As it turned out I didn't get accepted at either Harvard or MIT because I had not majored in economics as an undergraduate. I was advised to attend Tufts, obtain a Master's in economics, and reapply to Harvard and MIT. That was very good advice. If I had gone to MIT without the background from Tufts, I would have had a very difficult time.

During the year at Tufts I applied again to the PhD programs in economics at Harvard and MIT. I had an interview at Harvard with one of the senior economics professors, who should probably best remain nameless. He started out the interview with a most disconcerting question: "Are you normal?" I was stunned and asked, "What do you mean?" "Well," he said, "Do you want to get married and have children?" I told him I was already married. Then why in the world would I want to go to graduate school, he asked. I couldn't win. Either I was abnormal or I was abnormal! [*Laughter*]

139

My interview at MIT was much different; it was very positive. In the end, they accepted me, but I deferred the acceptance for a year. Actually they wouldn't defer it, so I had to apply again. The reason for the deferment was that my husband wanted to study at Oxford for a year.

Did you finish the Master's at Tufts? Yes.

How long did it take you to finish? I finished my course work in one year and then I went to Oxford. But I didn't finish my thesis until the following year.

I had a wonderful time at Oxford, because when I told the folks at the local school district that I had taught fifth grade in New York City, they offered me a job teaching third grade. I was given a special class of children who had failed to learn how to read in the first and second grades. It didn't seem to matter at all that I had no training in teaching young children. Fortunately for me, the vast majority did learn how to read. I also had a wonderful time teaching English history. But I was truly astounded at the class segregation in this school. Every single child had parents who worked at the Morris Motors factory just south of Oxford. One day, I took them on a field trip to see a fox hunt. I was an American; how did I know that working-class children were not supposed to be interested in fox hunts (as the other teachers later told me)? Of course, it turned out, the children were quite interested and we had a terrific outing.

Could you talk a little about your experience in the Master's program at Tufts? I had an excellent experience at Tufts. I had three really fine professors. One was Frank Holzman who was an expert in the Soviet economy. I had planned to have Soviet economics as one of my fields. I even took Russian at Tufts, but it was very difficult. I took several courses on the Soviet economy and wrote my thesis on Soviet trade unions. I had Dan Ounjian for micro theory. He was also excellent and very supportive. I was the only woman in the program but I never faced any discrimination. The faculty seemed perfectly happy to have me learn this stuff. The third person was John Cornwall, who was a macroeconomist and also very good. The Tufts program was altogether excellent.

Were there any woman faculty? None. The only woman faculty I ever had was Alice Cook at Cornell.

Including your graduate school experience? Oh, certainly. Absolutely none, zero. Alice Cook was it. But these three men were very supportive of my going on and getting a PhD and wrote me strong recommendations.

How about women students? Were there many at MIT? There were two other women in the program: Ann Coffey and Heather Ross. Heather stayed in the program, but Ann left at the end of our first year. She continued graduate school in economics, but got married and moved elsewhere. So there were two women in my class, three women in the class ahead of us, and two in the class behind us. That was it. There were probably about twenty-five to thirty men in each class. The MIT program was tough, especially since I had not taken any mathematics since high school and had never had trigonometry. I had some quantitative economic theory at Tufts, but not math. So during the first year at

MIT I took math for economists [*laughter*]. I had a lot of math to learn in a very short period of time. But I did extremely well in all my courses.

What kind of community of peers did you have? Well, I was part of a group interested in labor. There were probably four or five people from each year in that group, and that was my peer group. I also knew some of the guys in class. We had a fixed first-year program, so we took the same courses. But I was not part of that group at all. I was married, lived in Boston rather than in Cambridge, and most of my friends were the wives of medical school students. We did little socializing with people from MIT. In fact, given how hard we both worked, we did little socializing with anyone.

Were most of the students single? Some of the guys were married, but most were single.

Are you in touch with anybody from graduate school? Occasionally, I'm in touch with some. Sometimes I see them at the economics meetings.

Do you know what happened to them? Heather Ross worked in the Department of the Interior. Alice Kidder and Jeanine Swift are professors. But I was not close to them in graduate school and am not in touch with them now. I know the whereabouts of some of my male classmates because many of them have become well known: Joe Stiglitz, Bill Nordhaus, Ray Fair, Bob Gordon, and Bob Hall.

Tell us a bit more about your experience as a female graduate student. I was not aware of much discrimination. Although, on the first day I walked into a labor seminar, the professor, Charlie Meyers, looked at me and said, "I think you are in the wrong room." I said, "No, I don't think so. I'm Myra Strober." "Oh," he said, recovering quickly. "Well, hello and welcome." In other words, because there were so few women, I was already "famous." It was a very strange experience. It made me feel special in both senses of the word: protected, but also odd.

MIT was an incredibly male place. I mean, at that time, in the late 1960s, there were no women undergraduates. When I think back, I realize that I used to periodically get on the subway and go downtown to Filene's Basement just to try on clothes, see women, and have a female experience of some kind [*laughter*]. I never bought much, because we didn't have much money, but being with other women felt good.

Actually, the woman that I talked to most was the janitoress. She was an absolutely wonderful Irish woman. She and I used to stand in the ladies' room and have long chats. She had numerous children and would tell me about her family. She was always interested in what was going on in my life. I sometimes talked to the secretaries too, but they didn't know quite what to make of me. By contrast, this Irish woman had absolutely no value judgments about what I was doing.

So basically, the "maleness" of MIT did not bother you very much, is that right? Consciously, it didn't bother me. Although when I look back now, I see things differently. There were things that I did to indicate that at some level I was bothered. It's interesting, I didn't want to attend an all-girls college because I wanted boys in my classes. Well, MIT certainly went too far in the other direction. I craved female companionship, peers, perspectives, professors, etc.

Do you think that your marriage helped you or hindered you in that situation? It was definitely a support system. It was a hindrance in the sense that I didn't make any real friends among the guys in my class. But I am not sure what that would have looked like anyway.

To give you a sense of how male the place was, when I became pregnant and wanted to tell my advisors, I was never able to do it. The notion of mentioning pregnancy in this male environment seemed like an impossibility. Of course, pregnancy has a way of making itself known [*laughter*] and eventually I did "show." I still remember Abe Siegel, one of the professors in the labor group, who later became Dean of the Sloan School at MIT, congratulating me. In retrospect, his positive attitude was more important than I realized at the time. Even today, not all professional women who become pregnant get congratulations from their male colleagues. For instance, when my female colleagues at Stanford became pregnant, they were told by the senior male professors that they had shot themselves in the foot; they had ruined their career chances.

Did you have a mentor in the department at MIT? None.

Who did you write your dissertation under? Charlie Meyers was my dissertation advisor. The other committee members were Doug Brown (also in the labor group) and Richard Eckaus in economic development. The labor group supported me financially. For example, I spent one summer as a research assistant looking at the effect of employment on parole success. I had good financial support the whole time and was able to present my work at labor seminars.

What was your dissertation on? I did my dissertation on manufacturing wages in fifty-three countries. I got the idea from a paper that I did for Evsey Domar's course on the Soviet economy. Stanley Lebergott had written a paper that showed that the wage structure across broadly aggregated manufacturing industries (at the two-digit level) was remarkably similar across all industrialized countries, including the Soviet Union. Then, in the course of doing some other research, I learned that the Soviet wage structure had in fact been different earlier in its development process. So I wondered if the manufacturing wage structure of the currently developing countries was different from the manufacturing wage structure of western industrialized countries. I also wondered to what extent the rankings of manufacturing industries by wage levels were determined by their ranking by productivity levels. In those days we didn't have to write a thesis proposal. I found data from the United Nations and the International Labour Organization that would let me study wage and productivity structures across two-digit manufacturing industries in fifty-three countries. I simply told them I wanted to use these data to look at wage and productivity relationships for my dissertation; all three on my committee agreed.

What inspired you? What made you believe that you could do a dissertation at MIT that was not highly mathematical? I think my advisors helped me. They, themselves, were not highly mathematical and that is why I chose them. Richard Eckhaus was, but Charlie Meyers and Doug Brown were primarily interested in labor relations. Evsey Domar was interesting. Even though he had certainly mathematized growth theory, he was also interested in Soviet institutions and wasn't purely a mathematician. Although I took courses from people like Paul Samuelson, Karl Shell, and Frank Fisher, who were primarily mathematical economists, I had little to do with them and certainly never worked with them. It's funny, I knew that the discipline was becoming highly mathematized and I knew that I was at a place that was leading the charge, but I decided to stay in the discipline because there were interesting problems that I wanted to work on. I was probably at the tail end of people who could avoid doing a mathematical dissertation. Shortly thereafter things changed, and students were forced to play the mathematics game.

Did you finish your PhD in what you would consider a reasonable amount of time? In looking back, from the vantage of thirty years of experience advising doctoral students, I can see that I did. But when I was in the "thick of it," back in the late 1960s, I felt I wasn't moving fast enough. It is interesting, my husband had wanted to have a child earlier than I did. But I couldn't see how I could have a child and do the course work at MIT. I wanted to postpone having a child and he agreed. But as soon as I passed my general exams it was like a curtain fell, an era was completed, and I was ready to move on. Just a day or so later, I began to feel strongly about having a child. Shortly thereafter, I became pregnant.

My plan was to finish my dissertation at the end of my third year because I had already done a year of course work for my Master's degree and I had my dissertation topic pretty well in hand by the end of my second year. We knew that my husband was going to be going to Washington, DC. This was the late 1960s and at that time physicians had to either serve in Vietnam or go to the public health service. He had received an opportunity to be part of the public health service by going to the National Institutes of Health to do medical research following up on the research that he had done in Oxford. So, we knew that we were going to DC at the end of his internship year and our plan was for me to finish my dissertation by the end of that year [*laughter*]. What I didn't realize was how tired I would be during pregnancy. I was just exhausted! I would come home and be asleep by 7:30 or 8:00 p.m. So, my thesis did not make much progress at all.

In January of 1967 I interviewed for jobs, still thinking that my dissertation was going to be done. I interviewed while I was pregnant, but I wasn't showing yet. I got a job as an assistant professor of economics at the University of Maryland and I was to begin in September of 1967. Who should be at the University of Maryland but Barbara Bergmann. So, I finally had my first mentor. When I was interviewed, or shortly thereafter, Barbara told me that she was also pregnant. Her daughter and my son are just a few months apart. She said that she was planning to have the baby and continue to teach and that gave me encouragement to do the same.

My mother was horrified that I had accepted a job when I was pregnant and wondered whether I had any idea what it was going to be like to be a young mother and have a full-time job. I told her that I didn't really know how I knew, but that I knew for sure that I wanted the job and that I didn't want to stay home full time with my child, especially having worked so hard to get a PhD.

You still hadn't finished your dissertation at this point? I still hadn't finished my dissertation. We moved to DC on July 1, 1967, because my husband had to report for active duty. Jason was born July 17. When we moved I was nine-months pregnant, I had an unfinished dissertation, and a job that was starting in September. And I had never taught before (except for fifth and third grades)! [*Laughter*]

How did you deal with child care? I had the baby and found someone to take care of him, which was very difficult, because we had just moved to the area and knew no one. In 1967, there were no agencies for child care workers, and there was no day care. So I knew I myself had to find someone to take care of him. Here I was, 26 years old, having never interviewed anybody for anything, interviewing a child care worker. I put an ad in the paper. Only one person, Jean, answered the ad. I interviewed her and she seemed nice. She gave me a reference, but I didn't know if it was a real reference or just a woman she had lined up to vouch for her. Making the decision to hire Jean was the most terrifying thing I have ever done. I worked with her for about seven days before I went to work, trying to make sure that she knew what she was doing. Then I kind of climbed up the ladder, walked out on the diving board and jumped in. I left Jean with Jason and went to work. It all worked out fine. Jason seemed to be doing well and I loved teaching.

But, of course, I wasn't getting my dissertation done, because how can you have a new baby, be in a new place, be teaching courses you've never taught before and write a dissertation? [*Laughter*] Impossible. Then the summer came and I took out the dissertation. I had done a fair amount while I was still at MIT and thought I would be ready to finish writing that summer. But, as soon as I started looking at the materials, I realized that, because I hadn't planned to be away from it for so long, I hadn't left myself any clues as to what I had done [*laughter*]. I had all this statistical output, and I had boxes and boxes of punch cards. But I couldn't reconstruct what all of it was for. Since I hadn't written a dissertation proposal, I had no road map. I spent the entire summer unraveling what I had done earlier. By the end of the summer I still had no dissertation. But I realized that I would probably not be able to look at the materials until the following summer. So this time I left myself some clues. Then I became pregnant with my second child.

In your second year of teaching? Yes, and that's when I realized that if I didn't get this dissertation done, I would be in real trouble, having two children. So the following summer I finished the dissertation.

Was the baby already born? No. I went back to MIT in August of 1969, as pregnant as I had been when I left [*laughter*] the first time. I defended and got the degree.

What was that experience like? The MIT system of dissertation defense was very humane. The only people at the defense were the candidate (me) and the three readers. We had a great discussion about the work and its implications and it was basically stress-free. Watching students at Berkeley and Stanford sweat their orals for weeks, wondering what questions the outside people would ask, I was always grateful for the MIT system for basically putting its trust in the three faculty members. After the defense, Charlie Myers took me to lunch at the MIT faculty club and then I decided to visit my old haunts in downtown Boston. This time I had money to buy something. I celebrated my new economics PhD with a bargain maternity outfit from Filene's Basement.

Liz was born in November of 1969. With Jason I was home for six weeks. This time I was home for only three weeks because I was teaching; we needed the money; and the University of Maryland had no maternity leave. One of my colleagues, Bob Knight, a fellow labor economist, took my classes for three weeks. Liz came early; she was supposed to be born after Thanksgiving but came three weeks before. So Bob taught until Thanksgiving. Then I came back and taught between Thanksgiving and Christmas. After Christmas I finally had a little breathing room.

So you were in the economics department at Maryland. Did you feel pretty settled in the DC area? Oh, no. We knew DC was not permanent: Sam was supposed to be there for two years. As it turned out, he was there for three. The third year was not required, but he was so much into the research that he didn't want to leave. So, I was at Maryland for three years.

Were you on a tenure track? I was a lecturer until I got my dissertation done and when I finished my dissertation, I became an assistant professor.

Can you talk about your department? I believe that Barbara Bergmann was the only other woman there. I knew I wasn't going to come up for tenure there and didn't really have much to do with other faculty in the department. Most of the time I was working on my dissertation and once I got it done, I wrote an article based on it. But I didn't start any new research. At one point, I seriously considered going part time, because it was really very difficult to do what I was doing. First of all, I was commuting because we didn't live near the University of Maryland. Second, my husband was doing nothing around the house. He had a very demanding career in an extremely competitive field. He was trying to get work done so that he could go on the job market and be really marketable. So I didn't get any help in child rearing from him. I was also teaching a lot. I wasn't getting a whole lot of sleep with two little ones. I thought that maybe I should go part time. Barbara Bergmann was her usual honest self. She told me that I could not have a career by working part time and to my credit I listened to her. I don't even think I argued with her! In looking back she was absolutely right. I coped by working even harder [*laughter*].

What was your strategy for going in the job market? It is amazing to me that my husband and I never considered going on the job market jointly. We decided, no, we didn't even decide, we didn't make a conscious decision about it! He simply went on the job market and found a terrific job at Stanford. In fact, I was more enthusiastic about moving to California than he was, even though I didn't have a job lined up. I tell you this because I am stunned by my own naivete. I already told you about my decision with regard to whether I should be a historian or an economist. Now, I have to remember how unsophisticated I was about going on the job market. After Sam got the offer from Stanford, I asked the people on my dissertation committee to help me find a job in the San Francisco area.

What did you do, then, once you got there? We knew we were going to live close to Stanford because the kind of biomedical research Sam was doing often required him to go back to the lab in the late evening, to check on experiments. We knew we had to live near the university. For me, then, there were a few options in the area: Stanford, Berkeley, University of Santa Clara, or one of the state colleges, San Jose State, San Francisco State, or Hayward State. None of the people on my dissertation committee knew anybody at Stanford. I made a "cold call" to Mel Reader, the labor economist at Stanford, and explained that I was coming there because of my husband and asked if there was a job. Mel was cordial, but said they were not in the market for a junior person in labor. I interviewed for jobs at Hayward State, San Francisco State, and Santa Clara. But no job offers ever came of those interviews. There was also an opening for an assistant professor in labor economics at Berkeley, which I interviewed for. It was first offered to someone else, who accepted it. But during the summer before he was to take up the job, he changed his mind, and I was offered the job.

Was it a tenure track job? No, I wasn't offered an assistant professor position. They asked me to take the job as a lecturer. In other words, even though I already held an assistant professorship at Maryland, Berkeley offered me a non-tenure track appointment without any commitment beyond one year. I had no choice but to accept. It was only then that I realized that, by not going on the job market at the same time as my husband did, I had left myself without any bargaining power. I was already living in California and either I could take this job or not have a job at all. So I took the job as a lecturer.

When I got to Berkeley I noticed that two of my former classmates at MIT were both assistant professors. I was truly upset by this. This was really the first time that my gender had done me in. Things were not fair. The job had been listed as an assistant professor, but I took the job as a lecturer. Yet these two guys were assistant professors. I also noticed that the economics department did not have a single woman faculty member who was either tenured or on the tenure track. There was another woman lecturer, Margaret Gordon, who was very friendly and welcoming. It turned out she was the mother of my former class-mate at MIT, Bob Gordon. She had been a lecturer at Berkeley for years while her husband, Aaron Gordon, was an economics professor.

What was going on at Berkeley at this time? This was the fall of 1970. The last round of student demonstrations and tear-gassings by the police were coming to a close, but a new kind of revolution was brewing at Berkeley, a gender revolution. The same month that I arrived, there was an article in the campus newspaper about the fact that so many women at Berkeley were in lecturer positions. I remember reading that article. I was horrified. But I was also comforted. I was not alone. This outrage was not just about me. And so I started looking up some of the women lecturers in the other departments. They were a fabulous group. We met frequently for lunch at the women's faculty club. This was the first time I had a group of women colleagues!

What did you do? I finally got my courage up and went to see the chair of the economics department to ask him why I was a lecturer while two of my former classmates were hired as assistant professors. He told me it was because I lived in Palo Alto. (It is about an hour's drive from Berkeley.) I was stunned by his answer and didn't know what to say. After all, it was true; I did live in Palo Alto. I thanked him and I left to drive home [*laughter*]. I always say that I became a feminist on the Bay Bridge (the bridge that connects the East Bay and Berkeley with Palo Alto), because it was only as I drove home that I realized how ridiculous it was. I wasn't an assistant professor because I lived in Palo Alto! I was furious. When I got home, I called the chair's office and asked his secretary to speak with him again. She put me on hold for a bit, no doubt to consult with him. When she came back, she said that he couldn't see me for three weeks. He was busy.

Did you give up? What does an academic do when she's mad? Research, of course. In those three weeks I did all sorts of research: research about women in higher education, women at Berkeley, women in the workforce. I suddenly had a whole new career. I hadn't done any work on women's education and employ-ment. The work I had done was mostly my thesis and I had really not started any new research program. One of the things I found out was that the last woman to be hired on the regular faculty line in the department of economics at Berkeley was Jessica Pixoto, in 1936. In the thirty-four years between 1936 and 1970 not a single woman had been hired on the regular faculty line!

What happened during the gender revolution at Berkeley? A few months before I came to Berkeley, the group of women lecturers with whom I had been meeting had sued Berkeley. And not long after I came, investigators from the Equal Employment Opportunity Commission (EEOC) began poking around at the university. Apparently, they originally thought they would be investigating for a few weeks. It turned out they were there for several years.

When it was time to go back to the chair of the department, I felt much stronger. The research I had done and the presence of EEOC investigators on campus helped me to realize that being a lecturer was not just about me. When

I asked him again why I was a lecturer while the two men from my class were assistant professors, he told me that it was because I had two young children. When I asked him what that had to do with anything, he said that with two young children, "they just didn't know what was going happen to me." I told him that I wasn't asking him to *give* me tenure, but merely to put me on the tenure track so that I could work toward getting tenure. He said that he could never sell that to the department.

I left his office feeling very blue. After all, I was worried about myself. And hearing that the department was worried about me certainly didn't help. I had two children under the age of 2; I was commuting an hour each direction; I had a husband who wasn't doing any housework or child rearing; I had new classes to teach; I had to start a research program; and I had no support from anybody, except of course from the women I had met at Berkeley. They became my support group. I used to have lunch with them regularly. Except for one of my former male classmates and Lloyd Ullman, the senior professor in labor, I don't remember ever having lunch with any of the men in the department.

This is when I started to work toward developing a course on women and the economy. A colleague was willing to take one of my regular labor courses so that I could teach this course. He told me he deserved the Susan B. Anthony Award because he was letting me teach it. At first, he asked me if I really thought there was enough material for a whole course on women. I assured him there was. I taught the course, and started developing a research program on women and the economy.

Then the job for an assistant professor in my field was re-advertised and I applied for it again. It was extremely stressful to be there while they brought people for interviews. But guess what? They offered it to me. Ironically, at almost exactly the same time, I got an offer from Stanford.

How did that happen? My son was in a nursery school in Palo Alto. I met Ruth Franklin, whose son was in Jason's class. We started talking and it turned out that she was a Radcliffe alumnus and belonged to the Radcliffe Club in Palo Alto. She thought it was a shame that I had to spend so many hours each week commuting to Berkeley and that I needed to get a job at Stanford. She asked me to give her my resume. She passed it on to a woman economist in the Radcliffe Club, Rita Ricardo Campbell, who in turn passed it on to the dean of the Stanford Business School, Arjay Miller.

One night I was bathing my son. My husband knocked on the door to tell me that the dean of the Stanford Business School was on the phone for me. I said, "Right and the President of the United States wants to talk to me after that!" But my husband said he wasn't kidding. So, I got on the phone. Arjay told me that he had my resume and was very interested in talking to me about the possibility of joining the business school faculty as an assistant professor. The business school had never, ever, had a woman on the faculty before!

Was the economics department in the business school? No, but the business school had its own economists. Shortly after that, I had an interview and they made me an offer. So now I had two assistant professor offers. I chose based on the commute. The idea of not having to commute was enormously appealing.

Do you mean that otherwise you would have chosen the department of economics at Berkeley? Yes. But I decided that I had to protect myself and my physical well-being and not put myself through that commute. So I chose the business school. I was one of the first two women on the faculty there. The second woman was hired in organization behavior at the same time I was, but she was there for only four years. She had come to Stanford fresh out of a PhD program and had found the teaching very tough. I think one of the things in my favor was that by the time I went there, I had had five years of teaching experience.

What was the Stanford Business School like for you? It was a pretty stressful experience. Teaching MBAs is rough and teaching Stanford MBAs was particularly rough [*laughter*].

Why? Well, they were very demanding and it required a great deal of preparation on my part. Also, the atmosphere was even more male than at MIT (if that was possible). But I never found MIT rude. Some of my men students at Stanford were just plain nasty. I had men students who told me in class that they hadn't paid Stanford tuition (which was indeed extremely high) to be taught by the likes of me; meaning they hadn't paid all that money to be taught by a young woman.

Did you teach only MBAs or did you also teach undergraduate business students? Only MBAs.

Did you teach only economics? I taught labor economics and macroeconomics and also a course on women and the economy.

What was the gender composition of faculty at Stanford? There were ninety men on the faculty, many of them quite senior, and two young women. There were five women students out of 350 and they made a slide show called "What's a nice woman like you doing in a place like this?"

Who did? The five women students.

As time went on, more and more women applied to the business school and were admitted. The advisory board of the business school was very persuasive to the administration that they needed to train more women MBAs. Because of the legal climate, businesses were interested in hiring more women MBAs. The Class of 1974 had thirty-four women MBAs and Francine Gordon and I surveyed them just before they graduated. We wanted to know how they compared to the men in their class. We found that their average starting salary was approximately the same as men's, about $17,000. Also, their job goals and life goals were amazingly similar. But women compared to men ranked the accumulation of wealth as a much less important life goal, and the salary women expected at the peak of their careers was only 60 percent of what men expected.

Four years later, I resurveyed these same MBAs. The salary parity was gone! Women now earned about 80 percent of what men earned. The first major reason for the difference was that the women who had taken time out of the workforce paid a whopping salary penalty when they came back. No men had taken time out. The second reason was that some men, but no women, were employed in two very high-paying sectors – investment banking and real estate.

Going back to the fall of 1972, Stanford was very proud because that year the business school had four new "firsts" on the faculty: two women, a black man, a Hispanic man, and an Asian–American man. All in one year. In that same year, the Stanford Law School hired its first woman ever, Barbara Babcock, and the school of engineering hired its first woman ever, Lilly Young. Do you think maybe something was going on that year? [*Laughter*] What I think was going on was that just across the Bay there was a major lawsuit against Berkeley, and Stanford was trying to avoid a similar lawsuit. Stanford was so proud of their new women hires that they took Babcock, Young, and me in a van up to San Francisco for a press conference.

The good thing for me was that, as a result of that press conference, it was all over the local papers that I had come to Stanford and was doing research on women. Because of the newspaper articles, several undergraduate and graduate students came to see me. They wanted to start a center for research on women at Stanford. What they didn't understand was that I was a lowly assistant professor in my first year [*laughter*] and had no power to help start a research center. But they were so persistent that I finally decided to try to help them get some senior faculty interested in this idea. Ultimately Eleanor Maccoby from psychology and Jim March from the school of education applied to the Ford Foundation and got a $25,000 planning grant for setting up the Center for Research on Women. Jim and Eleanor were the co-directors for about three months. Then we had a board meeting in which they told me that if this Center was going to happen, it was I who would have to direct the effort.

I decided to take on the job. It was too exciting not to do it. So I agreed to head up the Center's policy board and went to talk to the Ford Foundation about parlaying the $25,000 planning grant into a major three-year grant. Lucky for me, the woman I went to see was another woman economist, Mariam Chamberlain. I have already told you that Barbara Bergmann was my first mentor; Mariam was my second. She taught me how to write a grant proposal, and how to negotiate with the provost at Stanford to assure that the Center would survive after the Ford money ran out. In 1974, Ford gave us $100,000 to set up the Center for Research on Women and I became its first director.

Even though I felt incredibly alienated at the business school, heading up the Center allowed me to feel very comfortable at the university. I developed warm relationships with a whole group of folks at Stanford. They all wanted to see the Center get off the ground: the president; the provost; and especially the president's wife, who helped me to put together a group of women associates who helped us raise funds among wealthy women in the Bay area. I also got to know the provost's wife, the dean of the law school (Tom Ehrlich), and the dean of the school of engineering (Bill Kays). Women students and staff from all over the campus contacted me to see how they could help.

I would never advise a new assistant professor to do what I did [*laughter*]. I got involved in university politics, I got involved outside of my own school, and of course, most cardinal of sins, I took time away from my own research. Getting the Center started was almost like having a third child [*laughter*]. It was a wonderful thing to do and I did it for about four years. Then I decided that I needed to go back full time to the business school and work on my research. I was coming up for tenure soon and needed time to write my findings.

Myra, how did your research interest affect your status in the Stanford Business School? Well [*laughter*], I was the first woman to ever come up for tenure in the business school. A year or so before I was slated to come up, I received invitations from some of my business school colleagues to go to lunch. They wanted to tell me how nervous they were about my tenure. I told them I understood my own nervousness about the process, but I didn't understand theirs. Of course, I did. They knew my work was solid, but they didn't want me in their exclusive male preserve. They were nervous about what excuse they were going to use to keep me out.

To make a long story short – I was turned down. In fact, of those who were hired at the same time as myself, two had already left (the African–American man and another white woman); one decided to postpone his tenure (a Hispanic man); and the remaining four were denied tenure (myself, an Asian–American man, and two white men). The dean of the business school was very upset that I and the Asian–American man were denied tenure and resigned shortly thereafter, in part because of the tenure decisions. Two male associate deans told me that I was denied tenure because I "hadn't hit a home run" and my work was not "seminal." They seemed completely unaware of the male metaphors they were using. They also "explained" that the faculty were unable to evaluate my work because my field was too new.

Several of my colleagues in the business school had advised me early on that I shouldn't work on women's issues, at least not until I got tenure. That always seemed odd to me, because I was already working on women's issues when I was hired. I was a known quantity. In any case, Stanford was not paying me enough to sell my soul. I never changed my research agenda. Of course, with hindsight, I now realize what these men were really worried about. It wasn't that my field was "new." The problem was that my field was threatening. It was questioning men's power, and they didn't like that one bit.

How did you find your way to the school of education at Stanford? After I was turned down for tenure, my colleague David Tyack went to the dean of the education school and explained my situation. He told the dean that he thought the business school faculty had made a mistake and recommended that I be considered for tenure in the education school. David was a historian and a very respected member of their faculty. The dean accepted his suggestion, and they voted to offer me a tenured position, and the dean worked out a deal with the provost. I got a position with half-time tenure in the school of education and a half-time position without tenure as the director of the Center for Research on Women. It was not until ten years later that I received tenure in the other half of my position.

What did you teach in the school of education? I taught the economics of education and a course on women, education, and work. For a long time, I also had a "courtesy" appointment in the business school. I always thought that was an odd title! [*Laughter*] Many women from the business school always took my courses.

Could you talk about your "threatening" research? What are some of the major themes of your work? My main focus has been occupational segregation. My experience at Berkeley, knowing women had not been on the tenure track in economics for more than thirty years, made it painfully clear to me how the world was divided into jobs that were female and jobs that were male. I wanted to understand the source of that situation and why it persists.

My first research project focused on teaching school in the nineteenth century. I wanted to know how and why teaching had become a female occupation. A doctoral student in my class on women and the economy, Katharine Poss, told me that David Tyack was also interested in this issue. She also told David about me. It's interesting how students become conduits for the intellectual collaboration among faculty.

Did you collaborate with David Tyack? Yes. We had the same intellectual agenda, but his was from an historical perspective and mine was from an economic perspective. We wrote a grant proposal and received a fair amount of money from the National Institute of Education to study how teaching became a woman's occupation. We put together a wonderful team of research assistants, including Kathryn Poss, Ted Mitchell, Suzanne Greenberg, and Audri Lanford. Poss, Mitchell, and Greenberg were all history students. Lanford was a quantitative sociology student. Together, we had terrific discussions about what constitutes "evidence." With much enthusiasm, the historians would present diaries to show that Miss So-and-so was thinking about the same issues we were. Lanford and I would pooh-pooh the diaries as "anecdotal" evidence from a non-random sample. We would then wave our computer output and argue that our R-squares showed that we had explained 50 percent of the variance – a triumph as far as we were concerned. In reply, the historians argued that the data were unreliable (which they no doubt were), and anyway, *they* were interested in the other 50 percent of the variance. This was all done with good humor, and we learned a tremendous amount about the joys and tribulations of interdisciplinary work.

What are some of the main points that you make in your work? Although we talk about the feminization of an occupation, which focuses our attention on women coming into an occupation, we should really be paying attention to the role that men play as well. It's my theory that women move into an occupation when men no longer want to be there. In our society, because the social norm is that men need to earn a family wage in order to support their wives and children, men are given the first choice of occupations. Men make occupational choices based on their relative attractiveness, including salary, benefits, working conditions, prestige, and opportunity for advancement. If an occupation's relative attractiveness diminishes, either because the occupation itself has changed or some other competing occupation has become more attractive, men will leave that occupation and move to another. Only when men do not want an occupation any more does it become available for women.

Although changes in family structure and increases in the number of working women have somewhat weakened the norm that men should be the primary providers for their families, the norm remains very strong. Men still get first choice of the better jobs. Even within occupations where women have made great inroads, like law, medicine, and academia, men are over-represented in the high-paid specialities and women are over-represented in the low-paid specialities.

Although my theory is supply-side-oriented, in the sense that it relies on men to decide which occupation they will inhabit, it's also demand-oriented. How the job is structured (which is determined on the demand side of the market) determines whether men will choose to take a job and stick with it, or not. Given the structure of a job, men get to choose first. If they choose not to take a job, or if they choose to leave it, only then do employers seek women for that job. The theory also heavily depends on societal norms.

What other occupations have you studied? Bank-telling was the second occupation I studied. Carolyn Arnold and I co-authored an article in 1987 on how bank-telling became a woman's occupation. During this study, I read something in the *New York Times* that absolutely intrigued me. The maquillas in Mexico during the late 1950s and early 1960s only employed young women workers. But around 1984 a huge number of men were employed. The explanation? Employers realized that hiring only young women was wrecking the Mexican family. I thought, this is odd. Why would multinational corporations suddenly care about the Mexican family? [*Laughter*] I talked about this with a student of mine, Lisa Catanzarite, who was fluent in Spanish. She was also intrigued and we decided to investigate the situation.

Several weeks later, without advance appointments, we got on a plane and flew to El Paso. We talked with some folks and got the names of some plant managers of maquillas in Juarez. During our first interviews, we were honest and told them that we wanted to know why maquillas were hiring more men. We got some of the silliest answers you can imagine. So we regrouped and decided that for the next interview we would say that we were from the School of Education at Stanford and were interested in the educational and training requirements for these jobs. As soon as we told them our interest, the first thing they told us was about the gender change [*laughter*]. Suddenly, we began to get reasonable answers to our questions. That was an interesting discovery about doing qualitative research.

We discovered two things. First, the Mexican economy had a meltdown, and men who would have disdained working in the maquillas under ordinary circumstances were suddenly moving into Juarez and looking for work. Once again we demonstrated that it's men's choices about where they want to work that is the determining factor of occupational segregation. We found men in sewing jobs, which are normally outside the purview of men. Most men were sewing paper hospital garments. We also visited a lingerie factory. They told us that they had hired men, but they wouldn't do it again because the men were unruly. The company made women's garments and apparently the men were throwing bras around, whooping it up, and in general disrupting production [*laughter*]. But they had hired men simply because men wanted to be hired. Moreover, within the maquilla sector, the industry mix had changed. Although sewing was the main product in the beginning, now the factories were producing electronics. In this sector, some jobs actually had job ladders that led to quite good higher-level positions. Men were getting the entry-level positions on those job ladders. Some were even attending community college to move up the ladders. Once again, the good jobs were reserved for men.

Have you also looked at professional jobs? Yes; I've looked at occupational segregation in medicine. My theory led me to suspect that women would be under-represented in the highest-paid specialities and over-represented in the lowest-paid specialities. I found that this was indeed the case, and presented my work at the meetings of the Industrial Relations Research Association. It was subsequently published in their Proceedings. Recently, Dr Frances Conley, a professor of neurosurgery at Stanford, wrote a book called *Walking Out on the Boys*. It details how occupational segregation takes place and how women become discouraged about moving into specialities where men are guarding the gates. I think women move into an occupation only where men do not guard the gates.

More recently, another student of mine, Jihyun Lee, and I have investigated academia. The highest-paid specialities such as computer science, engineering, and physics have almost no women, whereas the lower-paid specialities are becoming feminized. Again, male-dominated disciplines like engineering, computer science, and economics make it just uncomfortable enough for women so that they do not pursue academic careers in those fields.

What are the policy implications of your work? Can we "solve" the problem of occupational segregation? From a public policy point of view it is an interesting question. Occupational segregation has declined in the last thirty years, and most people are content to leave further reductions to changes in societal norms. And indeed, norms are changing. The notion that men should be the only wage earners may be on its way out. But even today, it seems that most people view men as the primary breadwinners. There is a belief that, in some sense, the dynamics of the relationship between the husband and wife are better if the wife works. If the man earns more, the man feels good about himself and the woman feels good about the marriage. The social message remains that, as long as women are married, they don't have to worry too much about their earnings. Of course, single women, single mothers, and lesbian women can't rely on men's earnings, but their experiences have not permeated our cultural norms.

I just finished a book on the earnings and employment of Stanford and Tokyo University graduates. We found that most large Japanese companies pay a premium to men who are fathers, but not to women who are mothers. The effect of this premium was evident in our earnings regressions. The family wage notion is certainly alive and well in Japan.

Most of my work, with the exception of bank-tellers, has concentrated on highly educated people. But we find the same thing at the blue-collar level. Most interesting is that women are now more than half of all college students. It is less important for men to go to college, in part, because men can still get good jobs without a college education. There are virtually no such jobs for women.

Public policy needs to be more cognizant of occupational segregation. Often we applaud the fact that women have moved into some occupation without recognizing that, if too many women enter an occupation, it will resegregate like bank-telling, and its rewards will fall. For example, it now seems quite possible that medicine will resegregate as a female occupation together with poorer working conditions, lower pay, and prestige compared with what existed when men had a lock on the occupation.

You always talk quite passionately about teaching. Could you talk about yourself as an educator? I do love to teach. I think I am an actress at heart. If I'd had the talent, I would have become an opera singer. Teaching satisfies some of my appetite for drama. I love to watch my audience when they "get" a complicated point I've tried to make. But increasingly, I recognize that the "sage on the stage" model is not the only one, and often it is not the best one for learning complex material.

I have done some research on my own students and how they learn. The main course that I taught in the school of education was the "Economics of Education." Most of the students had never had economics before. So I spent the first few weeks on an introduction to economics. After a couple of lectures I had two groups of students waiting to talk to me. One group said they understood everything I said, but were lost when I used graphs or equations. The second group said the opposite. They were technically trained. They didn't understand why I kept talking on and on. As soon as I used graphs, or better yet, equations, they knew exactly what I was saying.

I asked one of my colleagues, a cognitive psychologist, whether these two groups were learning the same thing. He suggested that I videotape a small group of students discussing a simple problem, and then ask them to graph the solution on the blackboard. He thought the videotapes would help me to better understand how my students learned, and what they did and didn't understand.

My teaching assistant videotaped ten small groups. In analyzing the videotapes, we discovered that none of the students, irrespective of whether they were qualitatively or quantitatively oriented, seemed to have a grip on the question. It was a very humbling experience for me to watch those tapes. After all, these were Stanford graduate students. They did well on exams, and they talked a good game in class. I thought they understood the material. But it was clear they did not understand the concepts. It also became clear that, if they couldn't graph it, they didn't understand it. Verbal and graphic understanding needed to go hand in hand. The graphic analysis provided a necessary framework for the analysis, because it required looking systematically at all the pieces in an orderly way.

I repeated the experiment using the same question with small groups of undergraduate students who were taking introductory economics at Stanford. The results were the same. For the most part, students simply could neither talk sensibly about the material nor properly graph it. When I showed the tapes to the chair of the economics department and the instructor for the course, they were also humbled. They have since used the tapes for training teaching assistants to anticipate student confusion. Anyway, as a result, I totally revamped my way of teaching.

How does your interest in teaching and pedagogy tie into your editorial work for the *Journal of Economic Education*? Bill Becker, the editor of the journal, asked me to be on the editorial board after I submitted my article on the videotapes. He asked if I would direct a new section of the journal on qualitative methods in research on economics education. I have been disappointed. Over the years, very few people have submitted articles in this area, and those that have been submitted were not very strong. I regretfully decided to resign after my efforts to get more people to submit high-quality papers were not successful. The journal no longer has a qualitative methods section. Economists evaluate economic education in the same way that they do their other empirical research, with regressions. I don't think regression analysis tells you much about the underlying mechanisms of learning. We need qualitative research to understand how people learn economics. Unfortunately, economists are simply not trained to do qualitative research; and they don't seem interested in learning the required skills.

How would you describe your evolution as an economist? Although I had a very mathematical set of courses at MIT, I was never mathematically inclined in terms of understanding economic problems. I am not sure I would have gone into economics if I had known the mathematical turn the discipline would take. For me, it is important to analyze things systematically. However, economics has almost become a minuet; everything has to be done according to a tight formula in order for it to be officially sanctioned. I find that extremely constraining. Trying to think about extremely complex issues with social as well as economic components, and boiling it down so it can be mathematized, is just not what I'm after.

I remember giving a seminar at the National Bureau of Economic Research on how teaching became a women's occupation. Ten minutes into my talk an economist stood up and nastily remarked, "I've been here for ten minutes and you haven't put a supply or demand equation on the board yet." I replied that I would talk for another 20–30 minutes and that I would not put a supply and demand equation on the board at all. I suggested that, if that was all he was after, he might wish to leave. So he left. This anecdote is emblematic of what is wrong with our discipline.

I have always done my own thing. I came into the discipline for reasons that interested me. I've stayed and worked on problems that interest me. Somewhere along the line I noticed that I was different from other economists. In part, my evolution was simply noticing that difference. Fortunately for me, I have not been in an economics department since I left Berkeley in 1972.

What about your evolution in your personal life and how that has influenced your career? Well, my divorce and subsequent remarriage have certainly played a big role in my life. In 1982 my husband of almost twenty years and the father of our two children decided that he wanted a divorce. This really took me by surprise.

How old were the children? They were 12 and 14 years old. I was pretty shocked. Going through the divorce was very difficult for both me and the kids. But I began to see other men and learned how to date again [*laughter*]. It was a very difficult time. I had to figure out my life financially and how to be a single parent. It was an extraordinarily painful time in my life.

In 1989 I got together with Jay. I had known Jay for more than thirty years. He had been a classmate of my ex-husband's at Columbia and Harvard Medical Schools. Our families had been friendly for years. He had gotten divorced about the same time as I, and was living in Hawaii. Suddenly, in 1989 our relationship changed, and we realized that we wanted to spend our lives together. Our relationship has been the most wonderful gift. We got married in 1990, and he moved back to California. We have been very happy. We have put our two families together and healed as many relationships as we could. His ex-wife and my ex-husband and his new family all join us and our kids for Thanksgiving and Passover.

Changing the topic once more, how do you feel about the emergence of feminist economics and IAFFE? How did you become familiar with it? A paper by Julie Nelson on feminist economics crossed my desk one day. She wrote that economics ought to be about provisioning rather than about making choices. I was really excited about her paper. It showed me some possibilities for analysis that I had been groping towards but had not really seen. I called Julie and drove up to Davis to meet with her. I asked her how she had put this together. She told me that, as a graduate student in Wisconsin, she not only did a PhD in economics, she also took courses in women's studies. The combination of the two intellectual domains got her involved in some path-breaking work. Julie's work and the birth of IAFFE came to my attention just about the same time. Suddenly there seemed to be a real chance of revolutionizing economics.

What needs to be done in the next few years is to come up with an alternative paradigm in economics. We will not bury neoclassical economics until we can replace it with something. I am excited about working on that "something." How will we take the notion of provisioning and move it forward to develop a new economics exactly? How will we theorize not only how individuals make themselves better off, but also how will we as a community, indeed a set of communities, make ourselves better off and sustain the planet?

Myra, do you have any advice for young women entering the economics profession? How can they survive in the profession while contributing to the development of an alternative paradigm and helping to change the profession? There are several different possibilities. I do not encourage most of the women who come to see me to enter economics. I am not interested in simply increasing the number of women economists if all they will do is the same stodgy work that most men do. I suggest to young people that they should only go into economics if they have a burning desire to answer certain questions and those questions are squarely in economics. I tell them that, if they do become an economist, they will either have to play the game of mathematical economics and make it in the mainstream, or they will have to devote themselves to the kinds of changes that heterodox economists are seeking to make. People who work toward change have bumpy careers. On the other hand, if someone is willing to fight the mainstream and work for change, I welcome them into the profession. The discipline needs a lot of help.

Is there anything you would like to talk about that we haven't discussed? Yes, increasingly I am occupied with what has come to be known as spirituality. For me, spirituality means being connected to the larger universe, to something greater than oneself and greater than the material world. One of the problems in economics is that it is so individually oriented. When I tell people that I am both an economist and interested in spirituality, they often see this as a major contradiction. Perhaps this contradiction is what makes me uncomfortable with neoclassical economics' emphasis on individuals. I certainly think that one of the strengths of the United States is its concern with and protection of individual liberties. However, economics does not ask enough about the collective, either in terms of the family or the community. It certainly does not ask enough about other human values. It seems to me that economists in particular have to be the voice for values in life that go beyond material things and things that we can see.

Why economists? Because, in a certain sense, we have a great deal of credibility. We are not seen as dreamers. We are seen as realists and people who are concerned with the bottom line and the practicalities of life, such as earning a living, providing for retirement, and so on. If we point out that there is something else, I think people pay attention in a way that they don't when the art or the English professor points it out. I feel that this is a particular responsibility that we have. For instance, many people discussing retirement are basically focused on the economics of retirement. For economists, such matters are a "no brainer." We have formulas for figuring out what the inflation rate or the payout rate on investments will likely be in the future. But conversations about retirement also provide an opportunity for us to ask about more than material matters; to ask questions about human values, quality of life, payback to the community, and the large moral and spiritual questions of our time. To me it is very important to communicate to students as well as to professional colleagues that there is much more to life than maximizing utility functions.

Plate 8   Top left: Barbara Jones's main portrait as Dean of the School of Business, Alabama A&M (1998). Top right: In booth, John A. Brown's Department Store, Oklahoma City (1958). Bottom left: Standing at lunch counter, Katz Drug Store, Oklahoma City (1958). Bottom right: Family portrait (1984). 1958 photos: Courtesy of the Oklahoma Historical Society.

8

BARBARA ANN POSEY JONES

> If I had to compromise my sense of what was right or wrong – my
> sense of ethics and social purpose – I would forgo the [PhD]. The
> degree did not define who or what I was. Other things were more
> important.
>
> (Barbara Jones, 1998)

As a teenager, Barbara was a leader in the lunch counter sit-ins in Oklahoma City
during the civil rights movement. Today she is the Dean of the School of Business at
Alabama A&M. In the interim, she has taught at the University of Illinois, Texas
Southern University, Atlanta University, Clark College, and Ahmadu Bello University in
Nigeria, and has received numerous teaching awards as a reflection of her love for
teaching. She has also chaired two economics departments at Prairie View A&M
University and Clark College, and is the former Dean of the College of Business at
Prairie View. She has been an active member of the National Economic Association,
serving as President, Secretary–Treasurer, and as a member of the Board of Directors.
As a scholar, she has published several articles on African–American issues, edited a
book on unemployment, and has served as Assistant and Interim Editor of *The Review
of Black Political Economy* and remains on its Board of Editorial Advisors and Board of
Reviewers. She has also served on advisory boards for the Rockefeller Foundation's
Minority Scholars in Research Awards Program and the Center for Research on Women
at Wellesley College, among others. She received an AB in government, economics,
and mathematics from the University of Oklahoma (1963), an MA from the University
of Illinois (1966), and a PhD from Georgia State University (1973).

We began our conversation at the Gaslight Inn in Atlanta, Georgia, on a hot August
day in 1998. Then we toured her old neighborhood and the nearby campuses of
Morehouse and Spelman Colleges and Clark Atlanta University. We stopped by her
home and were introduced to her husband Mack and, after a late lunch, we went
grocery shopping for dinner. Barbara is one of those people who you feel you have
known all your life.

Barbara, let's begin with your family background. What can you tell us about that? My parents are both from the northeastern part of Texas; a rural area. My mother's family lived in a community called Roxton. They did some farming, but farming was not their major source of income. Her father was a carpenter and teacher. I doubt, however, if he had more than a fourth-grade education. Most black teachers in the early part of the century were self-taught. I remember as a child perusing his rather eclectic library. My mother's mother reared five children and took care of the house. The eldest daughter was sent to Paris – the nearest town with a high school for "coloreds" – after grammar school. The family was responsible for her room and board while she studied. She became a teacher and ultimately earned a Bachelor's and Master's degree.

And your mother? My mother and her brother (numbers three and four) finished grammar school at the same time. But since the family could not afford to send them both to high school, they sent neither. That ended my mother's education, except for some night school courses she took after she married and moved to Oklahoma City. After she completed the seventh grade, she worked in the fields and did things that were available for black women, which at that time was not much of anything except domestic service.

What about your father's family? His father was a farmer in Howland, Texas. Howland is about 10 miles [16 km] from Roxton, which was "walking distance" in those days. From what I gather, my grandfather was an established person in the area. My dad talked a lot about their car. It was not only their first car, it was the first car in the community for either whites or blacks. Unfortunately, he died early and everything went to pot. He had two sons (the older one died while away at Texas College), eight daughters, and a wife who knew nothing about the family's business affairs. So after my grandfather's death, the white bankers and others in the area walked away with everything. They'd say, "He owed me so-and-so. I'll take two cows." Others took pigs or farm equipment. Had the family resisted, they would have been burned out. Because there was a mortgage on the family home, they lost it and were forced to move into what had been the rent house. It only had about 20 acres [8 ha] of land. The family then became sharecroppers.

Did your father attend college? My father went to Texas College for a couple of years on a baseball scholarship. He must have been doing the equivalent of high school, because, as I said, there were no high schools in the area for blacks. In spite of his limited farming skills and total lack of interest in farming, he was forced to leave school and return to Howland to help the family with the crops. Even if he had gotten a degree, it didn't matter because an older sister who had finished college returned to Howland and ended up working in the fields and doing laundry for white families in the area.

When did your parents get married? In their early 20s. She was 23; he was 22. They lived on his family's property and farmed. About eight years into their marriage, mother's brother went to Oklahoma City. He got a job in a furniture factory (Oklahoma Furniture) and arranged one for my dad. When daddy opened the letter announcing the good news, he left his cotton sack in the middle of the field and said good-bye! He took the job in Oklahoma City, found a place to live, and sent for my mother. Mother did domestic work. Daddy advanced to foreman before Oklahoma Furniture moved to Guthrie, a little town about 10 miles [16 km] north of Oklahoma City. Because daddy didn't want to relocate, he went on the job market and soon found a job as a shipping clerk with Buck's Sporting Goods, a small independent business that sold sporting-goods equipment to the high schools and colleges around the state. It was the kind of business where salespeople went out and took orders. The next thing you would know the salesmen had opened their own businesses, taking their clients with them. Like a Baptist church! [*Laughter*] Daddy began making deliveries and, probably due to a shortage of salesmen, began taking orders. About 20–25 years later, they hired someone to help with shipping, and he did sales almost full time. So that's the way it was.

So both of your parents had little formal education? Daddy did not take any formal courses while I was young that I can remember, but he was an avid reader. Like his mother, he read the newspaper every day and enjoyed intellectual challenges. He routinely came home with a brainteaser for us and monitored our speech: pronunciation, word usage, grammar, etc. Church activities provided an outlet for his intellectual and creative activities and a chance to hone his organizational skills. He chaired the finance committee and directed the Sunday evening educational activities, among other things. My sister and I observed all of this.

You have one sister? Yes, my parents were in their mid-30s when they had my sister. She is two years older than I am. My parents remained together until my dad died in 1992. They were married sixty-one years. My mother is over 90 years old and still lives in Oklahoma City. My sister is also in Oklahoma City. She has three sons. She became an attorney and opened a law practice after teaching elementary school for almost twenty years. Her story is also very interesting.

What was your school experience like when you were young? We went to Douglass High School in Oklahoma City. It was about four or five blocks from our house. Oklahoma City public schools began desegregation in 1957, three years after the 1954 *Brown versus the Board of Education* Supreme Court decision, as I entered the tenth grade. They opened Central High School and many of the black students from the rather small black community on the west side of town enrolled there. One summer after my junior year, I took American history at Central High because I wanted the experience. We had no white teachers or students at Douglass High and no summer school either. I remained at Douglass where I graduated in 1960.

Do you recall a special teacher who influenced your thinking when you were young? The teachers at Douglass followed the pattern of those who taught me in elementary and junior high school. They were very "hands on." I ran into my third-grade teacher at a friend's daughter's wedding recently and we had a wonderful exchange. I always felt free to drop into their rooms before or after school and chat. I remember my eighth-grade teacher reading and commenting on my essay even though it was not for her class.

Do you remember a particular role model in those early years? The teacher who had the most influence on me did not teach at my school. She was Clara Luper, advisor of the NAACP Youth Council. The Youth Council and Mrs Luper raised my political awareness and social consciousness. The summer after my sophomore year (1958), I went with the Youth Council to New York. Mrs Luper had written a play about Martin Luther King and the Montgomery bus boycott. It was the kind of play you could do with fifty or ten kids, because there were scenes with marchers [*laughter*]. She was quite a phenomenal person; very creative and very energetic. She always worked with kids. The NAACP National Youth director saw the play and invited us to perform in New York City. This gave us the chance to see New York as well as other things we had never seen before.

Later that summer, on August 19, we were having a Youth Council meeting under a shade tree in Mrs Luper's front yard. There were probably eleven of us. I was the Vice-President of the Youth Council at that time. Sam Cornelius, who became the Under-Secretary of Agriculture under Reagan, but at that time was director of the colored branch of the YMCA in Oklahoma City, happened by. He had recently moved to Oklahoma City from Wichita, Kansas, where they had a sit-down. (After the events in Greensboro, North Carolina, we called them sit-ins.) He told us about black kids, our ages, who went to lunch counters where they didn't serve blacks and sat there until they were served. They just sat. After a couple of days or so they were served. One participant in the Wichita sit-ins was Ron Walters who is now a political scientist at the University of Maryland, and often on television as a political pundit. He ran Jesse Jackson's national campaign for president.

We said, "Ah ha! We ought to do that!" We talked it over with Mrs Luper. She was all for it. So we took off for downtown Oklahoma City. We decided that only one person would speak for the group. I was selected because the president of our Youth Council was out of town. We went to Katz Drugstore because it had the only lunch counter open on a Sunday night [*laughter*]. We went in and sat down in the vacant seats. They happened to be at the back. We decided ahead of time that if they told us that we couldn't be served, our response would be, "I'll wait." That's exactly what we did. The waitress would say, "We don't serve colored," and we'd reply, "Thank you, I'll wait." She began to panic. She called the manager. The manager told us, "Y'all can't be served." And we said, "Thank you, I'll wait." When the white folks who were sitting at the back end of the lunch counter had been served, they closed that section. So we took seats as they became available toward the front. They didn't know what to do. We stayed until the store closed, and returned the next morning.

Did your parents know what you were doing? Neither my sister nor I said anything to my mother or father. They got up and went to work; we got up and went downtown. On Monday, however, the newspaper was there. The word had gotten out: black kids were filling up the lunch counter at Katz Drugstore. The police came and stood there to protect us. That was certainly different from the pattern in most cities that followed us. There wasn't much to say to the newspaper.

Were there any adults involved? There were no adults visible at this point. As the spokesperson, I explained to people that we were with the NAACP Youth Council, we were there to eat, and that was all we wanted! This was the first sit-in movement that received national publicity (Oklahoma City, 1958). The sit-in in Greensboro was sustained and spread to other cities, but this one didn't spread. We continued our efforts and, after a couple of weeks, Katz began to serve us. We moved two or three doors down the street to Woolworth and then to S.H. Kress. Both served us fairly quickly.

How many children were involved? The group grew. We had over 200 kids before the summer's activities ended. When I say kids, I mean kids. The youngest was 7 years old. At 15 years, and about to become a junior in high school, I was one of the older ones. *Jet Magazine* did a multipage spread on the movement. There are lots of pictures of me walking and directing the protesters. By then we were at John A. Brown's Department Store, the largest department store in Oklahoma City. They had a cafeteria in the basement and we knew that, if John A. Brown would serve us, the whole city would open up. It was over a year before they did. School opened after Labor Day and we could only demonstrate on Saturdays. So every Saturday for a year, we sat in at John A. Brown [*laughter*]. We waited to be served! We mobilized the city. The adult chapter of the NAACP gave support. The Negro Baptist Ministers Alliance gave support. The principal of the black high school, F. D. Moon, spoke in support of the demonstration at a public meeting. Members of the white community joined the march and gave money.

But it was the children who really led the movement? Yes. Clara Luper called the shots. She was the advisor to the Youth Council. But we would meet and talk about it. The role of the adults was simply support. They drove the cars. None of us had driver's licenses. They also provided money for food and logistical support.

And did you remain the spokesperson for the group? Yes. As spokesperson, I was easily recognized not only in the black community but also in the white community. When I went to a Hi-Y camp in Estes Park, Colorado, with a citywide group, the other black girl in the group and I were the only girls housed with chaperons. One asked me if I was a communist. She knew about my activities with the sit-ins.

How did your parents react to your central position in the movement? My father was warned by well-meaning white men (who he knew through his job at the sporting-goods store and the mortgage company where he/we did janitorial work in the evenings) that there was a good chance I would have difficulty finding employment in Oklahoma City. He passed that warning on to me. Up to that time, we had never discussed whether or not I should participate. But when people he trusted predicted this would have a negative impact on my ability to get a job, he was worried. However, he was still supportive.

What about your sister? Did she face the same problem? Yes, but like the others, she was only a member of a group, and the media did not identify group members. Of the 250 kids who were marching, I was the only one who was singled out. After the talk with my father, I told Mrs Luper I would do everything else, but I would no longer do interviews. Mrs Luper was a very direct person. She said, "Barbara, you are going to have to decide. You are no use to us if you can't do the interviews." That evening daddy and I talked again. I told him, "This is important. If it means I can't find a job in Oklahoma City, I'll just have to move somewhere else." And I resumed my role as spokesperson. This marked a turning point in my life. I had to make a very important decision; what I now refer to as a grown-up decision. My dad never said – this is what you ought to do. He only pointed out what he thought was a constraint. But my parents were 100 percent supportive. They went to the meetings, and he never suggested that I quit. Indeed, it would have been irresponsible for him not to tell me his concerns. If he hadn't, it would have meant that he was making a decision for me which would have influenced my life. It would not have been fair. Once I had made the decision, it was fine.

Did your activities with the Youth Council detract at all from your high school work? When I finished high school I was one of the top students in my class. I received most of the top awards [*laughter*]. Most of the awards had the same criteria, so the same person would usually get most of them [*laughter*]. After high school, I went to the University of Oklahoma.

Did you always know you would attend college? There was never any question. However, where I was going, and what I would study, was a whole different ball game.

How did you decide to attend the University of Oklahoma? Oklahoma had a very small black enrollment in 1960, but the numbers had begun to increase. In fact, Prentice Gautt, an all-American football player who played with the St Louis Cardinals, was in the first class to have more than two black students. He graduated in 1960. Prentice also lived behind the house I was born and lived in until I was 8 years old. Sixteen students from my all-black high school class went to the University of Oklahoma in 1960; one or two went to the University of Kansas; and a small handful went to Oklahoma State University. Most of those who went to college, however, went to predominantly black colleges.

Did you have scholarships to attend college? Yes, between scholarships and family support, my expenses for school were pretty much covered. Tuition was just $7 per credit hour. I worked my third year as a dorm assistant, which covered most of the dorm cost.

Did you major in economics right away? No. In fact, I changed my major every semester and sometimes in the middle of the semester for the first year and a half [*laughter*]. At first I had a year's scholarship for majoring in math or science. When the year and the money ended, I majored in psychology and thought it was wonderful. Then I moved on to something else [*laughter*]. Fortunately, all the courses I took during my "shopping spree" satisfied the general education requirements.

You probably weren't worried, but were your parents concerned? One weekend when I was home, my dad was about to leave for a church meeting and he asked, "Do you have a major yet?" Rather nonchalantly, I responded in the negative. "Look, I want you to pick a major. Folks keep asking me about your major, it's embarrassing. By the time I get back I want you to have a major." We didn't have another conversation about it, but I did have sense enough to know that I needed a major.

Why did you choose economics as a major? One afternoon I took the university catalog and went through it, page by page, and listed all of the courses I wanted to take before graduation. My plan was to major in the area that had the greatest number of courses on my list. The two fields that satisfied my criteria were economics and political science. But while I was going through the catalog, I also discovered what was called a "planned program" – an individually designed program of at least thirty-six credit hours. I could select three fields and take at least six units in each field. This meant that I could earn a degree without actually limiting myself to one major. Wonderful! I knew I had a winner. There was a public affairs option under the planned program that combined economics, political science, and finance.

My program had to be approved by the dean of arts and sciences. He not only approved the public affairs option, he said rather flippantly, "I would even approve economics, political science, and mathematics." I said, "I'll take it." I then had a major that turned out to be a perfect background for economics at the graduate level. Although I took the same number of political science courses as economic courses, I had all As in economics, so the decision to study graduate economics seemed like a natural.

What did your parents think of your decision to major in economics? It's funny, but I'm sure you have had this experience. People would ask, "What are you studying?" I'd say, "Economics." In fact, this happened to me just a week ago. Their response was, "Oh, you know, I think it is so important that women do home economics." [*Laughter*] But my mother and dad were pleased. My mother has never understood what an economist is. And how do I explain it? Near the end of my undergraduate program, she asked me, "Barbara, when are you going to do your practice teaching?" I would explain, "I'm not an education major so I won't practice teach." She'd say, "OK." That's the way my mother is. She would never say – I don't believe you. Instead, a few months later she would ask again, and I would have to remind her that, because I was not an education major, I would not practice teach.

I hadn't planned to participate in graduation, until I realized that it was really important to my parents. I'm glad that I did. Otherwise, I don't think she would have ever believed that I had graduated because she has never known anyone who graduated without practice teaching.

What was your course work like as an undergraduate? I took labor, economic development, statistics, micro theory, and another twenty-four credit hours, but no macro.

Was there a particular professor who inspired you intellectually? It was the subject matter that fascinated me. But the professor who had the most influence on me as an undergraduate was not an economist. He was a political scientist named John Paul Duncan. I did three courses in the history of political thought. I was not particularly interested in political thought, but he taught it, and I would probably have taken physics if he had taught it.

How did he inspire you? He was a wonderful person with a tremendous sense of humor and a genuine love for his students. He was very interested in day-to-day political developments. He would come to class and spend half the time commenting on the news. And students loved him. His classes were always closed. We had to sign up for his classes early. Students would ask him a question about a current event and he would go off on a tangent. It was just fascinating! Then he'd say, "Look, I've got to cover this material." Eventually he would.

Did you have contact with him beyond the classroom? He was also my advisor. He suggested that I take intermediate micro because he knew it was required by the folks in economics. He had an office in the library. At night, we'd sit at the table in front of his library office and wait for him to come. With a little prodding and a couple of questions, he'd be on his way! He loved to talk, and we loved to listen [*laughter*]. One day he announced to the class that he could no longer hold conferences in the library. His colleagues were complaining that they couldn't do their work because of the talking. That night, however, we were there waiting for him as usual. He politely reminded us that he really couldn't talk. We promised we'd whisper. So for about five minutes we did, and then we were at it again. It was great! [*Laughter*] That was the first time I had a relationship with a teacher that stimulated me intellectually. Learning with him was totally unrelated to grades and credits. He raised political questions that I wanted the answers to.

Was he an African–American? No, in fact, I don't think there was one African–American professor on the entire faculty at that time. There was a black teacher in French, but he was a graduate assistant.

Were you the only African–American student in economics? I had two classes in my freshman year – German and anthropology – with an African–American male. Other than that, I had no other African–Americans in any of my undergraduate classes. Remember, this was before affirmative action. The Civil Rights Act wasn't passed until 1964. However, Mack (who became my husband) was in my very first graduate class. Not only was he black, he obviously knew more about municipal government than any of the other graduate students in the class. I was impressed! [*Laughter*]

Were you the only woman majoring in economics? I don't remember much about the economics students as an undergraduate. I related more to the political science students. It had more women.

Were there women students in your math classes? Very few to speak of. The engineers took the same math sequence I took. However, when you are black in an overwhelmingly white setting, the gender thing becomes secondary .... Oh, is there a problem in that area too? [*Laughter*] It's like when you have cancer and then you get a paper cut. You don't pay too much attention to the cut.

How did you go about deciding to attend graduate school in economics? First, I decided to go for a Master's in economics, mainly because I didn't know what I wanted to do professionally. Remember, I didn't "practice teach!" I asked one of my professors for a list of graduate schools he would recommend for economics. Out of the list of six schools, only Stanford turned me down. That hurt my feelings. I had no preference, I just didn't like the rejection. I know that one of my letters of recommendation (this was very common at the time) indicated my race. There was a statement, "This is one of the best black (probably said, negro) students I have ever taught."

You decided to go the University of Illinois. Why? They accepted me and gave me a tuition waiver, but not a graduate assistantship at first. However, on the day of my graduation in August of 1963, I received a letter from them offering a quarter-time assistantship. John Dew, who was in public finance, had just become head of the economics department, and I later learned the first thing he did as chair was to make this offer. He told me that they had never given a graduate assistantship in the College of Commerce to a black.

So you decided to leave Oklahoma? I had thought about staying there because they offered me a half-time graduate assistantship to work in student affairs. I received the offer because I was very active as an undergraduate in the student organizations – Student Senate, the Association of Women Students, International Student Association, etc. When I got the better offer from Illinois, I asked the Dean of Students at the University of Oklahoma for advice about what to do. I was told that the better offer would depend upon my interests; what I wanted to pursue. If I wanted a career in administration, Oklahoma was the better offer. If I wanted an academic career, Illinois was the better offer. At that point I had never considered a career in administration and, more importantly, I wanted to leave the state. I was ready for a different experience.

Can you say something about your experience as a graduate assistant at the University of Illinois? I was assigned to Professor Donald Peyton, who taught the principles classes via television and supervised all of the teaching assistants. The second semester they changed my assignment from a quarter-time to half-time position with regular teaching responsibilities. That's when I found out that I was also the first black to teach in the school of commerce. When my academic advisor told me, I said, "What took you so long?" Another shock at Illinois was learning that they were just getting around to inducting their first black member into the Mortar Board (1965). I had been inducted at the University of Oklahoma in 1963. At that time Oklahoma was "in the South" and Illinois was part of the "promised land." I also learned that the economics department at Illinois had only recently begun to give graduate assistantships to women. Prior to that, they had accepted women into the program, but they would not give them financial support because they felt it was a waste of their resources.

Do you remember how many women were in your graduate class? There were probably 100 graduate students in economics of which there were maybe three or four women.

How many blacks? I was the only black person with financial support. There was a black male my first year, but he only stayed through his Master's. ... Something else: of all the black graduate students at Illinois at that time, only two of us did our undergraduate work at predominantly white colleges. I thought to myself, there's obviously something going on at these predominantly black schools which is not happening at the predominantly white institutions. After talking to the other blacks there, I found out that they had had a more supportive undergraduate academic experience than most black students who attended the University of Oklahoma.

Barbara, can you say something about your overall experience in graduate school; what was it like during the 1960s? It was an interesting experience, being black, being female, and being an economist! At first, I wanted to do labor economics. That's where my interest was. So I enthusiastically registered for a course in labor economics and read everything assigned very carefully. That semester, I got two As and one B. I got the B in labor. I went to the professor who taught the course because I wanted to see my final exam and discuss my performance. Well, he told me he didn't have the exam in his office. I said, "Fine. Let's just talk about it." I wanted to take the second course in labor and I wanted to know what went wrong so I could do better. We discussed the exam. I asked about question number one. What did he expect in a good answer? He repeated what I had written. I asked about question number two. Again, he repeated what I had written. Then we got to the last question, which was about wage and price controls during World War II. It was a political question, so I created an argument *for* wage and price controls, the opposite of the position he had taken in class. But I had justified my position. He disagreed, and said the answer should have been negative. I said, "OK, fine." I dropped the matter and took his second course. Several students from the first course greeted me and said, "Well, I know *you* got an A!" I replied, "No, I got a B." They said, "What? How did you get a B?!" After I received another B in the second course, I knew this professor would not be my advisor for a Master's thesis.

Did you know what you wanted to do for a Master's thesis? I wanted to do something on blacks in the labor movement. For advising, they sent me to

Professor X who was doing research on women in the labor force. He was very nice. He loved me. He'd ask, "So how are you doing?" He'd have coffee and a Danish pastry for me when I came for my appointment to discuss my thesis. We talked, and had a wonderful time. My husband, Mack, also took a course from him. He thought Mack was bashful and said, "I'm going to have to draw him out." I responded, "Sir, I do not think that will be necessary." But he insisted it was necessary [*laughter*].

Anyway, I had written my thesis proposal. He approved the outline and the first chapter, which was a restatement of the proposal. Everything changed, however, when I took him my first substantive chapter, "Blacks in the History of the Labor Movement." I had a statement in the chapter that the founders of the early labor unions had helped institutionalized racism in society. He was pacing the floor when I arrived. He said, "That's a dogmatic statement. You can't say that!" He went on and on. He said, "This is all wrong. You will have to start over. This will not do!"

So I took what I had written to Professor Peyton. I asked him to read the proposal and the first chapter. After he read it, he agreed that I had written what I had proposed. And without my knowledge, he went to the chair of the economics department who arranged for me to do my thesis under a professor in the Institute for Labor and Industrial Relations. At that time, the institute and the department of economics were like oil and water. The university had established the institute with the War Labor Board without the approval of the department of economics. They had given the faculty in the institute both tenure and professorships in the department, but there was never any interaction between the two units.

How did that work out for you? None of the people in the department, except for the chair and of course Professor Peyton, knew what was happening. My new advisor at the institute, Professor Chalmers, understood the labor movement and was glad to take on my thesis. In fact, he had a grant that was compatible with my proposed study and was willing to share it with me. As a result, I was able to expand my study to include contemporary patterns of race and labor unions. Part II of my thesis was an analysis of the efforts of labor union locals to improve race relations. I went to three locals of three different labor unions in the Chicago area: the United Auto Workers, the Steel Workers, and the Ladies Garment Worker Union. I interviewed union leaders to find out what kinds of community activities they were engaged in and how they had been able to have a positive impact on the economic conditions of their black workers and/or the African–American community. The fieldwork complemented the work that had originally been proposed. As a result, it turned out to be a much better document than I had originally planned. Needless to say, the new project took much longer, but my name finally appeared on the list of prospective graduates.

Around this time, the labor professor (who gave me Bs and did not speak to me when I passed him in the hall) stopped me and said, "I've got something I think you may want to see!" I went to his office and he handed me an article. Then he said, "I understand you are finishing up your Master's degree this summer. Who worked with you?" I told him. He couldn't believe it! He couldn't deal with it. He couldn't figure out how I had finished without him or Professor X, the only two labor economists in the department. This is the same man who told me in my first year that I shouldn't be thinking about a PhD – that I could go South to some colored college and they would pay me good money for a Master's degree!

While you were in Illinois, were there any women faculty in the economics department? Yes, two. They shared an office. Marianne Ferber was one. She was not regular faculty, however, because her husband was a full professor and director of the Research Institute. Neither woman taught regular graduate courses. Consequently, I never had an opportunity to talk to her.

You said that you met your husband in classes at Illinois. When did you get married? On April Fool's Day of my first year in graduate school [*laughter*]. I told you, I saw a black man in class and decided this was it! [*Laughter*] Anyway, we got married and it was wonderful. Intellectually, he has had more of an influence on me than anyone else. Mack is very astute, bright, and knowledgeable. He also has a history of social protests. He was expelled from Southern University in Baton Rouge in 1960 for participating in the sit-ins. With the help of the SU faculty, he was admitted to Texas Southern University without losing any time. He graduated magna cum laude and went to the University of Illinois as a Fulbright scholar. I received a scholarship award from the Ladies Garment Workers Union in 1963 for student activists. (I shared the award with Stokely Carmichael, by the way.) I told Mack about the program and he got the scholarship in 1964. Mack was a graduate student in political science with a minor in economics. I studied economics with a minor in political science. As graduate students, I would type his papers. That was my moonlighting job [*laughter*]. I learned a lot from reading them. We've always had an interactive relationship in our scholarly activities.

How long did you stay at the University of Illinois? In my second year, I decided I had had enough. I would soon have a Master's degree. So I went to Professor Peyton and told him I was quitting. He told me, "I don't want to lose you as a teacher. You are my best teacher." He advised me to sign up for a couple of courses and teach. He said, "Let's face it. This job is going to pay as much as anything you could get in this town." Mack was getting the PhD in political science and had a year left, so it made sense. I agreed. The fall semester, I took French and one economics course. Then I took two economics courses in the spring and enjoyed both of them. The pressure was gone! I wasn't going to do the PhD and I was taking courses because I wanted to. I was studying what I wanted to learn. I enjoyed it.

By the end of the year Mack had accepted a position with Texas Southern University (his undergraduate alma mater), a predominantly black university in Houston. I didn't know what *I* was going to do. I was depressed, but Mack tried to reassure me by saying, "Why are you worried where you will work? I'll take care of you." [*Laughter*]

You were not reassured, I take it? It wouldn't do ... but as my labor economics professor had predicted, I was hired down South at a "colored school," Texas Southern University. Unfortunately, he did not predict my salary; I was paid the state minimum. But that year I discovered that I enjoyed teaching. I also got pregnant.

Can you say something about your experience at Texas Southern? We had a fifteen-hour teaching load, but I enjoyed it. It became very clear to me that I wanted to teach, especially in a predominantly black setting. However, we left after a year. Mack was the faculty advisor to the Friends of SNCC, a student civil rights organization. The group picketed the state highway patrol for beating a carload of black gospel singers. The singers had been stopped on the highway, dragged from their car, and beaten. Students were picketing the same day the university president was scheduled to attend the Houston Endowment to seek support for the university. The president canceled his visit and the administration fired Mack, who was faculty advisor to the student protestors. The point was to show they had taken action against the "inappropriate behavior of their students." Interestingly, Mack didn't know the students were protesting. However, he *would* have supported their actions. The administration wrote him a letter of termination saying, "Your contract will not be renewed because we have too many faculty in international relations." That was his speciality and they knew that when they hired him the year before. It was an obvious cover-up.

How did you and Mack respond to the firing? It was really funny because Mack had already signed a contract with Atlanta University. Meanwhile, the students found out that Mack was fired and began a major protest at Texas Southern. We left for Atlanta at the end of the academic year. I spent the next year at home with my son, who was born in October. The following year, I taught at Atlanta University and then went to Georgia State University to finish the PhD. Georgia State was the only option for a doctorate in economics in the Atlanta area. Neither Emory University nor Georgia Tech had graduate programs in economics at the time, and having a small child ruled out the commute to the University of Georgia which was over an hour away.

Were there any African–Americans on the faculty at Georgia State? There was one when I arrived, Ron Campbell.

Were there any women faculty? I had no women instructors at either the University of Oklahoma or Georgia State. Paula Stephen joined the faculty at Georgia State when I was finishing my dissertation. There was a woman in the Master's program. In fact, she and I were pregnant together. I was pregnant with my second child when I took my comprehensives. I finished classes in June and comprehensives were not until the end of August. When I left in June, no one other than Linda (the other woman in the program) knew I was pregnant. When I showed up for the exams I was conspicuously pregnant! [*Laughter*]

Everybody was quite surprised [*laughter*]. My daughter was born in late November.

Did anyone in the program have a problem with it? Not that I am aware of. But it never concerned me as an issue. After my experience at Illinois, I had decided I would take the degree if these folks would let me have it.

So it wasn't an imperative for you to have a PhD? That's right. If I had to endure unreasonable and unfair treatment, then forget it. I never felt that my life depended on having a PhD. It did not mean that I was not willing to work hard. I was simply not willing to put up with inappropriate treatment. I could have sucked up to the labor economist at Illinois (the one who gave me the Bs), and taken a political position which I didn't agree with and probably have gotten As. I could have also written a Master's thesis that would have satisfied Professor X and he would have been perfectly happy. But I was not willing to do that.

I remember once writing a paper for a political science class about state labor law. I was discussing the paper with a fellow black graduate student. The paper included a discussion of antidiscrimination laws. The student, who was considerably older, advised me, "Just leave that alone. Don't talk about race. Write a paper relating to oil wells in Texas or something." He explicitly told me to avoid writing anything with political implications or related to race or income distribution. He advised, "Just get the degree and get out of here." By the time I got to Georgia State I knew I was not prepared to sacrifice my principles. If I had to compromise my sense of what was right and wrong – my sense of ethics and social purpose – I would forgo the degree. The degree did not define who or what I was. Other things were more important. I was not willing to make the sacrifice in order to get the PhD!

So overall, how would you judge your experience at Georgia State? All my professors were white males. But I had no problems; none at all.

How did you choose your dissertation topic? I had read an article in a labor course about why black women chose to enter and leave the labor force. The explanation in the article seemed totally ridiculous to me [*laughter*]. It made absolutely no sense! Work had been done on white women, but very little had been done on black women.

Who were your committee members? The department chair was my committee chair. But I primarily worked with Larry Schroeder who had just finished his PhD and had recently joined the faculty. The chair was from the old school and was not familiar with the recent literature or econometric techniques, and I'm not sure that the third member of the committee even read it.

How did you deal with raising two children while you were trying to finish the dissertation? I had a housekeeper. Our standard of living was still at the level of graduate students. But housekeepers weren't that expensive then. We lived on Mack's salary, and used my fellowships to pay the housekeeper. I would get up in the morning and leave for the library. Going to school was my job. When I came home, I was home; although I still worked after the kids were put to bed and on weekends.

The housekeeper also took care of the children? Yes. She kept the older child while I worked and took classes. When our daughter was born, the housekeeper took care of her, and we put my 3-year-old son in pre-school.

You said you had fellowships to help pay for the housekeeper? This was the late 1960s or early 1970s and there was special support for black graduate students. I had two fellowships. The Southern Fellowship fund supported a year of classes and a year of dissertation. The National Research Council also funded a year of dissertation. So our standard of living was the same as it would have been if I had stayed home. We were still at that stage in life where boards and cinder blocks served as bookshelves! [*Laughter*]

Now this is interesting, when our third child was born, I was a full professor at Clark College and Mack was a full professor at Atlanta University. However, we could not afford a housekeeper [*laughter*]. I couldn't figure it out. How could we have afforded one when we lived off one income? What had happened was that my income did not keep up with the cost of living, and our style of living had changed.

When did you have your third child? Ten years after the second, in 1980. My youngest is a boy.

Did you enter the job market before or after you finished the PhD? Before. Clark College had about 1,100 students served by a three-person department consisting of business and economics. It had one economist who was ABD and two MBAs. After the ABD finished his dissertation, he received support from Princeton to do postdoctorate work. I saw him and mentioned I was working on my dissertation. He said, "If you're ready for a job, why don't you come over to Clark and take my spot?" I sent my vitae, met with the dean of the faculty, and they made me an offer. I started the fall of 1971 and stayed sixteen years. I became chair of the department while I finished the dissertation! [*Laughter*]. Not to mention everything else. It was crazy. It was wild. But it was so fun!

Would you like to elaborate on your experiences at Clark? Sure. Clark was a predominantly black liberal arts college. When I got to the department, things were really disorganized. There was not a ream of paper anywhere. There was nothing except a dirty trailer and one typewriter. I called the department of buildings and grounds and asked them to clean the floor. They cleaned it enough so that I was able to finish. I brought in my buckets and an electric scrubber, and I scrubbed and waxed the floor so that it was clean enough to work there. I bought some low-budget curtains and hung them up in the windows. Not only were there no filing cabinets, there were no files. The best part was that they allowed me to move in during the summer and use the office to work on my dissertation.

You didn't have a secretary? Of course not. In September, I found out what was required for graduation, set up a student file system, and started advising lots of students. For the first two weeks, I woke up in the middle of the night thinking about what I needed to do. I couldn't sleep. I was thinking about the chaos.

175

Were you teaching as well? Yes. The teaching load for the department chair was nine hours (three courses). The first semester I taught three sections of macro principles and the second semester I taught three sections of micro principles. I had only one preparation per semester which made things much easier. The level of the course also helped to make the load manageable.

Needless to say, I did not get a lot of work done on the dissertation. I worked on it the following summer. During the first two weeks of the fall session I thought, I can't do this! This is crazy. But I talked myself into staying until January because it would have been bad to quit an academic job in the middle of the semester. In January, I thought maybe I could hang on until May. I stayed sixteen years and loved it. I got things in order and chaired the department for nine years. I finished the dissertation in the summer of 1973, and I even managed to produce some articles.

What was the tenure process like for you at Clark College? When I started as an assistant, there were no written procedures for tenure or promotion. But when I finished the dissertation, I automatically was promoted to associate professor. At that time, there were a lot of non-doctorates on the faculty, unlike now. President Vivian Henderson, an economist, had a very positive influence on the college. He increased the budget, the number of programs, and the number of doctorates on the faculty, among other things. However, for a long time no one was awarded tenure. Jobs were not threatened, so the absence of tenure policies was not a big problem.

However, as faculty representative to the board, I brought it up. I argued that, "Having tenure does not matter, but not having tenure could be a problem." Although President Henderson died of a sudden heart attack, the new president charged a committee to propose policies and procedures relating to tenure and promotion. I was asked to chair the committee. The faculty and the administration approved our work, and I was in the first group to be granted tenure and promotion under the new system.

Were there white professors working at Clark College? Yes. Most historically black colleges were founded by white men, and initially many institutions had white faculties. Most of them opened right after the Civil War. Clark College was founded around 1869; Atlanta University in something like 1866. It was some time before Spelman College had any black professors. In fact, they didn't have a black president until the 1970s. The Rockefeller family founded it. Morehouse College was named for a white man. The white bishops of the United Methodist Church founded Clark College.

It sounds like you really enjoyed working at Clark College? In spite of what we lacked, working at Clark College was a wonderful experience. We were poor and the salaries were by no means competitive. But we had students with great attitudes and we didn't have the traditional academic politics. The faculty knew each other and worked together across disciplines. We all pitched in.

For instance, we had a writing proficiency committee that I worked on for years. We put together a program to foster writing across the curriculum and offered year-long workshops for the faculty. We did this years before it became a fad in higher education. We trained almost 100 percent of the faculty in our workshops. We worked hard with the students and created programs to improve the quality of education being delivered. The faculty complained, but faculty always complain. All in all, morale was high.

You said you chaired the department for nine years. What was that like? I became chair when I didn't even know what a department was. I saw what needed to be done and did it. There was no money for administration work-shops. In fact, I didn't know they had workshops or conferences for department chairs. I just did it. It was relatively easy in the beginning because there were only three of us, but the department grew. Business programs and economics programs grew nationwide, and so did ours.

You haven't mentioned a personal mentor at Clark; did you have one? The only mentoring I remember was Academic Council, a council of the depart-ment chairs. We met weekly and discussed issues relating to the academic life of the college. It was not a one-on-one mentorship. It was a matter of becoming friends.

And no political in-fighting? Right. I didn't need a person to help me over a political hurdle. The dean, Charlie Knight, was not a noted scholar, but he was very approachable. I could go in and chat and work with him. Clark College had a very collegial atmosphere. We all worked together for a common cause.

You went to Africa during the 1980s. How did that come about? I went to Nigeria to teach in 1983–4. Here's where my relationship with Mack, both professionally and personally, was extremely valuable. I learned how universities operate, not only from working at Clark, but from him. I also benefited from our circle of friends, who were primarily academics. I got the kind of enrichment I would not have gotten had my husband worked for, say, General Motors.

Anyway, Mack had spent five or six weeks in West Africa and had met people at Ahmadu Bello University (Zaria, Nigeria), the largest university in black Africa. They were interested in Mack because he had been instrumental in starting the PhD program in political science at Atlanta University (1973). As chair, he was able to get support from the Ford Foundation for the program. A number of Nigerian students had completed the program. Mack was also the first president of the National Conference of Black Political Scientists. He received a Fulbright to Nigeria to teach at Ahmadu Bello University. While negotiating his position, he also negotiated a position for me in the economics department.

We left home thinking all was in order. However, when we arrived, the economics department chair had taken ill and was not expected to survive. The new chair claimed he knew nothing about my appointment. He granted *us* an appointment to discuss me joining the economics faculty. The new chair talked to my husband for an hour. He explained to Mack why they could not hire me. At no point did he say anything to me. It was as though I was an infant in nursery school. The care giver doesn't talk to the 3-month-old infant. That is how I felt sitting there. I was the infant. I was dumbfounded!

How did you deal with it? I was trying to be respectful of other cultures. Finally, I said, "Would you like a copy of my vitae?" He responded, "You can give it to the secretary if you want." I walked out of the office and I cried. I was so crushed. I could not believe it. I had so looked forward to teaching in an African university.

Mack's major contact at the university, the chair of political science, had left to become Minister of International Affairs for the federal government in Lagos. Communication in Nigeria was limited; we couldn't send a fax or an email, or even use the phone. Somehow Mack finally got in touch with the former chair and told him about the problem. He, in turn, contacted the vice-chancellor (comparable to a university president) and I was contacted for another interview.

This time, did they meet with Mack or you, or both? I, alone, met with the chair (who was Nigerian) and some others in the department (another Nigerian, a Ghanaian, and a full professor who looked European). I went in and sat at the end of a very long conference table. They sat at the other end. If that interview had a title, it would be "Why you wouldn't fit this job and if you did, why you wouldn't want it." They explained to me how my research on the economic status of blacks in America and the labor force activity of black women was not relevant to the experiences of Nigerians. They asked why I thought my cultural background and interests would make it possible for me to teach in Nigeria. At which point I said, "I'm sure that my cultural heritage is closer to the students than the European gentleman's cultural heritage at the end of the table." That observation brought a quick response, "I'm not European." Turns out he was a Brahman Indian. I responded, "You are certainly not Nigerian. My point still holds." I was then told that all classes had been assigned for the year. Then they asked me how I would respond to teaching nothing but discussion sections. I said, "It is your job to make me an offer. Once it is made, it is my job to respond." That ended the discussion. By then I was angry. I decided if that was the way they wanted to play, I would play their way and whatever happened, I would go from there.

What finally happened? It all worked out. They gave me a second-year macro course, a third-year micro course, and a third-year public finance course. I was also appointed senior lecturer, one step below full professor. Since the university operated on the British system, the third year (Part III) is the last year of the undergraduate program.

Were you the only woman on the economics faculty? There was one woman, an Indian woman, who said nothing in faculty meetings. The men did not talk to her. It was almost as though she did not exist. I was told she was hired as part of a package because her husband was in another department. They gave her first-year courses. I never held a conversation with her.

How did they treat you in faculty meetings? I attended my first faculty meeting before I was assigned classes. No one said anything to me. They did notice, however, that I was there. One faculty member raised his hand and said, "Now that there are more resources for the department, how will they be distributed?" In other words, he wanted to know who would be partially relieved from their assignments now that I was there. After the meeting, they walked out. I walked out alone. I got an office and started teaching.

Did you have any interaction with the faculty at all? Initially, the faculty member across the hall would grunt back when I called, "Good morning." Soon, the Ghanaian who had studied in the US started a conversation. Others began to talk to me. One graduate student made regular visits to our home and invited the family to visit his uncle, the Emir of Kano. By the end of the year, attitudes had changed. Two things happened before we left. They gave me a good-bye party where they indicated how much they enjoyed working with me [*laughter*]. And the chair asked my husband if I could stay on another year [*laughter*]. He asked my HUSBAND if I could stay on another year! [*Laughter*]

I'm curious; what was the gender composition of the Nigerian students? In Part III, there were about 103 students. Five were women. But the students were no problem; nooooo problem!

Maybe because you were from the US? Yes. If I had been a Nigerian woman, I think things would have been less hospitable. After classes, the male professors hung out at the staff club and drank beer. Everyone would gather around a table and discuss politics. I would go over and meet Mack and join the group. Nobody was uncomfortable. There were also a couple of other African–American women on the faculty (one in social work, one in education) who also joined the group, but there were no Nigerian women.

You eventually left Clark College. Why did you leave? When I left Clark College in 1987, I was making $28,000. That was a problem because we had one child in college and another ready to enter. Two years earlier, Mack had left Atlanta University for Howard University in Washington, DC. Our family was split up. Our youngest son was 6 and we didn't want to move him to Washington, DC. In the meantime, I had read about dramatic changes taking place at Prairie View A&M University in Texas and I had met the dean of business at the AEA meetings. He was recruiting business faculty, and I had been recommended to him. A few weeks after our meeting, I was invited for a campus interview. I went because I wanted to see the university. Also, my parents' families were from Texas and some family members had gone to Prairie View. However, I did not anticipate accepting a position. After all, Texas is a lot further from DC than Atlanta. When I had my appointment with the vice-president for academic affairs, he must have sensed something, because he said, "What would it take to make you seriously consider coming to Prairie View?" I said, "I have a husband." I later learned that my offer came after the position was turned down by a man.

Did Mack join you in Prairie View? It just so happened that they had an opening for a chair in the division of social and political science. I sent his vitae, and in two weeks they asked him to come for an interview. They liked what they saw and made him an offer. Howard University was insulted that he would leave them for a less prestigious school. He stayed seven years in Texas until he got an offer as chair and distinguished professor at Clark–Atlanta University.

What was it like at Prairie View? We lived in Houston, which was 25 miles [40 km] away. To say Prairie View is a town is an exaggeration; it's the college, period. I was chair of the department of economics and finance. The dean became provost and asked if I would serve as interim dean. That's how I became a business school dean. I never planned to do that!

Did you teach as well? I taught one course each semester. As I've said, I love teaching.

How would you compare administrative work with teaching? Academic administration indirectly affects what happens in the classroom. I find teaching as an administrator to be very valuable. Teaching helps you to understand what you are responsible for managing. Also, if you change schools, you will not understand the culture of the new institution until you have taught. I may be rationalizing because I really, really like teaching.

You must, because you have several teaching awards! Students tend to respond well to me. I have also found, you do not have to give good grades for them to like you. In fact, at the end of my first full term at Alabama A&M, I turned in my grades and the economics secretary said, "Oh my gosh, these grades are terrible." But I gave my students a questionnaire asking what I could do to be more effective and about three-fourths of them said, "We appreciate the fact that you challenged us." They knew their grades were bad. The grades got better over the course of the semester because their effort increased, but I did not change my grading system. One student who got 69 on the first test and barely got a C in the course graduated magna cum laude in another program. I've heard from him four times since he graduated, thanking me. He said he had no idea how much he wasn't learning until he took my class.

What course was he referring to? An introductory economics course for non-business majors. I want to teach that course again. I love teaching. I find that I can reach students. I try to teach them how to approach knowledge, and how to use economics. I emphasize the importance of understanding the world as opposed to getting the correct answers for the test.

Overall, how do you perceive your professional decisions or the development of your career? My life has taken some rather unexpected turns, but basically I'm pleased. I see myself ten years from the finish line and I still wonder what I want to do when I grow up. I'm open to something different. I'm not sure if I want to keep doing this (administration) until the end. I know I like teaching better than administration, but I also see in administrative decisions the power to affect the quality of an educational program beyond what I can accomplish in the classroom. From student feedback, I know what I am able to accomplish in the classroom. I am not as confident on the administrative side.

As an academic administrator, we try to help the faculty improve how they deliver education in the classroom. The idea is to change the campus climate. But that means changing the classroom climate. It's difficult to know whether or not that is happening.

Do you feel that you have had any particular constraints in your professional life? Black colleges have always had a much more egalitarian perspective in terms of gender than white institutions. They have not had a choice. Indeed, the entire black community is much more egalitarian in terms of gender for similar reasons. This relates to the fact that the proportion of educated people within the black community who are women has always been higher than for the country as a whole. So black colleges have not had enough black men to fill all of the academic positions. Consequently, they have had to use women.

Also, women have always been a larger proportion of the black labor force than in the white labor force. I have no doubt, however, that if I had been male, I would have been considered for certain positions that I was not offered. As a woman, I have been considered for administrative positions because of the lack of male competition. For example, at Prairie View, if there had been an acceptable male among the department chairs, I would not have been asked to be the interim dean. I have no doubts about that. At black colleges, where the talent pool is less rich, they cannot afford to discriminate against women as much. The proportion of provosts and presidents at black colleges who are women is much higher than it is at white institutions.

Barbara, could you talk about the major themes in your research? My research in the last ten years has declined because I've been doing administrative work. But my main interest has been the various factors and forces influencing the economic well-being of African–Americans.

Right now I am working on a study of the pawn shop industry. I got into this in a strange way. A faculty member in the department of economics and finance at Prairie View A&M was doing a paper on pawn shops in Texas. He is from Bangladesh and had never been in a pawn shop in the US. I sensed from the earlier draft of his paper that he didn't understand the cultural context. He did not understand the questions to ask because he didn't know how traditionally Americans *feel* about pawn shops. We discussed these issues and he asked me to work with him. I agreed, but told him he would have to do the legwork. I didn't have much time because of my administrative commitments. I drafted a questionnaire for an initial survey of pawn shop owners. Then he wrote a proposal for a larger state grant. It turns out that he's been a good partner. He'll draft something, I revise it, we'll toss around ideas, and he'll rewrite it, and so on. Once we got started I added an analysis of neighborhoods to get at ethnicity and race. We're looking at San Antonio, Corpus Christi, Houston, and Dallas. We're interested in the patterns of pawn shops in different neighborhoods, how people respond to pawn shops by city and race, access to traditional avenues of credit, and to what extent pawn shops are a substitute for traditional financial institutions, a place to shop, and so on. My guess is that pawn shops are becoming a more middle-class phenomenon. I also have gender questions about the people who use pawn shops. Pawn shops in Texas can charge up to 240 percent annual interest (20 percent a month). This is happening all over the South and in other parts of the country as well! The highest interest is for $300 loans. But if you get a loan above $300, say $1,000, the interest comes down (to say 5 percent per month). But most shops do not give loans of that size. Instead, if you bring in the family silver, they will give you three $300 loans at 20 percent per month. They also have title pawns where you give them your car title in exchange for a loan. If you don't pay it off, you can lose your car for a $200 loan!

How would you describe your theoretical perspective in economics? That's difficult. I have an appreciation for some elements of the Marxist theoretical tradition and for some elements of the neoclassical tradition. I know I frustrate my husband because he moves much closer to a Marxist analysis than I do. He teases me and calls neoclassical economics that old "western stuff." When we were planning our stay in Nigeria, he thought they would not be interested in the "western stuff." When I got there, however, I taught micro theory. The courses and textbooks were straight from the US. But the economists, themselves, were much more Marxist in their analyses of development and contemporary economies. But the curriculum was the basic western stuff.

Much like your education, no doubt? Yes. Most of my professors were neoclassical. There was a Marxist here and there. In general, I am sensitive to Marxist issues, and I reject the pure neoclassical analysis, but I think there are certain insights that we can get from it.

Barbara, have you observed any changes in the economics profession over the years? Oh, definitely. When I was an undergraduate, I didn't consider economics to be a highly quantitative discipline. There were variables that could be best presented and analyzed quantitatively, and certain courses like intermediate micro that were full of graphs, but that was about it. The math was secondary in my undergraduate program. Now a student pursuing graduate work in economics is better off having an undergraduate degree in math or engineering than in economics. I think it's a weakness of the discipline.

I don't think, as economists, we are providing as many insights into real social problems or as many creative solutions as economists did at one time. And we are only talking to each other. Only another economist can understand what most of us write. People interested in economic problems affecting human beings are often turned off by the study of economics. Now we get a lot of frustrated engineers who don't want to do engineering. They know math, and find it easier to apply their technical skills to mathematical models with social names for $x_1, x_2, \ldots, x_n$.

We recently interviewed an economist who had his undergraduate degree in math. His graduate transcript showed three micro courses, three macro courses, one course in labor, and the rest were quantitative courses (econometrics and the like). That was it! A full graduate transcript and a degree about two years old. What does he know about the social aspects of economic problems? What *can* he know?

Do you think it is important that women and African–Americans are attracted to the economics profession? Of course. I still think economic issues are as important in our lives as ever before. I think the perspectives and concerns of researchers are very important in terms of what they are willing to address and the implications of their research. What you accept when the results roll off the computer is a reflection of what you were expecting. It is not uncomfortable for us to accept the conclusions we expect. Like I said, I studied black women in the labor force for my dissertation because I disagreed with what I read. Someone else had an explanation that wasn't consistent with my experience. So unless you have women and people from various groups doing research, certain things won't be questioned or researched.

Another example is the work of Darity and Myers on "the progress" of the black–white income gap. They discovered that in other studies, the zeros – people with zero incomes – had been eliminated from the data. When they added the zeros back in, it changed the findings. They knew something was wrong with the numbers when it rolled off the computer. So they continued to question it. Unless you have people like that, who view the world from a different perspective, the explanations that reflect mainstream thinking will not be questioned. What makes us uncomfortable, leads us to probe.

Do you think it is more or less difficult for an African–American woman to succeed in the profession today? Well, I entered the profession before it was *popular* to be an African–American or a female. I think things are better now than in the early 1960s. The world has changed. For instance, as I was coming here today, I saw a grubby-looking black man with a grubby-looking white man. I thought, racially, things are different. Thirty years ago a black man and a white man, particularly in that economic class, would never have walked together on the streets of Atlanta on a Sunday morning. Forty years ago, black kids and white kids went to different schools. We would not be sitting here, in this house, having this conversation. Things are not perfect, but the civil rights movement happened; the women's revolution happened. It was not without struggle. There is some back-peddling, but we are not going back to where we were, racially or as women.

What about within the economics profession; do you think it is easier or more difficult to succeed? Although racism and sexism are alive and well, a larger proportion of the economics profession now recognizes race and gender as issues worthy of consideration; as variables to be included in the equation. And it's no longer "a happening" when a woman or an African–American appears at a session or sits on a panel at an ASSA meeting. Many departments also find it useful to have one of each on their faculties [*laughter*].

Do you have any advice for women who are either going on the job market or trying to get tenure? My advice is – decide what is important to you and do not let anything force you to renounce your values. Stick to your ethics and be willing to accept the consequences of your actions so you can feel good about yourself. In the long run that will be very important.

The other thing I would say is that you cannot fight all battles. I have to remind myself of that. There are certain people who get sacrificed for progress, and often they are not the same people who enjoy the benefits. You need to understand that you may not be the person who reaps the benefits. You have to choose your battles carefully because people will stop listening to you. You can overdo it. You have to realize which battles you can win, and which ones are important.

I also think the race and gender battles are somewhat different. You definitely cannot live in gender isolation. And compared to thirty years ago, society is clearly more racially integrated. It was easier when I left graduate school for a black person to live in a predominantly black setting than it is for the generation coming out of school now. And although some predominantly black institutions will continue to thrive, they are more integrated than they were forty years ago. Prairie View is about 10 percent white. Likewise, Alabama A&M has a higher proportion of whites than it did twenty years ago. What this means is that the yardstick by which Alabama A&M is judged is not according to what other predominantly black institutions of higher education are doing, but according to what institutions of higher education are doing, in general. So even predominantly black schools and their graduates are not as racially isolated as they were in the recent past.

Barbara, do you consider yourself a feminist? I think I am, but not in any theoretical sense of what I have studied or set out to be. It's more in terms of my attitude; what I expect of myself; the kind of things I demand in terms of respect. When I decided I was interested in economics, I didn't know that "women couldn't do it." It was never an issue for me. But even if it had been, I would have done it anyway.

I remember when I first learned about civil engineering. I thought it sounded interesting. Engineers build roads and bridges and design things. My mother said, "Barbara, don't be crazy. They are not going to hire a black woman to do something like that." I was highly perturbed with her for saying that. I told her, "I'll do anything I feel like doing." The fact that she suggested that I couldn't do certain things because I was black or a woman made me very angry. That is a feminist position. But no one had ever said anything to me about feminism. This was the 1950s, before the feminist movement and the debate over the equal rights amendment. I never had any question that the equal rights amendment should be passed. There has never been a question of which side I was on when presented with a feminist political question.

Are you familiar with the scholarship in feminist economics? Somewhat. I have had some exposure at conferences.

What kind of work do you think that feminist economists should be doing? Feminists should be doing for women the same kind of things that racially sensitive economists should be doing for blacks. That is, they should look at economic issues that affect the well-being of women, and take a broad perspective to make sure that the questions raised and the way those questions are approached allow us to illuminate and explain the status of women in the contemporary period. We need to understand how various policies affect women differently from men; how various practices within society affect women differently from men; how economic theories may not adequately reflect women's experiences; and make appropriate policy adjustments to more accurately reflect their reality. Of course, women will be affected differently depending on their race and class. Race, class, and gender are wrapped up together, but first you must understand what those class differences are; what those racial differences are; otherwise you don't know what you are looking for.

The same thing is true for blacks. We need to ask questions that help us understand the conditions of black people. We need to understand their conditions, and the forces that lead to those conditions, so we can change things.

Do you think feminist economics can have an impact on the profession? [*Pause*] **Do you think heterodox economics, such as say Keynesianism or Marxism, has had an impact?** Clearly, Keynesian economics has affected our view of macroeconomics. In economic development, classical economists are forced to address the issues raised by the Marxists. Even if people reject Keynesian or Marxist economics, they are still reacting to it.

For instance? The resurgence of classicalism tries to address Keynesian issues as a way of revising classical explanations. Had Keynesian or Marxist issues never been raised, neoclassical economics would not have changed.

I think each person tries to find their own niche. We do this by refuting what others have said. The act of refuting can be influential. Likewise, feminist economics raises questions which would not have been raised in the absence of feminist economists. Those who disagree with their arguments must react.

One sign of irrelevance of much economic work is the fact that other social sciences, such as sociology and political science, are beginning to address what were traditionally economic questions. And their work is being read by policy makers. It's influencing public policy. At some point, economists are going to have to come to terms with that; to consider the negative effects of isolating the profession from educated debate.

The number of Americans, black and white, going into economics, is declining. What has increased is the proportion of foreign-born students in the profession who do not understand the culture, but who can crunch the numbers. I am not arguing against them studying or teaching economics. I do argue, however, that they cannot replace those who better understand the culture; who understand the economic issues in this country. There can be severe costs.

Barbara, if you could do it over again, would you have gone into economics or done something else? I would do it again. But I would not rush out of school. I went to graduate school two months after my twentieth birthday because I was unsure of what I wanted to do professionally. Would I do it again? Yes, if economics was the discipline it used to be. Since I decided early on to avoid the study of pure mathematics, there is the possibility that I would not have pursued economics in its present form. The technical emphasis in graduate school today would have turned me off. But my interest in economics persists. My advice to every student seeking advice on their career, love life, or religion is to take at least two courses in economics. I suppose this means that I still feel pretty good about the value of the experience.

9

LOIS BANFILL SHAW

> At the end of my first year in graduate school, I felt I had come to a crisis point. I was asked to believe many things that I didn't believe. ... There were concepts that I found personally disgusting. One was the idea of choice between labor and leisure. ... I was simply offended. The idea that economists called what I had been doing for years (raising four children) – "leisure" – was just too much!
>
> (Lois Shaw, 1998)

After eighteen years of a life devoted to care taking, Lois entered graduate school. Ten years later she received her PhD. For the next twenty-plus years, she worked as a researcher and teacher at various institutions. She has written books, articles, and published reports focusing on women's low-wage work and poverty. She has explored such issues as the relationship between women's earnings and child poverty, the impact of social security reform on women's retirement, the unplanned careers of working women, and the impact of restructuring on women and minorities, among other things. She is a former Staff Economist at the Gary Income Maintenance Experiment at Indiana University Northwest; former Research Associate at the University of Illinois at Chicago; former Research Scientist at the Center for Human Resource Research at Ohio State University; and former Senior Economist at the General Accounting Office. Currently, she serves as a Senior Consulting Economist at the Institute for Women's Policy Research in Washington, DC. She has taught at St Mary's University in Halifax, Nova Scotia, and at Ohio State University. She has served as reviewer of grant proposals for the National Science Foundation as well as for numerous scholarly journals. She received an AB with honors (1946) from the University of California at Berkeley and MA (1965) and PhD (1973) from the University of Michigan.

Lois was an engaging storyteller and a generous host. I was particularly struck by the combination of her gentle demeanor and great sense of humor. Unlike the other stories in this volume, her story is somewhat unique, in that it will surely resonate with those who have followed a non-traditional educational and career path.

Plate 9   Down left side: Lois Shaw with husband Dick (1945); with mother Lessie Banfill (1925); with sister Dorothy and father William Banfill (1929); high school graduation (1942). Top right: Main portrait (1990s). Middle down: with children Wayne (in arms), Rachel, Alan, and Sarah (in front) (1961); a young girl in 1932. Bottom right: Lois presenting paper at IWPR conference (1998).

Lois, could you begin by talking about your family genealogy? I guess my family qualify as WASPs (white Anglo-Saxon Protestants). Both sides of the family came to America very early, during the colonial period. We were among those who continued to move west. My father was born in Illinois. His father was a small-town lawyer, but probably not a very successful one, and not terribly interested in law. He put more energy into his large orchard. But my father, as the oldest son, attended college. Just before World War I, my father moved to Montana where his brother was homesteading. He took up a homestead on a high ridge of land with a good view of the mountains. But it was unsuitable for farming and cattle raising. So he ended up supporting himself by teaching school and working for other farmers. During World War I, he served in the army. After the war, he returned and got a teaching job on the Crow Indian reservation.

My mother was born in Kansas into a farming family. They probably homesteaded, but I'm not sure about that. They were very poor, but her mother wanted all three girls to go to college. She found a Presbyterian college that allowed them to work their way through both high school and college. This was important because there was no high school in the little town near their farm. My mother attended for many years and finally got a college degree. She became a teacher.

Do you mean she attended high school and college in the same institution? Yes.

Where was this? Park College in Missouri.

She left home for high school? Yes. She was nearly college age by the time she attended Park College, so she was a little older than most students by the time she graduated. She taught school in a number of places in Nebraska and Iowa. Then, for whatever reason, she decided to take an adventurous step and moved to Montana to teach on the Crow reservation. This is where my mother and father met.

What did your mother study in college? She studied English.

What did your father study? He studied biology, but he was always interested in writing. I actually have a few, but unfortunately not all, of his diaries when he homesteaded, which are very interesting. After my parents got engaged, I guess they decided that he could not raise a family as a school teacher. He had worked in an advertising agency before he went west, so he applied for a job as a reporter on the *Billings Gazette*. At that time he didn't need a journalism degree, at least not for a small-town paper. That's what he did, and he really loved it. He became a full-time reporter and didn't teach after that.

Did your mother remain a teacher? No, in fact, that would not have been possible. Billings would not hire married women as teachers. My mother became a housewife, and as far as I can remember she really enjoyed it.

What year did they get married? 1921. My mother was already 37. She was actually a little older than my father. They had two children; I was the oldest and I had a younger sister.

Can you talk about your experience growing up; what kind of expectations were there for you girls? We were certainly expected to go to college; there was no doubt about that. Just what was expected of us beyond that I am not sure. My father took great delight in my good performance at school. Both of my parents felt that I should get as much education as possible and believed that I should do what I wanted. But I don't know if they really felt that I should have a career. I vaguely remember asking my father whether I could become a newspaper reporter like him. I can't remember exactly how he answered me. I think he said something like it would be pretty difficult for a woman. This, of course, was realistic and accurate at the time. My father died when I was 9 years old, so I don't know how things would have developed between us if he had lived.

How did your father die? We've never been sure. He had a severe attack of the flu from which he seemed to have recovered. But he was never actually well after that. He had trouble sleeping and heart palpitations. This was in 1933. I think he was very frightened because the newspaper had already laid off one reporter. My father was a good reporter, but he kept his job partly because he had a family. I think that really frightened him.

So you think that had something to do with his illness? I think it's quite possible. He had a lot of tests with inconclusive results. Finally, he became so frantically worried that he couldn't sleep. He got really frantic and had to be hospitalized. They thought he had calmed down by the time he died. It was a great shock because nobody expected it, and we never exactly understood why he died.

What did your family do after that? Well, my mother was very strong. She realized that she would have to support the family. Of course, she did have a career to return to. I don't know how we survived the first year after he died. But she managed to enroll in the local normal school to renew her teaching credential. She went for a year. There was no social security at that time, but my father had a small life insurance policy and had paid off the mortgage on our house.

How did your mother juggle two children and work? Did she have a social network which she could depend on? My grandmother (my father's mother) lived with us. She lived with us as long as I can remember. She moved out to Montana after her husband died, and lived with various children. But after my mother and father got married, I think she preferred our family. She and my mother got along very well which is somewhat unusual. My grandmother thought that my mother made a great wife for her oldest son. She admired mother's housekeeping skills and had no reason to compete with her because she apparently hated housework herself. So my mother had built-in support. My grandmother was in her mid-70s when my father died and therefore couldn't do much around the house. But she would always do the dishes, and of course, she was there when we came home from school. If my mother needed to stay late for anything at school, my grandmother was always there.

And your father's family were in the area? Yes, they lived on farms outside of Billings about 40 miles [64 km] away.

Where were your mother's family? My mother had two sisters. One was married and lived in Iowa. The other was single and lived in New Mexico. None of my mother's relatives lived close by, but she was close to my father's family.

Did your mother ever see her relatives? They wrote regularly. They were very faithful about it. My mother's sisters also came to visit at various times. Surprisingly, my aunt from Iowa lost her husband the year after my mother was widowed. We went to Iowa and spent the summer with her.

It seems that it was very important for your mother and your aunt to have had their educations and careers to fall back on when their husbands died? Yes. My mother's first solution was teaching. But she found she didn't like it as much as she had before. She had always taught in small schools in small towns. Billings may sound like a small town, but its population was about 16,000. In the past she had taught in a town of 600 where everyone knew everyone. Billings was an urban setting where the children were not very well behaved, and she was not a good disciplinarian. So she began to feel like a failure at teaching. She taught for four years until her aunt asked her to come out to California to help manage her beach property. My mother agreed.

So you moved to California? Yes.

Did your grandmother go with you? No. She felt she couldn't leave the rest of her children behind. By then, of course, my sister and I were older. I was 14 and my sister was 12, and it wasn't essential to have somebody in the house. Besides, my mother's aunt in San Diego lived nearby. We rented out the house in Billings, and had that income and her insurance. But we did not live as well as we did in Billings because she was not earning a regular teaching salary. We lived rent free in one of her aunt's cottages, but without a regular salary.

Let's talk about you now. Did you go to high school in California? Yes.

Are there any memories of Billings that you would like to share? I was a good student. My girl friend was always a little better [*laughter*]. My main memory is that I always enjoyed school.

Did the move to California affect you in any way? It was very hard to move at that age. The high school in California had a diverse population and they were very class conscious. There were some very wealthy kids who lived in Loma Portal near the school. We lived in Ocean Beach which was lower-middle to working class. There were also Mexican kids from Old Town. They were considered even more inferior. There was a little Portuguese group whose parents owned fishing boats. Some of them were quite wealthy, but were not part of the white elite.

Was the community bigger or smaller than Billings? San Diego was somewhere between 100,000 to 200,000 at that time.

Was the high school considerably larger as well? No, because Billings's high school served an entire area, including some rural areas. In San Diego there were a number of high schools which were relatively the same size. It wasn't so much a matter of size as class differences. This was exacerbated by the fact that the school had a tracking system for English and social studies. Somehow the elite kids were always in the best classes and the other kids were not. I was initially placed in the slowest class. I suppose it was because I was from Montana and lived in Ocean Beach. But the teachers soon realized that I didn't belong there, and I was put in the top class. I was the only student from Ocean Beach. Because of this it was difficult to make friends with the kids in my classes, and I didn't meet many kids from my part of town.

What kind of political background did you come from? My parents were probably Republicans. Because my father reported on all sides of the debates, and died when I was young, I'm not sure about him. But my mother was Republican, and the California relatives were very conservative.

Did anyone in high school influence or mentor you? Yes. What really saved me in high school was my second-year English teacher, Miss Clark. She had no qualms about declaring herself a Roosevelt liberal in conservative San Diego. She was an excellent teacher who was well regarded despite her politics, because her students usually got into good colleges. Another change that year was that a small school run by the Theosophical Society in San Diego closed. The kids were transferred to our high school and placed in Miss Clark's class. I became good friends with some of them.

What was special about Miss Clark? She was very interested in politics and in anything intellectual. She considered herself an intellectual and was proud of it. She wanted students to see what fun it was to learn, and she expected a lot from us. My senior year I took a creative writing course from her. We wrote everything from diaries and letters to essays and short stories, after reading examples from world literature. She was very good at pointing out what you were doing well and where you needed to improve. It really helped my writing. We were also expected to do a lot of reading beyond what was assigned at our grade level. One year we chose countries we were interested in, and read novels and non-fiction about them, and wrote a final essay. This was my introduction to Russian novels. At lunch time if you went to Miss Clark's room, she would talk about one thing or another, or comment on a book she was reading or the Congressional Record, which she read regularly. I suppose I also began to be much more interested in politics because of her, and began to feel that her politics made a lot more sense than those of my relatives. It wasn't just national politics either. She encouraged us to campaign for one of our classmates, a Mexican–American boy. He ran for student body president and won the campaign.

She also influenced my college decision. I had assumed when we moved to San Diego that I would live at home and attend San Diego State University since it was close by and not very expensive. But Miss Clark encouraged me to apply for a scholarship at the University of California at Berkeley. I did and was accepted. It was also very inexpensive to attend Berkeley in those days. So that is where I went.

Did you graduate from high school as an honor student? Yes, I was Valedictorian.

Did you have much of a social life in high school? By the time I was a senior I had quite a few good friends. I and many of my friends belonged to Toastmasters. It was a school club that Miss Clark sponsored. We had a debate team, and gave talks at PTA meetings and other school functions, but our meetings were also social occasions. I didn't date much in high school. I had a lot of male friends in Toastmasters and my math and physics classes, but I didn't date. The summer after we graduated I started seeing more of my future husband. He was in Toastmasters and my graduating class, and also planned to attend Berkeley. He had been interested in a friend of mine. But during the summer he finally gave up on her when she became interested in somebody else [*laughter*]. We began dating.

This is the summer before Berkeley? Yes. I was actually tutoring him. He had to make up a second-year algebra course in order to be accepted by the premed program. He was taking a correspondence course.

What was Berkeley like in 1942? Well, Berkeley had a reputation for being quite radical. Of course, the men were beginning to be called away by the draft, but the student body population was still enormous. We often had classes of 700 or 800 people, not exactly easy to get acquainted with people.

Did you have a major, or did you make up your mind after sampling some courses? I thought I wanted to major in math, so that is where I started. There were many other distribution requirements, however, in the social sciences, natural sciences, and languages. So I took a variety of courses other than math.

What did your peer group look like as a math major? There were not very many women. It was primarily enlisted men in the armed forces.

How about professors – any women? In my second semester, my most successful semester as a math major, I actually had a woman professor for calculus. It must have helped, because I remember enjoying her class very much. I didn't know what I would do with a math major. I didn't want to teach because of my mother's experience. However, I realized that I needed to apply the math to something, so I took economics. I also took the undergraduate statistics course in the economics department during my first year.

By the end of that year, Dick and I were engaged, but he got drafted. It was difficult seeing him leave, but it made me pay a lot more attention to what was going on in the world. Before, it was much easier to block out the war and be a self-absorbed teenager in college.

What was life like at Berkeley? Most of the men at Berkeley were in some kind of military training. To accommodate the trainees, classes were year around on a trimester system. Each term was four months. I continued, but it was difficult. Three terms in a row was not bad, but by the fourth term it was just too much. I was also losing interest in math. Math wasn't helping me understand the causes of the war. I followed the war and was very distressed with the whole situation. The fact that I had a couple of bad math teachers didn't help either. In one class I was the only woman. The professor wasn't necessarily hostile, but he couldn't refrain from calling me Mister Banfill when he called roll (which he was required to do for the military trainees). I would say, "Here," and everybody would laugh. It was his joke all term. I got a B, but I didn't learn much. In another class, the professor was clearly not interested in teaching the relatively elementary material. By that time, I was fed up with math. So, I think in my fourth semester, I decided to change my major. I wanted to change to either political science or international relations, but I had no courses in those subjects. On the other hand, I had already taken all the prerequisites for economics.

What was your experience as an economics major? I enjoyed economics. It was a very different field from what it has become. It was not nearly so neoclassical. My first course in economics was taught by Professor Ira B. Cross. I learned later he had been a student of Veblen. It was an introductory micro and macro course. In those days, we also took introductory courses in the applied areas of economics, such as money and banking, labor, industrial organization, etc. These courses had an institutional emphasis, so I found economics quite interesting and had no complaints about it.

One of the professors I really enjoyed was Professor Robert Brady. He had his own brand of economics that didn't fit any particular school. He inspired people to ask questions and he himself asked a lot of questions. He wasn't exactly a Marxist, but he was very enthusiastic about planning. We were divided into teams to design river valley projects, like the Tennessee Valley Authority. This was very interesting. I also took a history of thought course from him. We got as far as Aristotle [*laughter*]. I also took a labor economics course from Clark Kerr. This was very institutional and an advanced statistics course. It was not yet called "econometrics."

Did you have any intellectual and career aspirations as an undergraduate? I was not at all sure what I was going to do. I actually started the Master's program in economics, but it never occurred to me that I might pursue a PhD and become a professional economist. Then the war ended and Dick came home. Soon after, I became pregnant. For a while I tried to fit in some graduate work, but I wasn't sure of my direction at that point.

I took a graduate seminar with Professor Brady. We wrote papers on various topics which he chose. In one project, I compared the view of human nature in economics and anthropology. This had a big impact on me. I read Ruth Benedict's *Patterns of Culture*. I was a naive, small-town person, and had very little experience with people of other cultures. I didn't realize how very different their world views could be from mine. I was beginning to think about the customs that we take for granted and to compare them with other customs. This was a very liberating experience for me. Then, of course, I began to ask myself what was missing in economics, with its emphasis on a certain kind of rationality and a western European world view. I read a lot of anthropology including Margaret Mead and a multitude of other studies about a variety of cultures, and I started to have doubts about whether economics was something I wanted to pursue.

In the meantime, we had a family, and Dick was finishing his AB and starting graduate school. It became apparent that we couldn't both attend graduate school, so I dropped out.

How big a family did you have? I have four kids. Dick and I came from two-child families, but we wanted more children for ourselves. We ended up with two boys and two girls.

How many years did you stay home to raise your children? Well, like my grandmother, I was not suited to being a housewife and, on a couple of different occasions, I worked outside the home. Of course, this was not the acceptable thing to do at the time. I worked for the agricultural economics department while we were still in Berkeley. I did regression analyses on a desk calculator. This work actually came in very handy when I did graduate work. I did so many regressions that interpreting regression coefficients was familiar territory.

How long did you stay in Berkeley? For six more years and then we moved to Davis, California. Dick had a research position at the College of Agriculture at University of California. After that we began our wandering. First, we were in Puerto Rico for a year, and then Pittsburgh for a postdoctoral year. Finally he obtained a faculty position at the University of Virginia. This is when our youngest was born, and I went through a very bad time.

Charlottesville, Virginia, was not a great place to live. The schools had just been desegregated, but the movie theaters were still segregated. I belonged to a group that boycotted the theaters. It was a bad time. We were there for six years. I was a Girl Scout leader. I attended faculty wives functions, and that sort of thing. But I didn't know what I was going to do with the rest of my life. I guess it was fortunate (although it didn't seem like it at the time), but Dick was denied tenure.

Dick had a research grant and had spent a lot of time collecting data on muscular dystrophy in Virginia. He took the grant to the University of Michigan. We moved to Michigan and I thought – this is my chance. I always read a lot when I was at home, but not necessarily economics. I read anthropology, and I was quite interested in demography. I was interested in why my generation was having so many kids [*laughter*]. I wrote to Ronald Freedman, a demographer in the sociology department at the University of Michigan. I sent him a list of what I had read, and asked him if I could study demography at the graduate level. He wrote a very encouraging letter, and asked me to come and see him. I did, and he told me that his wife had gone back to school and was getting her PhD in economics. In trying to decide what to do, I looked at the sociology curriculum and the textbooks. But I didn't want to start a whole new discipline. Finally, I decided on economics. Michigan also required a field outside of economics. Most people took math, but I took demography. I started graduate work in 1964 at the age of 39. I had been out of school altogether for eighteen years.

What was your experience as a graduate student at the University of Michigan? There were several problems at first. I was told by my graduate advisors in the economics department that I needed to take the graduate record exam first. I argued I had been out of school for a long time, and it wasn't fair that I was forced to take the GRE along with students who recently completed four years of economics. They looked at my record and noticed I had an honors degree from Berkeley. So they agreed to let me try. Then I pointed out I had family responsibilities and, therefore, I wasn't prepared to attend full time. They said they had no provision for part-time students. So the first semester I took the least amount of credits to qualify as a full load. I did all right, but it was difficult, very difficult. Fortunately, I was taking a demography course, econometrics, and macro. I had a pretty good background in those, except for the macro, so I could do well without too much worry. But macro was very hard. In the meantime, economics had changed a great deal; it had gotten more rigorous. At Berkeley, they were just beginning to teach Keynes in macro. I think we used Joan Robinson's new book on Keynesian economics.

At Berkeley – as an undergraduate? Yes, at Berkeley. That was before they had developed the Keynesian IS–LM curves. This type of macro was new to me.

What was the relationship between graduate students and faculty at Michigan? Well, it depended on the individual professor. Some of the faculty were quite accessible and some were not.

Did you feel that you had support among the faculty as a non-traditional student? Once I completed the first semester, I signed up for a partial load, and no one objected. I don't remember them as supportive. It was more like a hands-off attitude [*laughter*]; as long as you were maintaining the required grade point average they left you alone. But you could have a good relationship with certain faculty members who you got to know.

Did you have any mentors? Yes, when I got to the dissertation stage and decided to have Eva Mueller as my advisor. Earlier, John Parker, a young professor in labor economics, was also very helpful. I actually did a Master's thesis under him as insurance, in case I wasn't able to continue in the PhD program. I had planned to do my dissertation under him too. Unfortunately, he died of leukemia before I got to that stage. When I was searching for somebody else, people recommended that I work with Eva Mueller. I was using census data and was interested in doing a study of migration. She had just written a book on migration, so it seemed like a good fit.

So you chose a topic before finding an advisor? I had pretty much decided on what I wanted to do. She was shifting fields. She had taught macro. She was also associated with the Survey Research Center and had done research in consumer economics. But she was moving into the field of development and had an appointment at the Population Studies Center. Because I had a fellowship at the Center during the dissertation stage, it seemed like a good fit for both of us.

So you enjoyed working with her? Yes, very much so. Her reputation was well deserved.

How many women graduate students were in the PhD program at Michigan? Not very many [*laughter*]. In my first class I think there were three of us, out of a class of probably thirty. Because I was attending part-time, I slipped behind and was not always with my entering class. As a result, I met few women. I met my demography professor's wife, Deborah Freedman, as I entered the program, but she was taking her qualifying exams. Although she was ahead of me, it was still helpful to know her. She was also at the Population Studies Center working on her dissertation on development in Taiwan.

What was the relationship between the graduate students at Michigan? Well, I felt quite distant from the other students because I was so much older. Most were about 22, whereas I was almost 40 when I started. I was also very busy and couldn't stay around and talk to students in the graduate student lounge. If I wasn't in class, I was in the library because I had to go home at a certain time to relieve the babysitter or take someone to an appointment. I had to study whenever I had free time. I got acquainted with a few foreign students who were also older. But I rarely had access to the network of students to discuss faculty and the courses, which could be an important part of graduate school.

Were there any less formal intellectual networks? Not until the dissertation stage. I became acquainted with people at the Population Studies Center. The Center was quite a friendly place, but, of course, most of the students and staff were not economists.

How long did it take you to get your PhD in economics? It took nine years, partly because we moved away. We moved to Canada because Dick was offered a research position at Dalhousie University in Halifax. I arranged for a teaching assistantship there so I would have access to a computer to finish my dissertation. However, the summer before we moved, I was offered a faculty appointment from Saint Mary's University, also in Halifax, teaching principles courses. I accepted. I never did much research while I was teaching. But during the summers, I worked on the dissertation under fellowship with the Population Studies Center at Michigan. I went back to Ann Arbor every summer for four years. The fellowship involved a stipend, access to the facilities, and my tuition.

How did you do it with four children and teaching responsibilities? Well, by the time I started teaching my children were much older. Two of them had left home. Of the two who went to Canada with us, one was 10 and the other was 15, so I didn't have little children anymore.

Did you take the whole family with you back to Ann Arbor in the summers? I always took our youngest son. He attended day camp in Ann Arbor while I worked. One year my teenage daughter came too. My husband stayed in Canada because his job was year-round with only one month of vacation. He would come for that month. My two grown children lived in Ann Arbor, so I got to see more of them during the summer months.

How long did you stay in Canada? I was in Canada for five years: four years in Halifax and one year in Quebec. Dick thought the position in Quebec was going to be better than the one in Halifax. This proved not to be the case. I also thought I would do some research with an economist in Quebec. However, it turned out he just wanted me to write a proposal for a joint grant. So I spent that year finishing my dissertation, and returning to Ann Arbor to use the library and to consult with my committee members. This turned out to be a better use of my time.

Can you talk about your dissertation? Yes. My dissertation was on immigration in and out of metropolitan areas. I only used a male sample, which seems strange in view of the fact that I've done research almost exclusively on women since obtaining my degree. Today, I might be more likely to compare men and women.

So what was your hypothesis and what did you find? It was a kind of neoclassical model. Wages would play an important role in migration, but labor market imperfections like unemployment, discrimination, and non-economic preferences would also play an important role. I studied flows into and out of metropolitan areas, and my data were disaggregated by occupation, race, and the origin of workers. I found some interesting differences between groups of migrants. For example, blue-collar migrants from non-metropolitan areas were moving primarily to nearby cities and were strongly influenced by the city's unemployment rates. By contrast, white-collar migrants were more strongly influenced by wage rates, not because they were more likely to move to areas with high wages, but because they didn't move out of high-wage areas.

Was Eva Mueller still there when you defended? Yes, Eva prodded me along. I don't know whether I would have finished without her because I was too much of a perfectionist. I could always think of one more thing to do, and I would postpone writing. She would assure me that what I had done was fine, and I needed to move on to the next chapter. This is exactly what I needed.

Did you ever publish anything from your dissertation? No, I didn't, and that was a mistake. It took me a long time to gain enough self-confidence to become a "professional." This was the result of being away from school for so long. When I returned to graduate school, I felt that the other students were too far ahead of me. I hadn't thought about economic theory for years, and I was out of practice in taking exams. I was also working at something that I was not very good at.

Which was what? Housework. I couldn't keep a neat house, and in the climate of the 1950s, that made me doubt my competence. It took a long time to get my confidence back. Eva Mueller wanted me to present one chapter at the American Statistical Association meetings. If I had followed her advice, I would have had an automatic publication, and it would have been cited. For a long time, I recognized that my dissertation had relevance. But I went on to other research and didn't go back to the dissertation, and, of course, the data were soon out of date.

Let's talk about what happened when you finished your degree. Were you in Quebec? We were in Sherbrooke, about 90 miles [144 km] from Montreal. First

I looked for a job at a small English-language college. Then I looked at junior colleges in Montreal, and didn't find anything. I decided that, at my age, if I got the PhD and didn't immediately get a job, I would never be taken seriously. So after I defended my dissertation at Michigan, I got the *Job Openings for Economists* from the department office and started applying. I received a job offer from the Gary Income Maintenance Experiment in Gary, Indiana, in research. Then I had to decide if I could leave my husband and son in Quebec and live in Chicago – a really difficult decision to make. We were both afraid that it would be a strain on our marriage and that was frightening, but I finally decided to take the job. Dick was dissatisfied with Sherbrooke, but he was obligated to stay there for another year and was willing to move after that.

How old were you by now? I was 49 when I got my degree.

How long did you work in Gary? The experiment ran for two more years after I got there. Then they moved the project to Mathematica Policy Research in Princeton. They arranged an appointment for me at the University of Illinois in Chicago. John McDonald in the economics department was also using the Gary Experiment data. They gave him a research grant that funded part of his salary and my full salary. I didn't want to go to Princeton because Dick had followed me to Chicago, and had a research job at the University of Chicago. In fact, a number of other people from Gary who were still working with the data went to Chicago instead of going to Princeton.

What exactly were the income maintenance experiments? This was a time when the government was still interested in doing something about poverty. The experiments were meant to study the incentive effects of guaranteed income on the labor supply of different groups. Different groups were offered a certain amount of income, taxed at a different rate. If they worked, they lost some but not all of the guaranteed income. There were several different treatment groups, including a control group in which participants were paid a small amount for regular interviews. At Gary, we also had a child care experiment which studied the impact of different subsidy rates.

What were the group dynamics like at Gary? There were less than ten people in the core professional group: five or six economists and a couple of sociologists, as I recall. The Gary Experiment managed and conducted its interviews in-house rather than contracting them out. Consequently, there were a lot of other staff members engaged in training and supervising interviewers or acting as liaison with community and funding organizations. I was the only woman in the research group, but I became good friends with one woman in administration.

Was this work personally satisfying for you? Yes, it was very interesting. It was a good group to work with, and I learned a lot more economics and econometrics in this practical situation than in school. The director oversaw the research and interviews, but the work was collaborative.

How was your experience at the University of Illinois in Chicago? In some ways, it was very good. In other ways, I was a bit more isolated. I was in the economics department, but not "of it" because I wasn't teaching. I liked working with John MacDonald, and I sat in on a graduate econometrics course. But I knew it wasn't going to last.

How long did it last? I was there a little over a year. I went on the job market at the annual economics meetings before my first year ended. My resume got the attention of Herb Parnes at the Center for Human Resource Research at Ohio State. He interviewed me at the meetings. He wanted me to work on the National Longitudinal Surveys of labor market experience. At that point the NLS included four surveys: one on older men, one on middle-aged women, and two on younger cohorts. Herb was the same age as the older men, a cohort set up to study men's transition to retirement. What particularly intrigued Herb about me was that I was the same age as the women, a cohort set up to study women's transition to work after raising children. I had first-hand experience and a background in labor economics, so he thought that I would be a good person to direct that survey. I wasn't thrilled about moving to Columbus and away from my husband again, but both of our positions in Illinois were temporary, and this offer was too good to pass up. So I went to Columbus. Dick stayed in Chicago for a while and then followed me again. I was in Columbus for close to nine years. Dick never found an academic job there. Most of the time he ran a used book business in the sciences and conducted research with a friend in the genetics department.

What was your experience in Columbus? Well, it was the ideal job [*laughter*]. It was the ideal job for *me*. I am more of a researcher than a teacher. I enjoy all aspects of working with data. I am not as much a theoretician as an empiricist. I liked helping to decide which questions to include in the interviews as well as interacting with and troubleshooting for the data users who call in with their problems.

Who were the users? Almost exclusively academics.

What kinds of questions were you asking? We typically asked the standard questions like those asked by the Current Population Survey: whether people are employed, unemployed, keeping house, etc. We also kept a running work history of what the respondents did between interviews, at one- or two-year intervals. We would also ask about family and personal income, assets, marital history, children, child care, and health. We also had special modules on things like volunteer work, housework, attitudes, and eventually, as the respondents got older, plans for retirement.

In the context of this data set, what were your interests or what kind of things did you pursue? I was interested in looking at the entire work life of women in the cohort. I was interested in how long they stayed at home after having children, and what their patterns of work had been. I had done research on women's labor supply in Gary. But in Columbus, I was particularly eager to use the NLS data to add "attitude towards women's roles" to the standard labor supply models. Along with other researchers, I also looked at the effects of work history on wages. The NLS was among the few sources that had detailed work histories, including good measures of years of work experience, work interruptions, and job tenure.

Using these data, did any of the findings surprise you or resonate with your experience? It was interesting that the survey was supposed to look at women returning to work, assuming that they returned once. The first survey participants were women 30–44 years of age. We found that this was too late. Many of these women had returned to work earlier in their lives. The data also suggested that women did not take years off to have kids, and then returned to work once and for all. Instead, many women were alternating between spells of time in the labor force and spells at home.

My interest in women returning to work led to what was probably the most enjoyable project I have worked on: namely, the research I did in collaboration with Shirley Dex who was a lecturer at the University of Keele in England. Shirley contacted us. She wanted to compare the work experiences of British and American women, and to compare women's return to work after child-bearing in the two countries. She was using the British Women and Employment Survey, which fit with what I was doing with the NLS, so I agreed to work with her. We met several times in Ohio and England to plan the research, to compare our findings from the respective surveys, and to decide how to report the results. The end product was our co-authored book *British and American Women and Work: Do Equal Opportunities Policies Matter?*

Why did the job in Columbus come to an end? Federal funds were cut for research projects. Some of the interviews have continued, and some of the older women continue to be interviewed after twenty years. But there are no research funds to accompany the interviews. The staff at Ohio State remain, but only the director, the people who process publications and tapes, researchers with faculty appointments, and others who have their own research funds. Most of the former research staff were dispersed.

What year did you leave Columbus and where did you go? We left in 1985 and came to Washington, DC. Because the funding for NLS came from the Department of Labor, I had made some contacts in Washington and Dick received a short-term grant at Georgetown University. We thought we would come to Washington, and see what we could find. I had been at Ohio State long enough to get a pension, and I was entitled to unemployment compensation, so we had something to fall back on in addition to our savings. We came here and started applying for jobs. The project officer at the Department of Labor had moved to the General Accounting Office, and she told me that they were looking for economists. I applied and got a job, and was a federal employee for the next five years.

What did you do at the GAO? I worked in the human resource division. The GAO, besides auditing government-funded projects, also reports on topics requested by Congress (Congressional committees or members of Congress). Sometimes at the GAO, we could do self-initiated reports, if they had policy relevance. My group worked on pensions, social security, and welfare. For that we used the NLS data from Ohio State. We looked at the potential earnings that a welfare recipient could be expected to get if she went to work.

How satisfied were you with this job compared to what you did at Ohio State? It was less satisfying because it was more constrained. You had to get layer upon layer upon layers of approval before publishing a GAO report. There were other bureaucratic annoyances, and the hours were less flexible.

Is that why you left after five years? Yes, basically. I was turning 67 that summer, and I thought I was ready to retire.

You thought? Yes, I *thought* I was ready to retire. But, at home, I felt isolated again, like I had before I began my professional life. I had met Heidi Hartmann some time back when she was starting the Institute for Women's Policy Research. I had mentioned something to her about volunteering after I retired. But I had forgotten about this until I saw her again at the first IAFFE conference in Washington, DC. She reminded me and asked if I was still interested. I was. I've been at IWPR for seven years now.

Is this on a volunteer basis? No. It started that way. Heidi promised that whenever she got enough projects funded, she would pay me. I probably volunteered for a year, helping to get reports out or advising on some of the research projects. I thoroughly enjoyed that. Then we received a small grant from the Department of Labor for a project on the glass ceiling. Heidi asked me to do that project.

You became the project director? Technically yes, but it was a small project. We were supposed to look at the effects of industrial restructuring on the glass ceiling. This wasn't a topic I knew much about, so we recruited Dell Champlain who had a better institutional background and more familiarity with restructuring issues. Dell and I worked on the project together.

After this project, we did a grant proposal for the Social Security Administration. We wanted to study poverty among elderly women using their New Beneficiary Surveys. I had used these surveys at the GAO. We received the grant, and I was project director for two years. After that I volunteered until we received funding from various sources to work on social security issues. I also do a fair amount of advising and troubleshooting on other projects. It's mostly paid work.

What is your experience like at the Institute for Women's Policy Research? It's been very satisfying, although it is not quite as free as the atmosphere at Ohio State. In Ohio, I could do almost anything that was of interest to me, whether or not it had policy significance. I can't do that at IWPR. I have to work on projects that have been funded or will be. The scope is not quite as wide to do what I want. But, on the other hand, we do research that could have some policy effects, and this is very satisfying. Another thing I like about IWPR is the association with young women who come in as fellows, interns, or new professionals. Sometimes I'm a mentor, and I can stay in touch with the concerns of young or would-be professionals.

Lois, you have had many different experiences in academia and research in both the public and private sector. Can you compare these experiences for us? I don't think I was especially suited to teaching, at least teaching economics. In different circumstances, I might have felt different. At St Mary's where I taught, the great majority of the students were in business administration, and the only required economics course was principles of economics. The students didn't think it was useful, and did not understand why they had to take it. They were focused on working for a business and had trouble seeing, for example, how a formalized version of supply and demand would help them. I had many students who were taking the course against their will. If this reality is added to the fact that I was not always pleased about what I had to teach (because I didn't believe some of it myself), then it's not a very good combination [*laughter*]. So I didn't find teaching all that satisfying and, compared to the research positions I've held, not nearly as much fun. Partly, I think this is because I am not a person who thinks very rapidly on her feet. I prefer to go off and ponder ideas for a while before I decide what I think about an issue. So writing is more satisfying for me. Having to perform in front of a class, especially when I had doubts about some of the material (but couldn't go into these doubts with inexperienced students), made for an uncomfortable situation.

Can you also compare your experiences in different kinds of research institutions? It's harder to do anything approaching academic research in the federal government, although there are some exceptions to this, such as at the Census Bureau and Social Security Administration. Also, not all research interests academics because it is not sufficiently theoretical. But nevertheless it can be important for policy purposes. There were many different disciplines represented at the GAO. In particular, there was a preponderance of accountants who didn't understand research. As a result, it was difficult getting reports approved. But some interesting research does come out of the GAO.

Would you compare your experience working in an organization run by women versus working in an organization where things are essentially run by men? Working in an all-female environment which shares my values is very satisfying. But it is also challenging to work in a small non-profit organization working on issues of social change and social justice. You continually have to look for grants which are not often easy to come by. What tends to happen is that everyone is under pressure so frictions can develop. Still, working at IWPR has been one of the most satisfying experiences of my career.

If you had to do it all over again, would you have been an economist? I'm not sure [*laughter*]. At the end of my first year in graduate school, I felt I had come to a crisis point. I was asked to believe many things that I didn't believe. It is probably easier for a discipline to impose its way of thinking on students if it can get them into the program early. They can proceed through graduate school without other experiences. But that didn't happen to me. There were concepts that I found personally disgusting. One was the idea of choice between labor and leisure. This was before Becker's third choice of home production. I was simply offended. The idea that economists called what I had been doing for years (raising four children) – "leisure" – was just too much! [*Laughter*]

Aside from that, it seemed to me that there were ethical judgments underlying many of the implications and conclusions of economics. I couldn't quite figure out how this happened, but I felt that economics led to conclusions that I couldn't accept from an ethical standpoint. I certainly didn't have time to study ethics and philosophy at that point. Nor did I have time to closely analyze what I was learning to see where the value judgments were creeping in. I didn't have anyone to talk to about my concerns in any depth. John Parker and a young radical student in one of my classes were somewhat sympathetic, but they encouraged me to learn orthodox theory first. They argued that you have to know it well before you could critique it. They were correct of course, but I needed some counter-arguments which graduate school did not provide. Otherwise, I had an uneasy impression that I was being brainwashed. I spent one summer reading as many critics as I could find. This is how I became convinced that I could continue in economics. Others disagreed with the parts of economics I objected to. I could continue and see where it led.

I'm glad I became an economist. It has helped me to understand the world I live in, even if not always in the way intended by the profession. But if I was a young woman now, I probably would not. It would be important to understand the economic perspective, but it would be difficult to find a congenial place to study. I might want to enter a program offering a PhD in public policy that combines economics with other disciplinary approaches. I would also want to start out with a good background in philosophy, especially ethics and political philosophy. But because I am such a data-oriented person, I would probably go into a closely related field, if not economics.

Can you talk more about some of the changes in the profession? It seems to me that the role of various institutions was emphasized more in the past. This was certainly true when I was at the University of California as an undergraduate. Even at Michigan. For the qualifying exam in labor economics, we had to have a fair knowledge of the history of the labor movement. We had a required course in comparative labor movements together with a neoclassical course in labor economics. I believe the institutional approach is increasingly difficult to find. It might occur in places like the University of Wisconsin if you get your degree in conjunction with industrial relations. But it seems to me, at least in the field of labor, the field I know best, that the approach is increasingly reduced to microeconomics. This is too bad. When there are a variety of voices, it makes for a much more lively field and more questioning of what passes as economic knowledge and advice. It seems to me that economics has gotten ever more narrow, with increasing emphasis on formal mathematical models. In applied fields, to get something published in one of the best journals, you have to do something on the "cutting edge." This means econometrics. It is not that we shouldn't be doing this at all; some of this work is quite interesting. I just don't think it should be the only thing that counts as research. The tendency in the profession has also been to become more and more theoretical. Empirical work is not required. Instead, we can just infer what people would do, given the simplistic motivations we have assigned to them.

Do you think it is easier for women today to succeed in economics relative to when you were a student? Well, I suppose there is a greater expectation that women will be around. If you are comfortable with economic thought as it has developed, it may be easier. But it may be more difficult than ever to question mainstream economics, especially if you are a woman.

Why do you think more women are not attracted to economics? Although I don't like to over-generalize on the basis of gender, there are probably more women than men who find it difficult to consider that "rational" calculation of costs and benefits describes human behavior and what the world is all about. Maybe they don't agree with some of the conclusions that economists come to either; for example, when we put efficiency before any other goal. I met an undergraduate at the last IAFFE conference, a mature woman returning to school. She wrote me that she was changing her major. The lack of humanistic considerations in her courses was just too difficult to handle. Also, there might be quite a few women who are turned off by Becker's analysis of the family.

Lois, how would you describe your evolution as an economist? As an undergraduate, I majored in economics to gain a better understanding of unemployment and poverty. These seemed to be important contributors to World War II. As I told you, I've had problems with economics since the beginning of graduate work. Mainly I was bothered by some aspects of microeconomics, especially labor supply theory and its description of housework and child rearing as leisure. Some of the conclusions of welfare economics were also troubling. Nevertheless, I decided to specialize in labor economics because poverty depends to a considerable extent on how people fare in the labor market.

The year I started graduate school the new feminist movement was just beginning; Betty Friedan had just written the *Feminist Mystique*. When I read it I thought, she is describing me. I was surprised to learn that there were other dissatisfied housewives out there. This strengthened my view that labor supply was also influenced by social norms. What had kept me and many other women from working, it seemed to me, was mainly social disapproval and the lack of support for working mothers. Aside from my objections to labor supply theory though, I didn't apply feminism to economics. While I was teaching in Canada, I remember to my sorrow that I taught something about the special importance of a high male unemployment rate.

About the time we moved to Columbus I began to read the feminist literature: the histories of the suffrage movement and the biographies of women who had pioneered in the professions often over much opposition. Although I had quite good relationships with my male colleagues, I also became aware that some of them were treating me differently. For example, I started noticing that a colleague who I considered a good friend wouldn't think to introduce me to visiting economists. But he introduced our male colleagues who were sociologists. This is when I became more interested in finding women colleagues. Although at Ohio State I was the only woman economist on staff, I collaborated with one of the sociologists, and we still keep in touch. I was the research center's representative to the National Council for Research on Women and met many women academics in other disciplines. I also started attending CSWEP coffees at the AEA meetings. It was nice to meet other women in the profession. I met my good friend Marianne Ferber at one of the coffees. Then in the last seven years I got involved with IAFFE, the International Association for Feminist Economics, which I consider my intellectual home.

How would you describe yourself as an economist? I certainly consider myself a feminist economist. I have always leaned towards institutional economics, but I don't quite relate to the Association for Evolutionary Economics. I have friends in that group and sometimes go to their sessions, but their orientation seems a bit specialized. I am also very interested in the relationship between economics and philosophy, especially questions of ethics. I also feel comfortable with social economics.

What is it about feminist economics that appeals to you? I am interested in social issues that concern women particularly. Feminist economics offers insights that are often lacking in conventional economics. Although women are the majority of recipients of old-age benefits, it has been primarily women economists who have asked how the proposed social security reforms will affect women. I also think that feminists, along with other social economists, are less wedded to the view that economics is a value-free science, and more willing to consider equity to be as important as efficiency. IAFFE also offers a place where feminists can exchange ideas and work out our critiques of mainstream economics in a supportive environment.

What kind of impact do you think feminist economists can have in economics? I want feminist economists to be a strong voice representing women in policy debates. I also think we have to build alliances in order to change the profession. We should be working with others who question "the market" as the supreme evaluator of everything. We should be emphasizing in our writing and teaching that markets work well in certain circumstances, and analyzing when and why they do not. This isn't only a feminist agenda, but I think it's a particularly important goal for feminists. After all, there are always lots of conventional economists ready to explain why there is no discrimination against women or minorities in the labor market, why the market works so well, or why everyone is paid what they are worth.

Another important goal for feminist economics is to highlight how our backgrounds influence the way we see the world, and that we can't become objective by ignoring our own backgrounds. This is not a new message; Gunnar Myrdal advocated this critical stance long ago. But I think it is a point women can make very well. We see so many instances where men make assumptions or draw conclusions that are influenced by their experiences, which may not be valid for most women.

Do you have any advice for young women who are starting in the profession? There are a few places that are somewhat more congenial for mavericks. But if you're determined to attend one of the top schools your math background should be first rate. You also need a support group if you want to keep your values intact and if you want to question what you are taught. You also need to know the critiques of neoclassical economics even if those are not presented in the textbooks. It is also worthwhile to have a background and some allies in related fields.

Do you have any advice for women who have their degrees about how best to survive in the profession and keep their values and integrity? How do they find the balance between the demands of the profession and what they think is important to do? It is important to have a clear view of your capabilities, what you enjoy doing, and what you would like to accomplish. If you like to teach, you should aim for a smaller school that emphasizes teaching. If you are interested in policy-oriented research, you should probably look for a job in a non-profit organization or possibly work for the government. If you want a more prestigious position, you have to ask yourself whether you are willing to devote most of your time to achieving tenure, even at the expense of other things you value, and whether you are willing to suppress any radical opinions until you are well established.

Lois, could you possibly summarize your intellectual work in terms of the history and the themes in your work? There are probably two main themes in my work. As I said, in my early research career I was particularly interested in women's labor supply. I felt that the standard labor supply models were just too simplistic. It's not that I think women are not influenced by wages or income. Instead, I felt that there are other important influences that were ignored. Having personally felt the social disapproval aimed at working mothers during the 1950s, and having read many biographies about women's hostility to women entering the professions and skilled trades, I felt these were also important influences. In fact, using the NLS data, I was able to show that women's attitudes towards their "proper roles" and how well they personally liked housework, influenced whether women returned to work when their children reached school age. Labor supply models are useful for narrowly focused research like the work incentive project in the Gary Experiment. But for a broader historical understanding of women's work (and men's as well), we need to consider social norms and the intrinsic interest associated with different kinds of work.

Since leaving Ohio, I have turned to another major theme in my research: namely, the causes and prevention of poverty. I have been particularly interested in policies affecting single mothers in the context of welfare reform and low-wage labor markets. At the GAO I analyzed what welfare mothers could expect to receive in wages if they went to work, and whether they were likely to move out of poverty because they worked. I concluded that most would need free or heavily subsidized child care to be better off. As a result of welfare reform, many more welfare mothers have paid work, but we have little knowledge about the effects of losing their benefits. In the event of a serious recession, I think we will see big problems.

For the last few years, I have mainly focused on older women and poverty, and I've written about the dangers to women of a privatized social security system. Women, because of their longer lives, should have a life annuity indexed to the cost of living, which private companies provide only rarely and at great cost. In addition, there is great uncertainty in privatization. It's one thing to invest your discretionary funds in the stock market, but quite another to depend on investments in the stock market as your main source of income.

Most of my research has been empirical, and I have enjoyed it. But as I get older and near the end of my career I would like to write more general articles on some issues that concern me. I have just written a piece on the measurement and analysis of poverty for the *Elgar Companion to Feminist Economics*. It is, of course, related to empirical work, but on a different level. I would like to do more of that type of work. I would also enjoy writing more book reviews. I often read books that I would like to study more closely. Reviewing books requires this.

Is there anything else you would like to talk about? I'll end by saying that I feel very fortunate to have been able to start so late in a career that has been so satisfying. Not everyone knows at age 22 what they are best suited to do. I hope that the kind of unconventional route I followed will continue to be open to others in the future.

10

MARGARET CONSTANCE SIMMS

If I were to think about the impact of the things that I have done,
I would say that it has been less about my research, and more
about my contributions to building institutions.

(Margaret Simms, 1998)

Margaret's story begins during the era of racial segregation. By the time she entered college, the legacy of institutionalized racism was still evident. Out of 1,400 students at Carleton College, she was one of four African–Americans during her freshman year. Today, she is Vice-President for Research at the Joint Center for Political and Economic Studies and a member of the board of *Economists for Black Enterprise* magazine. She is the former Chair of the Economics Department at Atlanta University; former Editor of the *Review of Black Political Economy*; former Brookings Economic Policy Fellow at the US Department of Housing and Urban Development; former consultant to numerous organizations, including the National Urban League, the National Institute of Education, the National Urban Coalition, the US Department of State, and the Rockefeller Foundation; former Senior Research Associate at the Urban Institute's Program on Research on Women and Family Policy; former Director of the Urban Institute's Minorities and Social Policy Program; former Director of Research Programs at the Joint Center for Political and Economic Studies. She has also served as an advisor to numerous committees, including a Congressional Advisory Panel on Financing Elementary and Secondary Education. She received her BA from Carleton College (1967), and an MA (1969) and PhD (1974) from Stanford University.

We met Margaret at her office in Washington, DC. We were late for our appointment because we misread the map, and were quite embarrassed when we finally arrived. She was gracious enough, however, to spend two hours with total strangers who were interested in her story. It was a cold evening in February of 1998 and all of us were quite hungry. We decided on a delightful Thai restaurant. The following is our conversation during dinner.

Plate 10 Clockwise from top left: Margaret Simms at age 2 with father Frederick T. Simms; with aunt Constance Simms Green during Christmas holidays (early 1990s); as Senior Research Associate at the Urban Institute (1981); on camelback in Timbuktu, Mali (1998); main portrait, as Vice-President for Research, the Joint Center for Political and Economic Studies (1997).

Let's begin with your family genealogy. What can you tell us about that? I'm the youngest of three children, the only girl. I was born and grew up in St Louis. My parents were both college-educated. My mother had a Master's degree in social work and my father had a Bachelor's degree in chemistry. When he was young, his parents taught at Virginia State University which was a normal school at the time. His father studied at the University of Chicago at the turn of the century. My family was very academically oriented. One of my uncles taught in the medical school at Washington University and was part of the Nobel prize-winning team that discovered how DNA replicates. My father's sister was an accountant who worked at different historically black colleges and universities over the years. When I was young, she worked at Tennessee State University, but she finished her career as the controller at Fisk University. It was expected that my brothers and I would do well in school and that we would go to college. I went to a segregated school up until the fifth grade. In the sixth grade, I transferred to a city-wide program and attended my first integrated school.

Did your brothers attend the same school? No, my brothers were substantially older. One brother had graduated high school the year immediately after *Brown versus Board of Education*, so the whole question of integrated schools was a non-issue. Missouri was a border state; they had, in essence, *de jure* segregation until 1954, and *de facto* segregation for the rest of the decade. I went to Carleton College in Northfield, Minnesota, which was a broadening experience. When I left for college, I was going to major in chemistry or physics.

Why those subjects? I think because, in part, my father's side of the family was very scientifically oriented, and in part, because I did very well in those subjects in high school. But when I got to college, I found out these subjects weren't that attractive to me; they did not relate to real-world events. I did spend the first year taking calculus, physics, chemistry, and German. However, I decided that I didn't want to major in any of those. I spent my sophomore year taking subjects that I had to take for distributional requirements anyway. One of the courses I took was economics. I discovered that I liked it. So I declared a major in economics.

Were your parents disappointed? Ummm ... no. Actually, my mother wasn't disappointed because she thought everybody was too scientific [*laughter*]. My father didn't express his opinion one way or the other. He did tell me when I went off to college that he thought economics was very dull. He really didn't think that I should take it, but he didn't have any other opinions to offer.

Do you remember if there was a professor who contributed to this decision? I had one undergraduate professor who was fairly entertaining and he talked about policy issues, both of which certainly made economics more attractive than math.

What about high school? Did you have any teachers who influenced you intellectually? Well, my math teacher did. My high school was integrated, but the faculty and staff were predominantly white. Some were openly antagonistic to

211

black students. The math teacher was one of the few black teachers. She taught an advanced math course. She was not a role model in the sense that I wanted to do what she did, but she was certainly supportive of my performance in high school. She was also someone to be proud of, because some of the faculty were willing to tell us that we couldn't perform. This was unlike the high school that my brothers attended, where the staff were black and they had very high expectations for all their students. The interesting thing at my high school was that the counselors didn't have very high expectations for any student. I guess they expected most students to go to work after high school. Consequently, when they counseled us about college, they discouraged students from looking beyond Missouri. In fact, the African–American students were probably more adventuresome in their applications for college than most of the white students. Most of the white students that I knew went to the University of Missouri at St Louis, Washington University, or St Louis University. It's not that they were bad schools, it's just that there was no attempt to match student interests and needs with the full range of their higher education options.

Today, there is an awareness of "campus climate." What was it like when you attended college? It was the 1960s. Carleton was a very liberal college, so most students supported the civil rights movement. Some even worked in the South during their summers. It was less about attitude and more about social interaction. There were few black students. There were only four when I was a freshman.

How big was Carleton? Fourteen hundred students.

And four black students? Yes, there was one person in the junior class and two guys in my class. Carleton had received some money from the Rockefeller Foundation to engage in special recruitment efforts. By my sophomore year they admitted about eight minority students (or eight matriculated), but not all of them graduated from Carleton.

Do you recall the percentage of female students at that time? The college was about 40 percent women. In economics, there were twenty-five majors, five of whom were women, and there was one other black student besides myself who majored in economics.

Were all the professors white? Yes.

And all men? No, not all men. In fact, the chair of the economics department was a woman. She had worked with the price stabilization board around World War II. She was quite a formidable figure.

In the positive sense? [*Laughter*] Mixed [*laughter*]. But being an economics major was not an issue or a problem. It wasn't a situation where people looked at you oddly because you were a woman.

How did you decide to get a PhD in economics? That was really an accident. I did not intend to go to graduate school. When I was a junior, I was most interested in economic development. I applied for and was admitted to a program called the Foreign Affairs Scholars Program. The program was designed to increase minority representation in the US Foreign Service. I came to

Washington, DC, during the summer of 1966. Part of the program involved working at the State Department or one of its sister agencies, the Agency for International Development or the United States Information Agency. The other part of the program involved seminars in preparation for the foreign service exam and meetings with high government officials including members of minority groups. The program operated for about five years. There were forty students in each "class," primarily African–Americans, but also a few Hispanics. [*Pause*] I don't think there were any Asians. If we completed the summer program successfully, we were offered an opportunity to do a year of graduate studies with fellowships at any school that admitted us. So I applied to graduate school less to get a PhD and more to take advantage of this fellowship opportunity.

Why did you choose Stanford University? I went to Stanford because, at that time, they had one of the strongest faculties in the development field, and because it was in California. I had never been to California and I had certainly had my fill of snow during the four years in Minnesota. The first year I was at Stanford, Martin Luther King was assassinated. Several riots followed. It was during this time that I became more interested in domestic economic issues. Stanford was not Berkeley, but it was still about addressing the issues of the day. The faculty made modest adaptations to the graduate curriculum by creating an urban economics sequence. I became more interested in that so I told the State Department I was not going into the foreign service. Ironically, two people who were working in or managing the Foreign Affairs Scholars Program then are currently connected with our Center (the Joint Center for Economic and Political Studies). One became the president of the Center, and the other was our senior vice-president. She retired recently. As they say – Washington, DC is a small town!

I stayed at Stanford and finished my PhD. There are two things to note, however. When I arrived, there were no African–American students, and very few women. No woman had completed the PhD program in economics and only one African–American had finished. There was one woman in my class, and we became roommates after the first year. She is now working for the International Monetary Fund here in Washington, DC, and we continue to be friends.

Were there any female professors? No. Myra Strober came to Stanford's business school in, I think, 1970 and I started in 1967. As I recall, when she arrived all the women students in the department went out to lunch with her. All of us fit at one table!

Were there any African–American professors at Stanford? The first African–American faculty member, Don Harris, came in 1971 after I had finished my course work.

Did you have a mentor or role model at Stanford? Not really. I was pretty much on my own. The women had a little informal network, but it wasn't a formal support group. I think that it probably helped that my roommate was also in economics, but the faculty did not particularly go out of their way to be supportive. It was not until 1970 that the first woman got her PhD from the economics department. I didn't know her that well, because a number of women (including myself) went away and taught and then finished their degrees some years later. Nancy Gordon and Sarah Gordon were the next two women to get their PhDs (they had the same last name but were not related). I think Pat (my roommate) and I were the fourth and fifth women to finish. We finished the same quarter, but we had both left California a couple of years earlier. After I decided not to enter the foreign service, I wasn't sure what I was going to do. At the end of the fourth year, before I finished my dissertation, I wound up teaching at the University of California at Santa Cruz.

It doesn't sound like you had very much support at Stanford, but did you face any blatant constraints? No. It was certainly very different from what I had heard about other graduate programs in economics. There was no active discouragement. It was more like benign neglect. The attitude was, you're here and we're not going to stop you from finishing; we might not help you, but we will not make it difficult for you to finish. I remember at one point I was trying to figure out whether my problems were related to race or gender. I did an informal survey among my graduate school cohort, which was a very diverse group. I found out that race didn't seem to matter; gender didn't seem to matter; religion didn't seem to matter. I realized that it wasn't something special about me. It was just a general kind of treatment that everybody was getting. But not everybody goes through that sort of realization or verification process.

Was the Santa Cruz position a visiting position? No. I could have stayed there but Santa Cruz was, and to some extent still continues to be, an unusual institution. At that time it was a fairly new campus, and most of the faculty were between 35 and 45 years of age. I was younger. I liked my colleagues, but there wasn't much else to life. Santa Cruz was small and mainly a retirement community, except for the university. There were also very few single women on the faculty. After about two or three months, I decided to have a conversation with the chair of the economics board. Because it was on the British system, there were no departments. We were spread out among the various colleges, so periodically we met as a board. The head of the board was Dan Suits who was from Michigan. I explained my problem to him. He said he understood why I might not want to stay because he was 55 and there were also very few faculty at his end of the age spectrum. So I opted to move east, and interviewed in several places. I wound up at Atlanta University where, initially, I taught in the business school.

What was it like at Atlanta University? That was the first time I found what I would call a mentor network. It wasn't like having one mentor. It was a group called the Caucus of Black Economists. The group was formed in New York in 1969–70. The founding members were a small group of African–American economists, mostly men, who were attending the national economics meetings in New York. They decided they needed an organization that would provide support, promote expansion and participation in the network and in the discipline, and push for more representation in the meetings. It was similar to what became, for women, the Committee on the Status of Women in the Economics Profession (CSWEP). But the Caucus chose to be outside the American Economic Association rather than inside it. I found out about the organization through a part-time faculty member in the business school at Stanford. At that time, the Caucus had graduate student members on their board. I was invited to be the west coast student member. This was a little strange because I immediately left the west coast [*laughter*] and moved to Georgia. Some of the people who were active in the organization were on the faculty at the Atlanta University Center (Atlanta University, Clark College, and Morehouse College). That was a very different environment. So when I say that the Caucus was more like a mentor, it's because people began looking out for each other, doing the recommendations, doing the introductions and so forth. It was also while I was at Atlanta University that I met Phyllis Wallace. She introduced me to the women's network. The interesting thing is that our early careers were similar. I held the same position Phyllis did after she graduated from Yale. She taught in the business school at Atlanta University and worked with Sam Westerfield; I also took her place on the CSWEP committee.

Were you active in the Caucus? Because it was a young organization (it later became the National Economic Association), it was easier to be an active participant or a board member. Indeed, I went from being the west coast graduate student member to being a "regular" board member along with one of my colleagues, Barbara Jones, who was at Clark College. At one point we were, in effect, running the organization. She was secretary–treasurer for about six or seven years, and I was the head of the organization for about sixteen or eighteen months.

Can we talk a bit about your dissertation? How did you choose your dissertation topic? After my third year in Atlanta, I came to Washington, DC, and worked at the Urban Institute for a summer. When I returned to California, I worked as a consultant for their project on equity and school finance issues. So I did my dissertation on resource allocation in a school district in California. Since I was working on a project for the Urban Institute that involved the San Jose Unified School District, that became the case study for my dissertation.

Did you work with anyone in particular on your dissertation? It was a time of transition in the department, which made it a little awkward. I wanted to work in public finance, but the professor who had taught the sequence did not get tenure and left about the time I was starting my thesis. In addition, my topic was somewhat non-traditional and somewhat interdisciplinary. I did get a lot of help from Henry Levin, however, an economist who taught in the school of education. He was the second member of my committee. He could not serve as the committee chair because he was not a member of the economics department.

Were all the members of your committee men? Yes, they were. There were still no women in the economics department. Mike Boskin, who had just joined the department, was my dissertation advisor. Lori Tarshis was the other member. He later went to Toronto. I finished the dissertation my second year in Atlanta – in 1974. Then in 1976, I left the business school and became the chair of the economics department. After a year as chair, I got a Brookings Institution Fellowship and left for Washington, DC.

Why did you leave Atlanta University? There were both negative and positive sides to leaving Atlanta. I had a really good support network, and I was able to get connected to local politics and local politicians. For instance, I was on an economic advisory committee set up by Maynard Jackson when he was Mayor of Atlanta. But there were few systematic opportunities to do research because of the course load, lack of resources, and a fair amount of thinness in the faculty. There were few senior faculty to work with. That was the downside of the environment. At one point, Barbara Jones and I worked on a project together, but there were not the kind of research opportunities you would have in a large department.

How long were you the chair of the economics department before you left for Brookings? Well, I was chair for about two years. I was chair for a year, then I was on leave for a year, and then I went back to Atlanta for another year as chair. I wasn't at the Brookings Institution *per se*. Brookings administered a program called the Economic Policy Fellows, which provided opportunities for economists who were within five years of getting their PhDs to have a public policy experience. Fellows worked in government under the Intergovernmental Personnel Act, which meant that you were not counted against the personnel ceiling. You were essentially free to the agency. Even though the agency paid your salary, that wasn't the important thing. The important thing was that you didn't occupy a permanent slot. I wound up working at the Department of Housing and Urban Development (HUD) in the Office of Policy Development and Research. It was headed by Donna Shalala. This was during the first year of the Carter administration. I was in the Economic Affairs Office, where Katherine Lyall was the Deputy. Another woman in the same division, Betsy Roistacher, worked on some projects with me.

Did you enjoy being chair at Atlanta University? It was a very small department. In fact, the economics department was originally absorbed by the business school because our numbers were so small. In 1976, I took advantage of an opportunity to get outside funding to build up the faculty. I participated in the development of a proposal to fund joint positions among the schools in the Atlanta University Center. I hired two people, one who held a joint position between Atlanta University and Clark College, and another between Atlanta University and Spelman College. One of them became temporary chair of the department while I was on leave, and then became, I think, the permanent chair after I resigned.

Were you the only African–American woman in the department? No. Atlanta University is one of the historically black colleges and universities. It is now

216

Clark–Atlanta University. Clark College merged with Atlanta University. Although all of the undergraduate schools in that area of Atlanta were historically black schools, the faculty was mixed. We had one white faculty member in the economics department. In the business school it was probably about half and half.

Did you ever go through the tenure process? They didn't have an automatic tenure process, which had its pluses and minuses. On the one hand, you didn't have the pressure to meet certain standards by the sixth year. But, on the other hand, you were never quite sure if you had tenure until you made it an issue.

So you were not tenured when you became chair? No, I had only been on the faculty four years when I became chair. I had my PhD for only two years. I was eventually given tenure just before I resigned my faculty position to move to Washington permanently. After I worked at HUD, I returned to Atlanta University for a year. Then I got an offer from the Urban Institute and decided to go there. I came to the Urban Institute in 1979. I've been in Washington, DC, ever since.

You became a researcher? Yes.

Have you taught at all since coming to Washington, DC? No, I haven't. I have research assistants and so there is a type of teaching experience, but I have not taught courses.

Do you miss the classroom? No. I enjoyed it when I was doing it, but I really don't have time to miss it.

How would you compare the two experiences, teaching and research? I guess there are probably several differences. Certainly in the kind of non-academic jobs that I've held, the interest is more on policy issues and their relationships to real people (as they say) as opposed to research that focuses primarily on theory and research methodology. In most of these jobs, you don't have the luxury that an academic position affords, such as the ability to work on whatever you want or the relative assurance that your job continues as long as you're doing a good job of teaching. I know that's an oversimplification. But for most research jobs, identifying and securing funding for the work you are interested in pursuing is always paramount. If there is something you want to do, but no one wants to fund it, it's very difficult to get support.

How does it work; how do you get funding support? It varies. There are some things that will never get support. You can only do that kind of work if your organization agrees to support it with general support dollars. If it's an idea similar to what someone wants funded, then you can revamp it to suit their needs. Hopefully, you'll have time to piggyback your own work. There is much more urgency in research jobs to prepare proposals that "funders" are interested in funding. The standards used by funders have changed over time.

Relative to when you began, is it easier or more difficult to get funding? It's more difficult.

Too much competition for funds? It's partly competition, but it's partly that funders are more likely to have specific funding agendas in order to have a noticeable impact and to justify what they do. They are less likely to give you money just because you do good work. It has to relate to their population groups or their interests, and it has to have an impact. In proposals, you have to spend more time explaining how the study's findings will be disseminated and the impact they will have on people and policy. These are not unreasonable requirements, but they are relatively new.

What type of research are you doing now? Currently, I am doing very little research and mostly administration. If I were to think about the impact of the things that I have done, I would say that it has been less about my research, and more about my contributions to building institutions. I have spent a great deal of time helping the National Economic Association reorient itself and move to another level. I also spent five years as editor of the journal *Review of Black Political Economy*. During that time, I tried to increase its financial stability and establish a schedule and a set of recurring activities, such as special theme issues which continue today. Danny Boston, who I originally hired at Atlanta University, is the editor now. He is putting together a twenty-fifth anniversary issue. I came into my current job (Vice-President for Research at the Joint Center for Political and Economic Studies) a year ago and we just completed a strategic planning process. Most of what I'm currently doing is changing how things get done, and building and expanding an integrated set of programs.

Do you miss doing the research? I do miss research. I'm doing a little bit. But, at this point, I am more likely to be presenting work that my staff have completed. I am proud of what they do, but I still want to be "hands on," I guess. A big advantage in my current position is that I've done many different jobs and have worked in a fair number of different fields, so I feel comfortable commenting on, reviewing, or relating to different areas of work. I've done work in housing, employment and training, minority business development, and welfare, among other things. Consequently, I feel comfortable reviewing documents or proposals that are prepared by my staff and think I make a contribution to producing even better products.

How is your position as vice-president at the Center different from other positions you have held? I've actually been doing administrative work for a long time. The difference is that I've spent more time in the last year trying to think about the big picture. I have thought less about the details of individual projects, and more about how they all fit together; what the organization should be doing; what is most important to our mission; who is our audience; and so on.

Can you talk a little about the mission of your organization? The Joint Center was founded in 1970. Its overall mission is to provide information and analysis that promotes the movement of African–Americans into the political and economic mainstream of American life. It started with the primary objective of assisting black elected officials in performing their jobs. At the time the Joint Center began, there were about 1,400 black elected officials in the entire country, most of whom were elected after the Civil Rights Act of the 1960s. Most had been excluded from any type of participation in the political process or government administration prior to holding office, and many were in small communities that lacked resources. Their constituents did not have sewers, paved roads, or other community services. They didn't know where to go for help. So the Center began to provide technical assistance to help them write grants, identify funding sources, and set up networks. It also facilitated the development of most of the caucuses of black elected officials that still exist today. There are seven key caucuses from the congressional black caucus to state legislators, local elected officials, mayors, etc. Most were developed as a result of the Joint Center's efforts.

Do you still work closely with these organizations? We do. It goes up and down. We currently work with them on an informal basis. Part of our strategic plan is to reconnect with some of these organizations and non-elected black leaders in a more formal way. We are also working to change how we deliver our information and define our audience.

About 1980, the Center underwent its first transformation. It became more of a research organization. The premise was that black elected officials no longer needed our basic support. They looked more like their white colleagues in the sense that they had similar experiences; they entered public office with similar kinds of knowledge and so on. What they really needed was someone who could provide analysis of the impact various policies have on African–Americans. While there are many organizations that sometimes studied African–American populations, we were, until recently, the only organization that consistently looked at issues from an African–American perspective. In 1990, recognizing the importance of economics and economic well-being, we changed our name from the Joint Center for Political Studies to the Joint Center for Political and Economic Studies.

The first area in which we did work was political participation. The work included some basic things, like counting the number of black elected officials (which has grown from 1,400 in 1970 to close to 9,000 today). We also analyzed black voter participation during key elections. Since 1984, we've conducted a national opinion poll. This past year (1997), we produced four press releases from our surveys: one on race relations, one on children's issues, one on politics, and one on devolution. We use both African–American and general population samples in our surveys for comparison. The Joint Center is also recognized for its work on voting rights and redistricting representation.

Sounds quite different from an academic job. Yes. The other thing that is different about this job (compared to an academic job) is our public representation in terms of testimonies, speeches, presentations, etc., before different audiences. It varies from the NAACP, to the Congressional Black Caucus, to my most recent engagement with the Office of the Comptroller of Currency. There is a fair amount of media in this work as well.

What has been your experience with the media? The media spend a great deal of time calling around. They preview you. Some people call you up and want you to talk on the spot. Others, particularly the larger stations, call ahead. When I was on the McNeil–Lehrer program, for example, they called a day ahead and asked what I would say about this and about that. They seem to decide whether they like the mix of people and how appropriate you are for the program. Then they call back and tell you whether or not you're on the program.

In order to make an impact, do you think that it helps to be in Washington, DC? Yes, in some ways. But now that more things are moving out towards the states, Washington is not as central to policy making as it was. This is one of the challenges facing the Center. In some ways, it's difficult being in Washington because you are distant from what's going on. For instance, last fall, we held a conference on devolution which included welfare reform, and a forum on medicaid and managed care. At these meetings, we talked with black elected officials from across the country, about what we could do for them as heads of various organizations in this new environment.

Is the Joint Center a not-for-profit and non-partisan organization? Well, yes, the two are not synonymous. Non-profit refers to your business format. In Washington, DC, there are people who assign non-partisan organizations to different camps regardless of what you say or how others view you. They'll say, for instance, that Brookings is a liberal institution. Others proudly identify themselves as one or the other. We like to say we are completely non-partisan. In fact, an example we use to illustrate our non-partisan nature is that, in one of the Supreme Court's "redistricting representation" cases, the information generated by the Joint Center was used by opposing sides in support of each of their positions.

How do people react to that? We have been viewed sometimes as too balanced. Some people have said that we are too neutral, too scared to take a position. But what we've done is to assume that good analysis can be used by people in ways that will promote the right outcomes. Although, last year, we ran into a real challenge. Our opinion polls said that the majority of African–Americans favor school vouchers. These data were not supportive of a political leadership that did not favor vouchers, and provided ammunition for a conservative leadership which used the information for their own gains. We were caught in the middle. Some people even accused us of taking a position just because we said, "this is what our polls said." It's always a challenge.

You've been in DC for quite a while. Can you tell us something about the relationships between the different organizations in Washington, such as between the Institute for Women's Policy Research (IWPR) and the Joint Center? There are relationships in several dimensions. The main relationship with IWPR is that I'm on their board. But in general, it's a question of inviting people to conferences, serving on advisory committees, and things like that. Right now we are entering into a joint project with the Center for Law and Social Policy and the Center on Budget Policy Priorities to do a project on devolution. I also serve on a technical advisory group for the Urban Institute's assessing the new federalism project. Occasionally, the Joint Center also has informal requests from the people on Capitol Hill. There are also other organizational relationships across the spectrum where people have connections. But often they are less formal relationships because it's difficult to sustain collaboration. It is very time consuming, especially because organizations have differences in pace, perspective, and overall agenda. And it's difficult to keep a number of projects going at the same time.

Switching focus here, do you have any thoughts on why economics doesn't attract more women and/or African–Americans? Without any information, my guess would be that at least part of the reason has to do with the increasing quantification of the profession. I say this because when the Committee on the Status of Minorities in the Economics Profession (which I used to chair) was reviewing a set of proposals to transfer the summer program for minorities from one institution to another, one of the factors that was very prominent in the applications of the various institutions was their view of whether or not to play to the increasing quantification in the profession. We realized that this issue was not only about minority students. It is certainly true that minority students are disproportionately impacted by the shift to quantification because they are more likely to be at undergraduate institutions that do not take this approach to the discipline. But even students at very good liberal arts colleges may not have a quantitative view of the discipline. It's both a big shock to go to graduate school, and a disadvantage to students who don't have a strong math background. So my guess is that the quantification of economics is a contributing factor.

Do you think it is a question of not having the appropriate math skills or that math is not seen as an appropriate tool for economic analysis by minority and women students? I don't think you can separate the two. The two go together. It's how students are viewed and how students view the discipline. You may recall why I shifted away from math as my major. It wasn't because I couldn't do it. It just wasn't interesting to me because I couldn't figure out how, in and of itself, it could be useful to me. That is the way I would view it.

I am not sure how this relates to women, but some early work I did on African–Americans in the discipline may shed some light on this. One year the National Economic Association conducted a survey of black economists. In analyzing the data, we found that, if you look at cohorts from the 1950s, 1960s, and early 1970s, you find diversification in specializations over time. Among the early entrants into the profession, you often see a stronger concentration in fields that most relate to the needs of the group. Issues like labor and poverty tend to be areas of concentration for both women and minorities in the earlier cohorts. But then there was a shift. People who entered the discipline later were more likely to branch out into industrial organization and micro theory, areas that others might feel are irrelevant. I wonder if part of the issue for women in economics is that women are more interested in things that have applicability to their lives and the people they know about. I don't know. I don't have any empirical evidence, and since I no longer teach, I don't know what undergraduates are thinking these days. But, those are some things that would occur to me.

Many who were mathematical were also attracted to economics because it dealt with social issues. Then they entered graduate school and it was heavy on the math and light on social issues. It's funny. This week we have a temporary secretary in the office who is doing some transcription. In a conversation with this student, she complained that the program wasn't anything like what she had studied as an undergraduate. She said, "It wasn't any of the stuff that I thought was interesting." It turns out that she is the sister of a guy who was two classes behind me at Stanford. I think there were four minority students who were admitted that year; one didn't even last a semester. The only person of that group who eventually finished the program was this student's brother. He had a Master's degree in math when he entered the program.

How would you describe your theoretical perspective? Oh, I'd say middle of the road, based on what others have told me. Some of my colleagues believe that I'm not nearly radical enough. I'd say I'm probably a modified neoclassical.

That's probably everyone to the extent that we have all been trained in neoclassical theory. Well, that's certainly true. There are some perspectives in the discipline that are so strong that people look at you a little strange. I know that on trade issues I find it very difficult to push a protectionist position. This doesn't sit very well with the labor movement people that I deal with on a somewhat regular basis.

Do you see any themes that have re-emerged in your research over the years? Equity has been a strong issue in my work regardless of the dimension; whether it's issues of employment, education, or business development. That has probably been the dominant issue.

Have you witnessed any significant changes in the economics profession over time? Well, I'd say on the negative side, the increased quantification of the profession. And as the discipline has reconfigured itself it seems less welcoming to the issues that are most important, at least to me. On the positive side, there's an increased acceptance of both women and minorities in the profession. It's certainly a lot better than it used to be. Some people are doing quite well through the regular mentorship networks, not in the numbers that they should be, but certainly in comparison to the past. During my early days in the Caucus of Black Economists, the only blacks on the program at the ASSA meetings were those who were put on the program through the activity of the Caucus. Now people appear throughout the program, and there are so many topics that it becomes difficult to decide what to attend. This is a real change. The same thing for women. If it wasn't for CSWEP, there would be very few women on the program. Before, you'd see Anne Krueger and, maybe, Barbara Bergmann, if she was behaving correctly [*laughter*].

Do you think economic thinking is still developing? Ummm, no. At least not fast enough. One of the differences between a hard science and a not-so-hard science like economics is that people find it difficult to separate the quality of the work from the focus of the work. Somehow doing a scientific experiment is considered purer than work that has social or group implications. This work is considered subjective. There used to be an unspoken premise that you couldn't do work on your own people because you couldn't be objective, like women who do women's issues. [*Pause*] This reminds me of an interesting comment about a famous white, male economist who did a lot of work on the progress of African–Americans. Upon spending a couple of hours with him, someone said, "Oh, it's easy to understand how he can be objective. He doesn't know any African–Americans. Therefore, he can't be biased!" [*Laughter*]

Margaret, you described yourself as a modified neoclassical. What is it about the neoclassical approach that needs modification? Well, I think there are certainly good analytical tools that one can learn from neoclassical economics, tools which can be applied to different scenarios. But there are clearly some things that are somewhat absurd, which leads to all the jokes about economists. I do not think it is useful when one abstracts so far from reality. The extreme neoclassical model is not useful when it explains away everything that is subjective; when everything is reduced to differences in tastes; when discrimination is explained away as rational economic behavior. For instance, it is assumed that people are paid less because they don't have the appropriate skills. Or, if they have the appropriate skills, it is assumed that they make less because their employers have "a taste" against them. It's this sort of analysis which is useless; it makes everything OK and outside the realm of solution in some sense. People somehow need fixing. That is not to say that, if someone has a poor education, then they don't require more education. But you can't necessarily only use people's lack of education to explain, in an objective way, differences in outcomes.

In other words, it is not always necessarily a matter of choice? Yes.

I guess to some extent, I accept some of the institutional stuff, but I am not an institutionalist. And I am certainly not a Marxist or a radical economist. I wouldn't call myself a feminist economist, or necessarily a feminist either.

What is it about feminism that makes you reject the label of feminist? I guess that, in some ways, it's the same as saying that I'm not a Marxist. I don't see the world completely through that lens. This is a simplification, but to the extent that Marxists see the world through a class lens, you could say that feminists see the world through the gender lens, and I don't see the world quite that way.

In what ways does the fact that you are African–American relate to your rejection of feminism? I just had a conversation with someone about how black women are not doing well. They are only doing well against other women. If the standard is white men, however, they are still way behind. So if I look at the dominant issue – it's really race. Race dominates gender. That's part of the issue for me.

Feminists, such as bell hooks, have argued that it is meaningless to discuss the category of gender independent of race, class, age, etc. Would you feel comfortable with that argument? There certainly are some intersections you could use in understanding people's experiences in the sense that people don't experience life in just one dimension, nor are people necessarily viewed from only one dimension. It's not as though you are viewed as having a certain race with no gender, or that class issues don't enter into people's experiences. Some work at the Joint Center is focused on generational differences in attitudes and opinions and how they relate to differences in experiences based on a particular time period, because each period brings with it a whole set of experiences. For example, people who grew up prior to or during the civil rights movement have very different experiences and viewpoints than people who grew up afterwards. Another classic example is the Great Depression. The people who grew up during the Depression have very different views on food and security than those who grew up after World War II when these were plentiful. In the latter period, the big issue was to be thin, not fat. That comes out of a very different set of experiences. There are many examples like that.

Would you encourage young people to get a PhD in economics? It would depend on what they want to do, and their tolerance for digressing from their real interest. It is probably true for any discipline, but certainly in economics, that the first year never seems to bear any resemblance to what you expected; to what attracted you to the discipline in the first place. I would say that persistence is a trait you need in order to survive. The difference between those who finish and those who don't is more about persistence than intelligence. People who are willing to take the rejection, and do not give up, succeed. A PhD in economics is more important if you want to remain in academia. If not, graduate programs in related fields might be just as useful, such as public policy, policy sciences, or something of that nature. But in academia, even if you end up in a department other than economics but work in the field, you need to have a PhD in economics because it's a better "union card" to have.

Would you advise women, in particular, to pursue a PhD in economics? While in some dimensions the discipline is less supportive, in many other ways it is more supportive than it used to be. For instance, there are more women and sympathetic males within the discipline who provide support, mentorship, and other kinds of support for young women. That's not to say it's perfect. There are still certainly many pockets of resistance in the discipline. But there is more diversity. Students are more likely to have support. Clearly, there are people who give a lot of themselves to help others. I think about people that I know; people who go out of their way to provide guidance and opportunity whether it's part of their job description or not.

Have you encountered situations where you were able to help young women in economics? There was a young woman, a graduate student, who received a fellowship from the AEA. Part of her fellowship involved an internship with the Federal Reserve (Fed) in Washington, DC. Just before she was scheduled to do this internship, she and I had a long phone conversation. I had never met her; I only knew her on paper. She was resisting the internship with the Fed because she believed it was going to slow her down in finishing her dissertation. I think she was also pregnant at the time. She was worried that she had too many things to juggle. I tried to convince her that it was a very important part of the fellowship. I advised her that it was an opportunity that helps many people complete their dissertation because they have someone who works with them. In the second conversation, I directed her to somebody I knew at the Fed who was also on the fellowship committee and was very supportive. She also had children and could talk to her about the kinds of experiences she might encounter at the Fed. Between the pushing and pulling she finally decided to do it, and she actually finished her dissertation early. In fact, she turned her second-year fellowship down and went on the job market. I finally met her when she was on the market. She told me that I was responsible for persuading her to go to the Fed. There are many people like that in the profession now. If I hadn't been able to give her a contact at the Fed, it may have been less effective. I would not have been able to tell her exactly what to expect. It's important to have somebody on the inside who says, "OK, I'm here. I know the people you will be working with. I know they will be supportive. I know they will help you get where you want to go." The implicit understanding was that, if they don't help you, call me and I'll see what I can do. That kind of thing didn't exist before.

In fact I was talking to Andrew Brimmer about this last week. He was trying to recall when we first met. I told him I was in graduate school and he was on the board at the Fed. (He was the first black governor at the Fed, appointed by Lyndon Johnson. He was also the fourth or fifth black to get a PhD in economics at Harvard.) I attended graduate school with someone who worked for Dr Brimmer and had asked me over to the Fed for lunch. That is how Brimmer and I met. It was a casual meeting. We were together for about an hour. Anyway, because there were so few blacks in economics, everybody knew everybody else. You knew that if you ran into them several years later they would still remember who you were. For example, Andy remembered the circumstances of our meeting, even though he couldn't remember the exact year; he was a year off.

Margaret, in retrospect, if you had to do this over again, would you have chosen to be an economist? You know, it is very difficult to say. We really are a product of the time in which we came along. If I had to do it over again, in the same time frame, then yes. If I was coming along now, I don't know. There are clearly many other options that were not real options then.

Plate 11 From top left: Lourdes Benería with sons Jordi and Marc (1984); in peace march (1982). Main portrait (1998). From middle left: at 3 years in Spanish Pyrenees; with son Jordi at Christmas in Ithaca, New York (1999); with two sons in New York (1968); in Accra, Ghana (1978). From bottom left: with June Nash at UCLA (1992); with son Marc in Riverside Park, New York (1982).

11

LOURDES BENERÍA

> The goal of gender equality, as important as it is, is insufficient
> unless it is contextualized within the wider objectives of human
> development. For me, as someone interested in development, this
> notion is basic for the work that I do.
>
> (Lourdes Benería, 1998)

In her earlier years, Lourdes found it difficult to speak in public. Today, she is a highly sought-after lecturer both in the US and abroad. She has authored, co-authored, and edited several books and published over thirty articles on such topics as women and development, international labor, Latin America, and globalization and the debt crisis. She is the former Acting Director of the Institute for Research on Women at Rutgers University; former recipient of the Program on Peace and International Cooperation Grant from the John D. and Catherine T. MacArthur Foundation; former Director of both the Latin American Studies Program and the Program on International Development and Women at Cornell University; former Coordinator for the Program on Rural Women, World Employment Program at the International Labor Office in Geneva, Switzerland; and she has served on the editorial board of several scholarly journals. She has also taught all over the world including Spain, Nova Scotia, Dominican Republic, Honduras, and Columbia. Currently she is a Professor of City and Regional Planning and Women's Studies at Cornell University. She received her BA in economics (1961) from the University of Barcelona and an MPh (1974) and PhD (1975) from Columbia University.

Our conversation took place on a cold but sunny winter's day in February at the Smithsonian Institute in Washington, DC. Lourdes was working on a book as a fellow at the Woodrow Wilson International Center for Scholars. We began in the morning and, although we had intended to take a break, the conversation continued through lunch time. That evening we met in a bookstore, went for dinner, and discussed the experience of remembering and the process of telling one's story. It was a relaxing evening with good food and laughter. It is times like these that make this book so special and such a rewarding experience.

Lourdes, let's begin with your background. Can you tell us something about your family? I was born in the Catalan part of the Spanish Pyrenees, in a beautiful valley of nine villages. We spoke Catalan at home and everywhere, except at school where the official work, including all textbooks, had to be in Spanish. Catalan is a language spoken by 5 to 6 million people in northeastern Spain and southern France. When I was born my village didn't have a road. We traveled by horse to the nearest town that had cars and buses. Now it takes twenty minutes by car, but it used to take almost five hours by horse. This should give you a sense of how my life has moved from pre-modern times to the new millennium. Although the valley has modernized a great deal and attracts a lot of tourism, it is still very rooted in the Middle Ages, with impressive eleventh- to thirteenth-century Romanesque churches and stone buildings, which easily remind us of what life might have been like in the past.

The first road was built when I was young, and maybe because of this experience, I have always had an image of modernity disrupting the peace and quiet of a more traditional world. Up until the early 1950s, my part of the Pyrenees Mountains had a subsistence economy. It was a big jump for me to live in New York City twenty years later.

How long did you live in the village? Until I was 13 years old. I was sent to boarding school in the capital city of my province. I was there through high school. Then I went to the university in Barcelona.

How typical was it to attend a boarding school during high school? It was typical for the part of Spain where I come from, and for families who could afford to send their kids away.

Talk a bit about your parents. My parents had some land, cattle, and a tourist-related business such as transporting people and goods using horses. My family was a typical traditional Catholic family. Although my father represented authority, my mother played the key role in daily life and family affairs. She was responsible for the subsistence work like taking care of the vegetable garden. But she also helped my father. He traveled quite a lot. My mother stayed home and took care of daily business. She was a strong person, although I have sometimes referred to her as "a woman of silence." That's because she was quiet; much quieter than my father. The household was rather large, in many ways an extended family. There were always other people in addition to the nuclear family. I have this rather symbolic image of my family sitting around the long dining room table. My father sits at the head of the table with my mother at his side. My older brothers and sisters sit next to them. Sitting at the end of the table are those of us who were younger, together with the male workers who helped with the cattle, the land, and the household chores.

How many brothers and sisters did you have? There were six of us altogether. I was the youngest by quite a lot. My oldest sister is almost twenty years my elder and there is a thirteen-year gap between my youngest brother and myself. My mother was 46 years old when I was born, so in some ways I grew up as an only child. Up until the late 1950s or early 1960s in Spain, a middle-class family like mine could afford a maid. I often identified with the maid since, as the youngest, I was also told to fetch things and run errands and never dared to speak up much at the table. One could do an interesting analysis of gender and class relations around my parents' dining room table [*laughter*].

Did your father do all the talking at the table? Not quite, but his authority was very present. My mother was a bridge between him and the rest of us. Often when the talk was about business, it was concentrated among the men, cutting across class lines between my father and the male workers, while the women tended not to say much.

What was the educational background of your parents? My mother had a general education which was very common among women of her age and social background. My father had some kind of commercial training. Today, we would call it vocational business training and accounting.

What kind of education did your siblings have? Two of my sisters did not attend the university. One took up educational training after she became a nun. My third sister got a university degree. My two brothers assumed my father's work. We weren't a highly educated family. Rather, we were business people with a rural background.

What happened with your two college-educated sisters? One became a pharmacist. In Spain, this is a respected profession, involving as many years of study as medicine. The other taught at a nun's school, and became a leader in her congregation.

Could you say something about your pre-college education. You said you went to a boarding school. It was a Catholic boarding school for girls.

Was it far from home? It seemed far at the time because it could take more than a day via public transportation. Now it takes less than three hours by car.

How often did you go home? Only during Christmas, Easter, and summer vacations. My boarding school experience was the first step towards understanding what urban life was like. It was also rather oppressive. After all, it was a Catholic school in the 1950s in Spain! But, despite the problems, it prepared me intellectually for the university. The religious part was the kind of thing that for years I had to undo in some ways, although the discipline proved to be useful during many times in my life.

Did you feel at the time that it was repressive? Well, some things were difficult such as keeping silent during mealtime, or getting up very early in the morning to go to church. It was an all-girls' school, and many of us had rural backgrounds. The nuns tried to prepare us to become members of the middle and upper-middle class. They held short evening classes on ladylike behavior [*laughter*]. I guess I was used to the indoctrination, but I also found it repressive and rebelled against it in various ways. It was during my university years that I became more rebellious. After all, my exposure to urban life was rather limited in boarding school, whereas once at the university in Barcelona, I was much more exposed to the intellectual, political, and cultural life of a big city. Barcelona was a mind-opening experience for me.

Were you happy at the boarding school in general? Quite happy. I was learning a lot and discovering wider horizons. It was not liberating, but it was instructive in some ways.

Were any of your teachers influential in your thinking? I would say that there were three teachers who were important role models: two women and a man. They were knowledgeable and aware of their important role and influence on us. One woman taught philosophy and the classics in a very effective way. The other taught Spanish literature. Her classes were really fantastic. The man taught math. He was a very controversial character, who treated students differently, tending to favor the good students in a very open way. I had mixed feelings about him. While he treated me well and I liked him as a teacher, his ways of dealing with female students were very questionable. Yet, he was instrumental in getting me to like math. I didn't like chemistry or physics as well, maybe because of the teachers I had. But I did like math.

Was it your attraction to math that led you to pursue economics at the university or were there other things in your high school experience or otherwise that influenced your decision? The way I got into economics was totally ridiculous and backwards [*laughter*]. I was not a feminist. I had never thought about its meaning. But I did not want to follow a typically woman's career path like my sisters. I wanted to do something different. It turned out to be economics, although I didn't quite know what economics was about.

During the time of Franco's Spain, in underground politics I often heard heated student discussions about capitalism versus socialism, and I remember thinking that economics would help me understand the difference between the two. The problem was that, when I told my family and friends what I wanted to do, I was told that economics was not a "feminine" profession. I remember having to justify my choice and arguing that there were several things I could do with economics, even as a woman.

How did you come up with economics as an option? I read about it in the newspapers. At the University of Barcelona there was no economics major until the 1950s. Before that, anyone who wanted to pursue an economics degree had to attend law school. When the economics major became institutionalized first in Madrid and then in Barcelona (when I was finishing secondary schooling), the newspapers carried the news. Also people talked about it, so this got my attention.

Does that mean you were one of the first economics majors at the University of Barcelona? Yes. I was in the very first class.

Were there other women in your cohort? There were three of us in a class of seventy or seventy-five. Later on, another woman joined us. Of the four, I was the only one who finished out the year. Eventually three of us graduated and one dropped out.

Did you know these women well? I was very good friends with one, and also friends with the other two. We did a lot of things together.

What was it like during your undergraduate years? For instance, how long did it take you to get your degree? It was a five-year degree. That's how long it took me to finish.

What was it like? It was interesting and frustrating at the same time. Remember, this was during the Franco regime, and some teachers were appointed from Madrid through a centralized system. There were some awful teachers – just awful. We even organized protests against a couple of them on the basis that they were incompetent. Luckily, we also had a few teachers who were inspiring.

But for the most part it was enjoyable. I lived in a student residence for women which was also administered by nuns. They required us to return to the dorm by 9:00 p.m. and 11:00 p.m. on weekends. But after boarding school, this was fine to me! [*Laughter*] I was a fairly good student, although I was behind compared to many of my fellow students who came from more sophisticated urban backgrounds. One vivid memory is how I often played stupid and under-played my achievements. God forbid that I might do better than my male classmates! I remember being asked how I did on an exam. I'd say "OK," even if I did better than OK. I do remember, very consciously, playing this game. I had the notion of women's traditional place in society totally internalized.

Were you accepted by the guys? Yeah, but I was accepted as a "nice girl." Perhaps they thought that I was a bit eccentric for doing economics. But I was not threatening in any way. For the most part, I didn't ask difficult questions and behaved the way I was supposed to behave. If there were any feelings of rebellion on my part (and there were), they were not manifested, nor was I very conscious of them.

Did you have anyone among the faculty who was instrumental in your success as a student? There were several faculty members who were inspiring to me. They were all men, of course, because we had absolutely no women teachers at any level. One that inspired me was the historian Jaume Vicens Vives. He was a true scholar with a critical mind and interesting work.

Did you know him and did he inspire you personally, or was he in general an inspiring person to observe? Everybody liked him as a teacher. He was very instrumental in making us question the type of history we had been taught in high school. He specialized in fifteenth- and sixteenth-century Spain, and was very critical of the Spanish conquest of America. He was especially critical of Queen Isabella. His course represented a clear shift from the government-controlled high school history we had been exposed to. Another inspiring teacher was Fabia Estapé who taught political economy. He was a critic of the Franco regime, although he couldn't say so very openly in class at the time. A third influence was Lluis Fina who taught international economics, which is what I ultimately ended up pursuing. I enjoyed the topic and, in retrospect, he might have been instrumental in my decision to travel abroad.

In any case, the most inspiring event was a summer stay in Paris during my junior year. I was able to negotiate this through the Association Internationale

231

d'Etudiants de Sciences Economiques et Commerciales or AIESEC, which I think still exists in Europe. It was a job-exchange program. I arranged to get a job in a French bank, Le Crédit Commercial de France. Its headquarters were at the Champs Elysées. I lived at a residence at the Cité Universitaire which was my first experience in international living. In many ways, these two months changed my outlook on life. You have to realize that Franco's Spain was very insular until the late 1960s. Living abroad, therefore, was very liberating and enriching.

Was this your first trip abroad? No, but it was my first stay abroad on my own. The second came when I finished my university degree. I went to England for a year before coming to the United States. This was my introduction to the Anglo-Saxon world. I had learned English in high school, but I was far from fluent.

What did you do in England? I attended the London School of Economics. However, I was not officially registered because my English wasn't good enough. I had a scholarship to learn English and study European integration. I made use of their library and got to know some students and faculty, Alan Day in particular. This experience turned out to be quite instrumental in helping me to obtain a Fulbright and to come to the United States to pursue a Master's degree in economics.

Where did you do your Master's? I did a one-year program at NYU. However, I had to return to Spain immediately after because of my visa. While in the States I had met my future husband, Marvin Surkin, who later joined me in Spain. I couldn't return to the US for two years due to my initial visa status. We got married in Spain and at the end of the two years we returned to the US. It was then that I registered for Columbia University's PhD program.

Would you like to talk about the Master's program and your first year in the United States before we talk about your PhD program? The important thing about that year was that I was in the United States, and in New York City. In the Master's program, I got a little deeper into economic theory compared to before, and I enjoyed the micro course taught by Benjamin Katz. He was an excellent teacher. I also became very interested in Latin American development through one of the courses I took. But it was just one year, and as a foreign student whose command of English was not that great, I don't know how I managed to do it. In terms of a learning experience in economics, it wasn't a very important year. But as an introduction to the United States, and living in New York City, it was a mind-boggling experience [*laughter*]. I remember looking up at all those buildings; they were so tall and I felt so small. Coming from a protected, traditional background, New York City was both scary and exciting. I had come from a soft and homogeneous society. New York City was harsh and multicultural.

What happened when you returned to Spain? What made you decide to come back to the US? We got married in the Pyrenees and I got a research job with a group of economists. It was poorly paid, but intellectually interesting. During the 1960s, it was clear that my American husband would have difficulty finding a job in Spain. I had also come to the conclusion that I wouldn't mind pursuing a PhD. I could have got a PhD in Spain, but it would have been much less interesting than a PhD in economics in the States. In addition, it seemed relatively easier to live in the US and visit Spain than vice versa. It was also easier to get jobs in the US. Everything pointed towards moving back to the States. But the decision was very difficult for me personally; excruciatingly difficult because I felt very rooted in my native place and culture.

What did you expect to do with a PhD in economics? My motivation for pursuing a PhD in economics certainly did not include teaching. I was not interested in being a college teacher. I wanted a research job in a public institution or a job as a writer on economics issues. I was very shy about speaking in public as a consequence of my background. We were definitely not encouraged to speak up. On the contrary, you were taught to keep a low profile. I remember how I hated oral exams, and how nervous they made me. I never thought of myself as someone who would end up as a public speaker [*laughter*]. I had to really struggle with that, believe me. When I came to this country I was totally stunned to see how comfortable American students were with speaking in class. This was not part of my learning experience. Contrary to the United States, there was little reward for women in Spain in doing so.

When you returned to the States had you already applied and been accepted at Columbia? Yes, I wanted to be in New York City. Actually, I was accepted by both the New School and Columbia. But I decided to go to Columbia.

What was your experience like at Columbia? It was a strong culture shock, more than at NYU. It was a very competitive environment and not a friendly one. One of the shocking things to me was that students didn't help each other. I had come from a tradition where students tended to work together, but at Columbia, individualism was the rule. However, beyond the competitive spirit dominating the program, I also didn't expect the hegemonic thinking of the department. It was a shock to me. The program was strictly neoclassical. I had not come from an alternative paradigm, nor was I clear about the view I wanted to take. I had studied orthodox economics in Spain, but it was within an environment that was much more political and critical. At Columbia, I had the sense that there was no room for any alternative thinking, and that made me feel uncomfortable. Perhaps naively, I didn't expect it to be like that.

Remember, I came from the pre-modern Pyrenees mountains. Rational economic man was somewhat of a stranger to me. My childhood was to a great extent immersed in a subsistence economy amidst a deepening transition towards the market in some areas and with well-established markets in others. Economic rationality was somewhat relevant in that type of transitional economy, but certainly not to the same degree that it is in a highly monetized market economy. I still remember being surprised that young people in New York City were paid to babysit. I had babysat many times for free! I still find the notion of "human capital" awkward. In a sense, it was easy for me to question the basic assumptions of conventional economics since I had lived in an alternative, pre-capitalist system.

Can you elaborate on what you mean when you say that you got an orthodox education in Spain, but within a more political environment? Well, for the most part we had neoclassical economics, but the department's curriculum also included some history, sociology, philosophy, and law. The specialization was narrow, but not to the same degree as the program at Columbia. The program was too narrowly defined. I was interested in social and political issues. The reason I wanted to study economics was to have better tools to answer some fundamental social and political questions. In fact, it turned out to be an end in itself, rather than a tool. The emphasis was on technical questions. The political questions were rarely asked and very consciously separated from economics. Yet, the political biases were inherently there.

Were there women students or faculty in the economics department? Well, in many ways I went to Columbia twice, during two different time periods. First before I had my children and later when my second son was almost 3 years old. There were no women faculty during either period. As for students, I barely remember my first year. Perhaps there were three women out of thirty-something in my class. When I returned after a prolonged maternity leave, I vividly remember that I was the only married woman in the program. My problems seemed to be very different from everybody else's [*laughter*]. Everyone, including the women, seemed to have more time than I did. I was unable to stay for many of the activities outside of class. I felt deprived and was little understood when I complained about my time pressures.

How did you manage child care during graduate school? Frankly, with a great deal of difficulty. I tried to return to school when my second son was 6 months old, but I barely lasted a month because I was a nervous wreck. There was not a single day-care center in the upper west side of New York City at that time. We had to rely on babysitters and we were unlucky in finding a good one. It was often heartbreaking to leave the kids at home, so I decided to drop out. I just couldn't handle the tension. I did not return to graduate school until two years later when the Columbia Day Care Coalition – a group of mostly graduate students and some community members – managed to get a day-care center established. Columbia gave us a beautiful building at the corner of West 106th Street and Riverside Drive, and the City gave us a permit. It saved my life. Marc, my youngest son, was one of the first to register. Jordi, my oldest, was in kindergarten. It allowed me to finish courses and other graduate work.

When you returned to graduate school did you want to continue in economics? Thinking about it, I really hesitated about returning to economics, but I did for several reasons. First, I realized that I would lose a year of course work by changing departments. Also I had become a member of URPE [Union of Radical Political Economics] in 1968 and found it very helpful as an environment. Many of the questions that had been in my mind were being discussed. That made a tremendous difference. There were several URPE members among the graduate students at Columbia who became my friends. I thought that, if they were surviving, so would I. I went back determined to finish. By that time, my initial shock was over and I understood American society better. Moreover, the women's movement gave me a new impetus to finish. URPE was very helpful in making me understand that I was not alone in feeling uncomfortable in a profession that seemed to be unwilling to draw the connections between the social, the political, and the economic.

Were there any faculty whom you respected in this context – faculty who viewed economics a bit more broadly and could make the connections between economics, social, and political issues? Remember, at that time, Columbia was considered the second Chicago. Gary Becker had been there; Jacob Mincer was there; Jim Heckman and Barry Chiswick were there for a while. I respected them all, but I never had an affinity with them. Although I was interested in their field (labor economics), I felt closer to other faculty members. One of my early advisors was Gary Hart who taught a course in Latin American development. I worked as his teaching assistant the first year I arrived at Columbia. He was a very gentle and interesting person with whom I initially developed a sort of patriarchal relationship. I also liked William Vickrey. I took two micro courses from him. His detailed analysis of competitive equilibrium which showed that competitive results, including the degree of equality and inequality, depended on the initial distribution of resources, left its mark in my mind. Alas, I think I disappointed both Hart and Vickrey with my connections to URPE. Although, many years later I saw Vickrey at a URPE meeting in Geneva, New York, and he told me he had been a member of the organization for years. This was one year before he was awarded the Nobel prize.

Somewhat later I got to know Michael Elstein, the economic historian who became my thesis advisor. Unfortunately, he left for CUNY's Queens College before I finished my degree. Last but not least, one of my favorite faculty members, originally from Poland, was Alexander Erlich. He was a great human being and thoughtful scholar. He taught a course on Marxian economics, and was very critical of the Soviet model. His European origin and personal history were reflected in his approach, treating economics as a holistic rather than merely technical, intellectual enterprise.

Did you have a mentor at Columbia? Not really; my experience at Columbia was rather alienating. It was difficult to establish connections with most of the faculty. I had little help with my thesis, partly because I chose a subject (education and growth in Spain) which fell outside of the field of interest of the faculty. Partly, I had little help because the economics department was not very nurturing, although I certainly learned a lot about neoclassical economics and other things, including the US system of higher education.

What was your dissertation about? I had become interested in the economics of education. I constructed an econometric model of the changes in Spanish economic growth and the educational system from 1940 to 1973. It was a rather conventional thesis using time series and cross-sectional data for fifty Spanish provinces, a macro approach to the economics of education. I showed that the educational system expanded significantly during the 1960s, a period of high economic growth in Spain, but there was little creativity or novelty involved in the thesis. In fact, I totally lost interest as my work proceeded. By the time I finished, I was very critical of the static nature of the model which did not allow me to ask the more interesting questions about the ways in which the educational system did or didn't function. However, it was a great lesson in the shortcomings of econometric models, particularly their static nature, and inability to capture the dynamics and qualitative aspects of rapid change. This was also a time of great change for me intellectually. The initial formulation of the dissertation project no longer corresponded to my interest in the Marxian paradigm.

The dissertation research was important for me in another way. I had made a conscious effort not to do a dissertation on women's issues. I wanted to show that women could write on other topics. But, while gathering information for my dissertation in Spain, I also collected data by gender, and this became a separate article from my thesis. It was the first paper I ever delivered at the ASSA meetings. This was in San Francisco in 1974. In fact, this was my first publication. I published it before I finished the thesis. Somehow it was more vital to me [laughter].

Were there particular students you were close to? My closest connections were the students involved in URPE-related activities. I remember Manuel Agosin, Leo Cawley, Diane Flahertly, David Gold, Anwar Shaik, and others. We organized activities and met quite regularly. Harriet Zellner introduced me to feminism. I remember seeing her one day wearing a button that said, "Feminism Lives." I looked at her with bewilderment and asked what it meant. She smiled as if she was way ahead of me, which she was [laughter]. She was attending the meetings of the Columbia Women's Liberation Group, a pioneering group that included people like Kate Millet and Rachel DuPlessis, both graduate students in the English department. I remember being very curious about their discussions and activities. However, my initial reaction to what we called "women's liberation" was quite negative. I dismissed it as an American phenomenon. It was my period of denial. As a nice Spanish girl [laughter], I didn't think I could identify with it. I was married and it was quite threatening. I was curious, though, and I always found the discussions with Harriet interesting. She was the first student I remember writing a thesis on women. She worked with Jacob Mincer, focusing on discrimination. It was one of the first articles I read on the topic. It was eventually published in the *American Economic Review*. Other women students were also writing on women's issues, such as Cynthia Lloyd and Andrea Beller.

Have you kept in touch with any of them? When Harriet finished her degree, she set up a consulting firm in New York City to provide economic analyses of feminist legal issues such as divorce cases. We kept in touch for a while, but eventually lost contact. I kept in touch with Cynthia Lloyd for a longer period of time. I saw her recently.

You said that the graduate program at Columbia was not very nurturing. Did you feel that you were treated differently because you were a woman and/or a foreigner? This is a difficult question to answer. I did feel that the male faculty treated me paternalistically. But primarily, I felt ignored. I was rather shy and not as aggressive as the average American student. In an American context, this was an invitation to be ignored. My English was, of course, not as fluent as it is now and this didn't help. Luckily, though, my determination and strong will compensated for it. However, I should mention a special treatment that Vickrey provided to foreign students. During the final exam in micro, he allowed foreign students to take an extra half hour. For me, that made a difference between getting an A or not quite finishing the exam, and I was always grateful to him for that.

Was your husband supportive? Yeah, he was. I had to struggle for an equal division of labor at home, but he was very supportive of my attending graduate school. It was difficult at first to share child rearing and housework. But it got much better as time went on, especially when I finished graduate school and started to work. We learned to share quite a bit, pretty close to 50–50. We eventually separated, but I don't think it had to do with household work and sharing.

How long after graduate school did you separate? I graduated in 1975 and we separated in 1979.

What did you do after you finished? I got a job at Rutgers University in the economics department and I commuted from New York City. I was there from 1975 until 1986. In 1977, I took a job for two years at the International Labour Organization (ILO) in Geneva as the coordinator of the Program on Rural Women. Ingrid Palmer was the first coordinator and I replaced her in May, 1977.

When I went to Geneva, I didn't consider myself a feminist economist in any way. Despite my increasing interest in women's issues, I thought of myself as a development economist and as a labor economist. It was really the ILO job that finally shifted the main focus of my work towards gender issues.

What did that job entail? The Program on Rural Women had been created a couple of years earlier under the umbrella of the ILO's World Employment Program. It focused on Third World women and my task was to put together a program of research and action related to rural women. We had consultants and researchers working in different countries and we had to raise money to continue this work. The job included research, some administrative work, and supervisory responsibilities.

How did you get the job? I learned that the ILO was looking for an economist from an anthropologist colleague of mine at Rutgers, Helen Safa. My first reaction was to say that I wasn't interested. I would have to move my whole family to Geneva. I was afraid it would be too complicated. But when I mentioned it to my husband, he liked the idea. His own job was in question because the School of Contemporary Studies, a CUNY institution associated with Brooklyn College, was threatened by New York City's fiscal crisis. I applied and got the job.

Please talk about your experience in Geneva. Well, Geneva was difficult at the personal level, but it was very interesting professionally. I learned a lot at the ILO about both economics and the UN system. One of the most important things I discovered was that the narrowness of our profession did not allow us to ask and analyze questions that I felt were important for a program on rural women. When I got to Geneva, I found that economists had not written much about rural women in the Third World. So I started to read what anthropologists, sociologists, and other social scientists had written on the topic. This was my first interdisciplinary jump. Because I was already coming from a critical view of the profession, it was not a difficult jump to make. I found building bridges between economics and other social sciences very interesting. I would have liked to have stayed at the ILO longer than two years, but Rutgers would not extend my leave of absence. So, I had to make a choice between staying in Geneva and my academic job in the United States. I decided that, in the long run, I preferred to remain in an academic environment.

Did you have tenure at Rutgers yet? No, I got tenure in 1980–1.

Talk a little about your experience at Rutgers as an assistant professor. Was it a big department? Rutgers had four major colleges: Rutgers (initially a men's college), Douglas (the women's college), Cook (the land grant college), and Livingston (the new college which was set up as a result of New Jersey's urban riots in the late 1960s). I was at Livingston, an experimental college. It was Rutgers' response to the fact that students from underprivileged backgrounds weren't making it into Rutgers. The faculty was mixed and the economics department was not your typical department; it was more unorthodox. Across colleges, the economics departments were all quite large, but at Livingston it was fairly small; about seven to nine faculty. Each college had a degree of autonomy. In 1981 there was a major restructuring effort, centralizing the college departments. Rutgers College, the largest and most conservative and orthodox of all, became dominant. Thereafter, those of us who were not neoclassical were a minority and, as a result, we lost many battles. Eventually, several of us left for other universities. Others didn't get tenure and the former Livingston department was decimated.

In what ways was the department of economics in Livingston unorthodox? It was unorthodox in a theoretical sense. We had Marxist economists, post-Keynesians, institutionalists, as well as neoclassical economists. When I arrived, I was the only woman, but Nina Shapiro was hired three years later. It had a larger proportion of women than at any of the other colleges. I became the first tenured woman at Rutgers, not just at Livingston. Several women who went up after me did not get tenure. I am not sure what happened, but at the time Rutgers had a terrible record in terms of keeping women faculty. Despite all this,

Livingston College was a very interesting place to be because of the mixture of the faculty.

Were there people of color among the faculty at Livingston? No, and this is despite the fact that the student body was quite mixed, racially and ethnically. In fact, there was no faculty of color in economics in the entire university until a Nigerian, Tamisen Hebeyegbe, was hired in the early 1980s.

What was the tenure process like for you? I thought I would not get tenure and I prepared myself for such an outcome. I assumed that the majority of faculty at the university level would argue that my work was on gender and not economics. This is what had happened in other cases. I had enough publications and I had worked at the ILO. This meant that my CV looked somewhat respectable and probably made them think twice. It would be difficult to deny me tenure. In addition, I did have some supporters among the faculty, and it was the last year input from the faculty was allowed from individual colleges. I am sure that helped me.

Others may have been concerned about denying me tenure. I could take action. When I took the ILO job, the department chair initially turned down my request for a leave of absence. He hoped I would quit and a new line would be open. But I took my grievance to the AAUP and found out that he could not deny me the leave of absence. I was advised to start a grievance procedure, and I was quite nervous about doing it. But I immediately got the leave without going through the process. It was a very empowering experience for me. I realized that fighting back works.

And indeed a viable option. Yes, and an option, absolutely. So luckily for me the tenure experience was not difficult. Other faculty at Rutgers had terrible tenure processes, including grievances that did not work out. I remember vividly when the chair called to tell me I had been granted tenure. I was so surprised that I kept asking whether it was possible there had been some mistake [*laughter*]. My friends organized a tenure party I will never forget. They made a banner which said, "Tenure on Your Terms." [*Laughter*].

You were tenured in 1980–1. How many more years did you stay at Rutgers? I stayed until 1986.

Were you a full professor by the time you left? No, I was an associate professor. Given the nature of the restructured department, I figured I was going to be an associate professor for a long, long time [*laughter*]. I had difficulty getting to teach graduate courses. Most of our teaching was in the undergraduate program. But we all wanted to teach the few graduate courses we had and to work with graduate students.

Did you? My most rewarding experience with graduates was in women's studies. I also had a good association with anthropology, political science, and history. I was very connected to women's studies, but felt frustrated in the economics department. My activities outside economics allowed me to be creative and to teach the interdisciplinary courses that I enjoyed. I became the Associate Director of the new Rutgers' Institute of Research for Women and worked with Katherine Stimpson, who was its director at the time. This was a very rewarding experience that expanded my networks at Rutgers. I also enjoyed teaching a graduate course with Martha Howell, a historian who did European economic history. We had a great time. We looked at economic change from women's perspective. She did the transition from feudalism to capitalism in Western Europe, and I did contemporary transitions in the Third World. We used both development literature and historical readings. We analyzed the parallels between economic change in the Middle Ages and the twentieth century from a feminist perspective.

What made you finally leave Rutgers? I was not planning to leave Rutgers. But with the merging of the departments and the marginalization of our heterodox group, we felt increasingly out of place. For example, Rutgers had a core group of post-Keynesian economists, people like Paul Davidson, Al Eichner, Nina Shapiro, and Ian Kregel. The *Journal of Post Keynesian Economics* was located at Rutgers and edited by Paul Davidson. We expected that an institute for post-Keynesian economics would eventually be established there. But the neoclassical economists in the department managed to block the funding for the institute. Paul Davidson left for the University of Missouri. Kregel, who had come to Rutgers from Europe with the assumption that the institute would be established, went back to Europe. Others like Robert Guttman, Michelle Naples, and Bruce Steinberg (more Marxian than post-Keynesian) also left.

When I was contacted by a member of the Cornell search committee to apply for a newly created position in gender and development at the university level, I knew that I still had to be housed in a department. My first reaction was that it would not work. The Cornell economics department would not hire me. I also wasn't convinced that I wanted to leave New York City. But they persuaded me to at least apply. Once I learned more about the job and its good fit with my research and teaching interests, I couldn't turn it down. I went to Cornell as a full professor. Just the thought that I wouldn't have to go through the promotion process again was an incentive [*laughter*].

Did you ever pursue it with the economics department at Cornell? No, I didn't, because the fit with the program on International Studies in Planning seemed to be better.

How did you become a candidate for this job? Was it solely your record that was speaking for itself or did you also know someone at Cornell? I didn't know anybody at Cornell, but by then my published work on gender and development was quite well known by people in the field and some of my articles had become standard reading. My book with Martha Roldán on Mexico was not published yet, but parts of it appeared as an article. I think that's why they contacted me.

What were your responsibilities at your new job? Besides regular teaching responsibilities, we developed a program called International Development and Women. It was eventually called Gender and Global Change (GGC). I was the director for five years. My main responsibility was to establish the program's presence at Cornell and elsewhere, and to organize activities of interest to faculty and to (mostly but not exclusively) graduate students.

That must have been exciting. Can you talk a bit about the development of this program, what you did as the director, and generally your experience at Cornell? Well, I had a joint appointment with women's studies and the city and regional planning department. The GGC program was (and is) a university-wide program which brought together the interdisciplinary interests and activities related to gender and international development, especially at the graduate level. Like similar programs at Cornell, the GGC is a thematic program and not degree granting. It functions as a channel to facilitate the work of faculty and students.

For an example of what we did, in September of 1988, we put together a workshop to look at the gender aspects of structural adjustment in Third World countries. This was the year after the book *Adjustment with a Human Face*, edited by Andrea Cornia *et al.*, was published by UNICEF. This book was clearly the strongest criticism of structural adjustment that had since appeared. The first structural adjustment programs had taken place in the early 1980s. The Mexico package had been adopted in 1982, following the 1980 Philippine package. The Mexican policies were far more comprehensive. Then Bolivia followed. By the time of the 1985 Nairobi conference, it had become obvious that women and their households were significantly affected by these policies. By the time the UNICEF book was published, we had come to realize that we needed an analysis of the effects of structural adjustment from the perspective of women. This was the main objective of our workshop which was funded by the Ford Foundation. It was quite a struggle. There were basically no studies on the topic yet. In fact, the workshop was the incentive for some of us to begin empirical research on the topic. Ultimately, a few papers from the workshop were published in the book *Unequal Burden: Economic Crisis, Persistent Poverty, and Women's Work*, which Shelly Feldman and I edited.

Are you still working with the Gender and Global Change Program? Yes, I have become a faculty member in the program. Others have taken on the director's tasks. However, I will begin a second term as director in the spring of 2000. For some time, I have negotiated for an increase in the program's budget and for administrative help.

What courses do you teach? At this point I teach a course on globalization and development, another on gender and development, and a third on global institutions. The latter deals with the so-called new global architecture. I have also taught a course on the political economy of gender and work which focuses more specifically on industrialized countries. Recently I experimented with a course on gender, markets, and planning, which was inspired by reading Polanyi's book *The Great Transformation*. Polanyi writes about how the growth of national markets in nineteenth- and early twentieth-century Europe generated tensions and inequalities which led to what he calls "the great transformation," which, in turn, led to the different left movements of the first half of the twentieth century. I found his work useful for analyzing the formation of global markets in the late twentieth century. Parts of this course were summarized in my article "Globalization, Gender, and the Davos Man," which is an effort to engender Polanyi's analysis.

Lourdes, if you could do it again, would you become an economist? That is a very interesting question which I don't quite know how to answer. My reply is yes and no. I think economics gives a lot of depth to our understanding of the reality around us and I like that. But at the same time I have often felt that the profession is frustrating. If I had been in another profession, I wouldn't have had to devote so much time to things that were not particularly meaningful – like teaching rather meaningless indifference curves and equations that often turn students off. Luckily, I no longer have to do this. I have the ability now to select and use what I find most interesting in our discipline.

When you say economics gives a depth to our understanding, how exactly are you defining economics? I mean we can look at the material world that shapes social reality; the eternal tension between resource availability and the satisfaction of human needs; the ways in which production and consumption are organized and what that implies for the satisfaction of human needs, labor markets, employment, and wages; the distribution of income and inequality; exploitation, and discrimination; development and economic growth (which are not the same); etc. These are the areas in which I think economics has a lot to offer; and I would like to be part of a discipline which focuses on these issues. Working on gender has allowed me to have a greater interdisciplinary outlook while being grounded in economics. So I am pleased about having been able to find a compromise between being an economist and simultaneously being able to work on questions of interest to me. I also think that development is not only about economic growth. In fact, this is the reason why development economics has been phased out of most economics departments. However, for me, it has been a good route to channel many of the questions I am interested in.

Was it your interest, then, in feminist theory and practice that moved you towards interdisciplinary work? I find it ironic that during the 1970s, feminists moved away from the disciplines because we felt that they were hopeless in dealing with the questions we wanted to ask: questions about inequality, discrimination, and exploitation, for example, and about gender and power relations. As a result, we tried to develop interdisciplinary tools to explore these issues. However, as time went on, I have felt that, at least academically, feminism has gone into directions which were not helpful for what I wanted to do. I also became frustrated with the fact that interdisciplinary work has not produced the depth that specialization can provide; the result has been either intellectually interesting work with little social relevancy, or socially relevant work which is rather superficial. Perhaps for these reasons, in the 1990s we have witnessed a return to the disciplines and here I think that, for me at least, IAFFE has been very helpful. Much of the work by feminist economists offers both the specialization of a discipline and the possibility of having a critical view from a feminist perspective, and asking wider questions that go beyond a narrow definition of economics.

How would you explain the intersection of your feminist interests and your participation in the Engendering Macroeconomics Project? This project was a response to the problems that feminists and others working on the effects of structural adjustment had identified with respect to macroeconomic policies. We realized that macro policies are not neutral with respect to who bears the social costs of adjustment. Instead, they can result in gender and class biases. Economists designing policy packages are often oblivious to this problem. Our effort was aimed at the need to incorporate gender (and class) dimensions into macro models from the very beginning. For me, the project meant a return to the discipline of economics, albeit from a critical feminist perspective. This does not mean surrendering our interdisciplinary work. In fact, I think we are more empowered now than during the 1970s, because we have developed tools and acquired skills which make us more capable of dealing with the shortcomings of the discipline. We are stronger and in a better position to exercise some influence in terms of transforming some areas of economic analysis. Other academic disciplines, like anthropology, history, political science, and others, have been much more transformed by feminism than economics. We have a long way to go.

On a theoretical level, what direction do you think IAFFE needs to go in order to contribute to the transformation of the discipline of economics? There are many areas in which feminist economists can continue making theoretical contributions: for instance, the significance of the care economy and the connections between paid and unpaid work. We also need a theory of rights and obligations that can be used to distribute care responsibilities. We need a welfare economics that is tied to a notion of economic justice. We need to trace the connections between efficiency and equality, rather than assuming they have nothing to do with each other, or that inequality leads to greater efficiency. We need to explore further the nature of markets and market failures, and the nature of capitalism, its points of tensions, and how to deal with them. We need to investigate how winners can compensate losers in international trade liberalization schemes, and much more. In addition, I agree with Bob Solow, in his note included in *Beyond Economic Man*, in which he says that feminist economists have to get their hands dirty with the nuts and bolts of economics. I do think that we have to get more involved in engaging with the profession, not only on theoretical issues, but also on policy grounds. We also have to keep in mind what we have learned in the past twenty-five years, which I think has been quite a lot. We know that we need to go beyond the "add women and stir" approaches, such as adding women to neoclassical economic models without transforming the models.

The question is how these efforts may have an influence on economics as a whole. For example, how does gender analysis influence our assumptions about economic rationality and about how people behave and make decisions? So far IAFFE has a solid record in representing critical thinking about the profession. But we need to incorporate feminist ways of doing and knowing into specialized areas in addition to continuing the more general work. Perhaps this will eventually make economics more humane and responsive to social needs. The goal of gender equality, as important as it is, is insufficient unless it is contextualized within the wider objectives of human development. For me, as someone interested in development, this notion is basic for the work that I do.

Given what you think needs to be done, what kind of advice do you have for a young economist who needs to survive the current realities of the profession while, at the same time, wants to contribute to the kind of transformation of the discipline that you have been talking about? Based on my own experience, I would advise young economists to do what they think is important, according to their conscience and objectives. Of course, that's easy for me to say. For the most part it worked in my case, but it might not work in all cases. I would also advise caution. But I think it's important to do what one feels strongly about, to find out what you feel passionate about, and to push and work as hard as you can to accomplish what you believe needs to be done.

I also think that it is important to do things collectively and not to be alone in this enterprise. I see feminism as a very collective endeavor. I would advise our younger colleagues to not forget that their work is part of a much larger project. Find other people to work with. It is much more fun, rewarding, and often more productive.

How would you describe the evolution of your own work? Well, I started with neoclassical training, and was not exposed to alternatives in any systematic way. From the very beginning, I felt uncomfortable with the assumptions and methods. But most of all, it rarely seemed conducive to asking the questions that I wanted to ask. My biggest problem has been the tendency of our profession to be the main apologist for the establishment and for disassociating economic analysis from social problems. At the core of the discipline is what Paula England has called the "separate self model." In the 1960s when I arrived in this very rich country, I expected to find a different society. I was appalled, for example, at the extent of poverty and racism I witnessed in New York City. Michael Harrington's *The Other America* had a greater impact on me than the books we read in some of my economics courses. The Vietnam War also made me question many things. Learning about Latin American development was also an eye-opening experience, in terms of understanding how the world worked. And through all this, I wasn't receiving help from my profession in terms of addressing some urgent questions, let alone finding answers.

This is why URPE was important for me; it helped me to formulate these issues more clearly. When the organization shifted toward Marxism in the early 1970s, I was not persuaded that Marxist analysis is what I would have chosen, but it helped me to understand a different paradigm, and to evaluate its usefulness to answer my questions. For example, the Marxian emphasis on conflict rather than equilibrium gave me a better way of posing some of the questions that I had been grappling with. At the same time, I never felt I could embrace orthodox Marxism. However, in terms of a general paradigm, I felt comfortable connecting with a left project. In terms of gender, I identified with the branch of feminism in the 1970s called socialist feminism, in which class and gender were central categories of analysis. This was reflected in my work on gender and development. Using this approach, Gita Sen and I wrote two articles critiquing modernization theory as expressed in Ester Boserup's book *Women's Role in Economic Development*. In the early 1980s, Martha Roldán and I did a study of domestic home work in Mexico City which also integrated gender and class issues.

Eventually, in the late 1980s and early 1990s, I took quite seriously the postmodern critiques of universalizing theories. I recognized the ways in which we had used essentializing categories and grand theory. However, I found it quite ironic that, although the postmodern critiques applied to neoclassical theory as well, it was only Marxism that took a real beating. But this followed from the post-1989 events. After all, neoclassical grand theory underpins the neoliberal world that became triumphant after the dismantling of the Soviet Union. As a result, Marxism was in political retreat, having lost the Cold War between economic systems. Perhaps for this reason, the neoclassical world has basically managed to ignore the postmodern critique. The only orthodox economists that have acknowledged and incorporated some aspects of postmodern thought into their work have been those who are interested in the rhetoric of economics, such as Deirdre McCloskey and Arjo Klamer, but the numbers are not large and I guess this automatically makes them nonorthodox.

A central focus of interest for me has been women's work, including nonmarket work. My effort to understand the gender division of labor across countries began with the concept of reproduction, which I began to use in the late 1970s when I was at the ILO. I wrote an article, "Reproduction, Production, and the Secular Division of Labor," followed by another on "Accounting for Women's Work," in which I questioned the meaning of work; why work has been defined as paid work; and why conventional statistics are compiled as we know them. At the theoretical level, the big debate here is between a conception of work that is connected only to the market versus (what feminists have been struggling for) a vision in which the economy is viewed as the production of goods and services for human welfare. It primarily implies that we should pay attention to three main areas of unpaid work: namely, subsistence production, domestic work, and volunteer work. Most economists see no problem in including subsistence production in the GNP because it is conceptualized as marketable production to which a market value can be assigned. The problem comes with domestic work and volunteer work because they fall within a separate sphere of production without monetary value, and the comparison with market work is more difficult to establish.

Since there are feminist economists who think a redefinition of work is at best a useless and at worst a dangerous endeavor, can you talk more about exactly how this kind of redefinition of our measures of work can be useful? Let me give you an example. In trying to document the gender biases of structural adjustment, we had to rely on case studies (because there were no statistics) to show that structural adjustment had resulted in the intensification of women's work at home and in the paid labor force as well. Girls were often affected differently from boys, for instance. However, because our findings were based on relatively small data sets, they have not been easily accepted on the grounds that we cannot generalize from them. If statistics on unpaid work were available, it would have been possible to use large data sets to analyze whether and how it was affected by structural adjustment. It seems obvious that this is an important project; the better we can document who works and for how long, the better we can understand who contributes to household and human welfare, and the better we can press for an equal sharing of paid and unpaid work along gender lines. This has a lot of implications for different levels of policy.

How is this project connected to the wages for housework movement of the 1970s? I think some feminists who have misgivings about our project are afraid that this is where it might ultimately lead: wages for housework. But improving statistics has nothing to do with paying women wages for housework. It is a mistake to assume that unpaid work is only done by women. In fact, it is increasingly done by men, especially in high-wage countries because, as wages go up, it is more expensive to hire help, for example, for home repairs. As a result, men tend to do these jobs. Studies in France and Germany have shown that the amount of unpaid work done by men is on the rise, whereas the amount done by women is decreasing even if a large proportion of unpaid work across countries is still by and large done by women. Wages for housework is a separate project. There is nothing wrong in principle with paying women for the work they do in the home. However, I have misgivings about it because it could lock only women into household work, and this is not the purpose of the accounting exercise. The purpose is clear: why include polluting production in GNP statistics and not the goods and services that feed and care for families? Of course, there are theoretical and methodological problems involved but much progress has been made along these lines.

Earlier you talked about your involvement in the Engendering Macroeconomics Project. What does it mean to engender macroeconomics and international trade? This is a project that is fairly recent. The first time I remember thinking about the greater dimensions of trade liberalization schemes was during the NAFTA debates. Marjorie Cohen's book about the effects of trade liberalization on women in Canada was a pioneer effort, even if it was not totally persuasive. Since then, there has been more work on the issue, particularly in setting up an agenda for the empirical work necessary to analyze these effects. But much remains to be done. In particular, we need to identify the specific gender effects at the local level, by industry, on women as consumers, etc. We also need to work on how to implement the compensation principle: winners compensating losers in international trade and the gender dimensions of this. For example, trade liberalization negotiations could incorporate a gender breakdown of sectors and industries in order to evaluate trade policy, and could design compensation schemes for those, women and men, negatively affected by trade liberalization policies. This is a complicated project which has not been seriously addressed. There has also been enormous work on gender and trade at the activist level, including women's groups who work on the WTO and other trade liberalization schemes.

How did the macroeconomic project group get formed? The three main organizers were Nilufer Cagatay, Diane Elson, and Caren Grown. They were instrumental in getting the project funded, inviting participants, etc.

How has the collaborative process worked? It has been a very good experience. Once the funds were obtained, the group met first to discuss different ideas for the individual papers. Based on those discussions, each of us made our own decision about our project. Some of us had individual projects while others collaborated on co-authored articles. At the second meeting, each paper was thoroughly discussed by the entire group and, based on those comments, we revised our papers. The final revision was done after we received comments from the reviewers.

Will the project continue after publication? Yes, in fact the Ford Foundation has already funded us for a second round; this will focus on trade and finance as well.

Why have you been interested in Latin America and Mexico, in particular? I have been interested in Latin America for a long time, since graduate school. I took courses and attended seminars. I did not begin the empirical work on specific countries until the early 1980s when Martha Roldán and I studied subcontracting and domestic piece work in Mexico City. My interest in Latin America came very naturally. I speak Spanish and I understand the culture, although there are enormous differences among countries and between Latin America and Spain.

Can you talk about your work in Mexico? Working with Martha Roldán was a very interesting experience in interdisciplinary research. She was a sociologist who had also been at the ILO. Earlier, I had done some fieldwork in Morocco for an ILO study and had found it very useful; direct contact with human subjects is more rewarding than working with cold statistical data. I learned a lot about qualitative versus quantitative analysis, and how much we miss when we only focus on the numbers. The Mexican study was also very important to me in this sense. We interviewed women in their homes. I learned a lot, not only about the problems of data collection, but also about the way poor women and their families in Mexico City lived their daily lives. I repeated the experience again in 1988, this time to study the effects of structural adjustment and their gender dimensions. If I had not collaborated with a sociologist, I probably would not have done this type of work. It helped me see structural adjustment from the bottom up instead of the top down. As with the previous study, it was a transformative experience. For the most part, I worked with very poor families and, believe me, if the economists who design structural adjustment policies took the time to have a similar experience, they would no longer assume that macroeconomics is neutral with respect to gender and the poor.

I am delighted that IAFFE has been open to this type of work using case studies. There was an interesting panel on the nature and methodological contributions of case studies at one of the IAFFE annual meetings in Washington, DC a few years ago. *Feminist Economics* published some of the contributions. The main impetus for this work has come from the gender and development field, and it has taken a long time to legitimize this work as economics.

Can you talk about your current work? I am currently working on a book on gender and the global economy. It brings together some of the work I have done in the past. I'm updating or rewriting it, but I also have some new material. In general, it emphasizes what we have learned from feminist analysis in helping us to understand the different aspects of the global economy; the significance of unpaid work, the contributions of the field of gender and development to our understanding of human development, the feminization of the international labor force, the gender dimensions of economic restructuring (in the North as well as in the South), among other things.

Do you envision this book as supplementary reading in certain courses? Yes. Although grounded in economics, it is addressed to an interdisciplinary audience. It is a book that could be used in courses on development, on globalization, or in courses on women and work. I hope that it will be useful to a variety of disciplines in the social sciences.

Lourdes, is there anything you would like to talk about that we haven't discussed? Well, there are parts of my work that we have not discussed. However, there is one study I would like to mention. It was a study of laid-off workers in Cortland during the mid-1990s, a community in upstate New York. We followed the labor market trajectories of a large sample of laid-off workers and showed that the impact of economic restructuring can be different for men and women. Although the majority of workers suffered financial losses as a result, women workers lost a relatively larger proportion of their income. Moreover, there were other gender dimensions at the individual, household, and community level.

In any case, this is enough. I want to thank you for giving me this opportunity to reflect on my life as an economist. There was a time in my life when I did not want to say I was an economist. Now I am happy to say it because we have found our own voice within the profession!

APPENDIX
Questions used for Oral History Project

Family genealogy

What is your family background (e.g., class, ethnicity, educational level of parents)?

Student of economics

What was the attraction to economics? Where did you go to school? What was your experience as an undergraduate and graduate student of economics? Did you have mentors or role models as a student of economics? What constraints, if any, did you face as a student of economics? Were there other women students in economics with you? Are you in touch with them? Do you know where they are and/or what they're doing? What was the focus of your dissertation? How did you decide on the topic?

Professional woman with family

Did you have children? How many? How did you balance your professional and family life?

Professional economist

How would you describe your perspective as an economist? How has your experience as an economist evolved over time, if at all? What kinds of jobs have you had as an economist? What constraints, if any, did you face in your career decisions? What strategies did you use to overcome the constraints in your career? What was your general experience as a woman in the economics profession? What kind of personal and/or organizational support have you had in your professional life, if any? How do you feel about the development of your career? How do you feel about your professional decisions? Have you observed changes in the economics profession over time? Why do you think more women are not attracted to economics? Do you consider yourself a feminist economist? Why or why not? Did you ever consider a different type of career? If so, what would you have done differently?

SELECT BIBLIOGRAPHY

Ackerman, F. (ed.) (1998) *The Changing Nature of Work*, Washington, DC: Island Press.

Albelda, R. (1997) *Economics and Feminism: Disturbances in the Field*, New York: Twayne.

Allen, R. A. (1961) *East Texas Lumber Workers: An Economic and Social Picture: 1870–1950*, Austin, TX: University of Texas Press.

Amott, T. and Matthaei, J. (1996) *Race, Gender, and Work: A Multicultural Economic History of Women in the United States*, Boston, MA: South End Press.

Amsden, A. and Moser, C. (1975) "Job Search and Affirmative Action," *American Economic Review* 65, 2.

Ashenfelter, O. (1998) "Report of the Editor," *American Economic Review* 83, 2.

Ausubel, L. M. (1991) "The Failure of Competition in the Credit Card Market," *American Economic Review* 81, 1.

Badget, L. (1995) "Gender, Sexuality, and Sexual Orientation: All in the Feminist Family?" *Feminist Economics* 1, 1.

Becker, G. (1957) *The Economics of Discrimination*, Chicago, IL: University of Chicago Press.

—— (1992) *A Treatise on the Family*, Cambridge, MA: Harvard University Press.

Bell, C. S. (1973) "Report of the Committee on the Status of Women in the Economics Profession," *American Economic Review* 63, 2.

Beller, A. (1978) *The Effect of Economic Conditions on the Success of Equal Employment Opportunity Laws: An Application to the Sex Differential in Earnings*, Madison, WI: Institute for Research on Poverty, University of Wisconsin.

Benedict, R. (1934) *Patterns of Culture*, New York: Houghton Mifflin.

Benería, L. (1979) "Reproduction, Production and the Sexual Division of Labor," *Cambridge Journal of Economics* 3, 3.

—— (1992) "Accounting for Women's Work: The Progress of Two Decades," *World Development* 20, 11.

—— (1999) "Globalization, Gender, and the Davos Man," *Feminist Economics* 5, 3.

—— (2001) "The Impact of Industrial Relocation on Displaced Workers: A Case Study of Cortland, New York," *Economic Development Quarterly* 15, 1.

Benería, L. and Dudley, M. J. (eds) (1996) *Economic Restructuring in the Americas*, Ithaca, NY: Latin American Studies Program, Cornell University.

Benería, L. and Feldman, S. (1992) *Unequal Burden: Economic Crisis, Persistent Poverty, and Women's Work*, Boulder, CO: Westview Press.

Benería, L. and Roldán, M. (1987) *The Crossroads of Class and Gender. Homework, Subcontracting and Household Dynamics in Mexico City*, Chicago, IL: University of Chicago Press.

Benería, L. and Sen, G. (1982) "Class, Gender Inequalities and Women's Role in Economic Development: Theoretical and Practical Perspectives," *Feminist Studies* 8, 1.

Bergmann, B. R. (1966) "The Cochabamba–Santa Cruz Highway in Bolivia," in G. W. Wilson, B. R. Bergmann, L. V. Hirsch, and M. S. Klein (eds) *The Impact of Highway Investment on Development*, Washington, DC: Brookings Institution.

—— (1971) "Effect on White Incomes of Discrimination in Employment," *Journal of Political Economy* 79, 2.

—— (1973) "Combining Microsimulation and Regression; A 'Preferred' Regression of Poverty Incidence on Unemployment and Growth," *Econometrica* 41, 5.

—— (1974) "Occupational Segregation, Wages and Profits When Employers Discriminate by Race and Sex," *Eastern Economic Journal* 1, 2–3.

—— (1981) "The Economic Risks of Being a Housewife," *American Economic Review* 71, 2.

—— (1986) *The Economic Emergence of Women*, New York: Basic Books.

—— (1994) "Curing Child Poverty in the United States," *American Economic Review* 71, 2.

—— (1996) *In Defense of Affirmative Action*, New York: Basic Books.

—— (1996) *Saving Our Children from Poverty: What the United States Can Learn from France*, New York: Russell Sage Foundation.

—— (1997) "Government Support for Families with Children in the United States and France," *Feminist Economics* 3, 1.

—— (2000) *Is Social Security Broke? A Cartoon Guide to the Issues*, Ann Arbor, MI: University of Michigan Press.

Bergmann, B. R. and Bennett, R. (1985) *A Microsimulated Transactions Model of the United States*, Baltimore, MD: Johns Hopkins University Press.

Bergmann, B. R. and Kaun, D. (1967) *Structural Unemployment in the United States*, Washington, DC: US Department of Commerce.

Blau, D. and Hagy, A. P. (1998) "The Demand for Quality in Child Care," *Journal of Political Economy* 106, 1.

Blau, F., Ferber, M., and Winkler, A. E. (2001) *The Economics of Women, Men and Work*, 4th edition, New York: Prentice Hall.

Boris, E. and Chaudhuri, N. (eds) (1999) *Voices of Women Historians: The Personal, The Political, The Professional*, Bloomington, IN: Indiana University Press.

Boserup, E. (1970) *Woman's Role in Economic Development*, London: Allen and Unwin.

Bye, R. T. (1924) *Principles of Economics*, New York: Knopf.

Cagatay, N., Grown, C., and Elson, D. (1995) Special Issue on "Gender, Adjustment and Macroeconomics," *World Development* 23, 11.

Cohen, M. G. (1988) *Women's Work, Markets and Economic Development in Nineteenth Century Ontario*, Toronto: University of Toronto Press.

Conley, F. K. (1998) *Walking Out on the Boys*, New York: Farrar, Strauss and Giroux.

Coontz, S. (1992) *The Way We Never Were: American Families and the Nostalgia Trap*, New York: Basic Books.

Cornia, G. A., Jolly, R., and Stewart, F. (eds) (1987) *Adjustment with a Human Face*, New York: UNICEF/Clarendon Press.

Darity, W. and Myers, S. L. (1998) *Persistent Disparity: Race and Economic Inequality in the United States since 1945*, Cheltenham: Edward Elgar.

Dimand, M. A., Dimand, R. W., and Forget, E. L. (eds) (1995) *Women of Value: Feminist Essays on the History of Women in Economics*, Aldershot: Edward Elgar.

Dimand, R. W. (1995) "The Neglect of Women's Contributions to Economics," in M. A.

Dimand, R. W. Dimand, and E. L. Forget (eds) *Women of Value: Feminist Essays on the History of Women in Economics*, Aldershot: Edward Elgar.

Dornbusch, S. M. And Strober, M. H. (eds) (1988) *Feminism, Children, and the New Families*, New York: Guilford Press.

England, P. (1993) "The Separate Self: Androcentric Bias in Neoclassical Assumptions," in M. A. Ferber and J. A. Nelson (eds) *Beyond Economic Man: Feminist Theory and Economics*, Chicago, IL: University of Chicago Press, 37–53.

Ferber, M. A. (1986) "Citations: Are They an Objective Measure of Scholarly Merit?" *Signs: Journal of Women in Culture and Society* 11, 2.

—— (1988) "Citations and Networking," *Gender and Society* 2, 1.

Ferber, M. A. and Bartlett, R. L. (1990) "A Feminist Approach to the Principles of Economics Course," in P. Saunders and W. Walstad (eds) *The Principles of Economics Course: A Handbook for Instructors*, 2nd edition, New York: McGraw-Hill.

Ferber, M. A. and Green, C. A. (1985) "Homemakers Imputed Wages: Results of the Heckman Technique Compared to Women's Own Estimates," *Journal of Human Resources*, 20, 1.

Ferber, M. A. and Loeb, J. W. (1973) "Representation, Performance and Status of Women on the Faculty at the Urbana–Champaign Campus of the University of Illinois," in A. S. Rossi and A. Calderwood (eds) *Academic Women on the Move*, New York: Russell Sage Foundation.

—— (1974) "Professors, Performance and Rewards," *Industrial Relations* 13, 1.

—— (eds) (1997) *Academic Couples: Problems and Promises*, Chicago, IL: University of Illinois Press.

Ferber, M. A. and Nelson, J. A. (eds) (1993) *Beyond Economic Man: Feminist Theory and Economics*, Chicago, IL: University of Chicago Press.

Ferber, M. A. and Spaeth, J. L. (1984) "Work Characteristics and Male–Female Earnings Gap," *American Economic Review* 74, 2.

Ferber, M. A. and Teiman, M. L. (1980) "Are Women Economists at a Disadvantage in Publishing Journal Articles?" *Eastern Economic Journal* 6, 3–4.

Ferber, M. A., Green, C. A. and Spaeth, J. L. (1986) "Work Power and Earnings of Women and Men," *American Economic Review* 76, 2.

Ferber, M. A., Loeb, J. W., and Lowry, H. M. (1979) "Faculty Patterns of Publications and Rewards," *Atlantic Economic Journal* 7, 2.

Folbre, N. (1982) "Exploitation Comes Home: A Critique of the Marxian Theory of Family Labor," *Cambridge Journal of Economics* 6.

Forget, E. (1995) "American Women Economists, 1900–1940: Doctoral Dissertations and Research Specialization," in M. A. Dimand, R. W. Dimand, and E. L. Forget (eds) *Women of Value: Feminist Essays on the History of Women in Economics*, Aldershot: Edward Elgar.

Friedan, B. (1963) *The Feminine Mystique*, New York: Dell.

Gatlin, R. (1987) *American Women since 1945*, Jackson, MS: University Press of Mississippi.

Gluck, S. B. and Patai, D. (eds) (1991) *Women's Words: The Feminist Practice of Oral History*, New York: Routledge.

Gluckman, A. and Reed, B. (eds) (1997) *Homo Economics: Capitalism, Community, and Lesbian and Gay Life*, New York: Routledge.

Gordon, F. E. and Strober, M. H. (1975) *Bringing Women into Management*, New York: McGraw-Hill.

—— (1978) "Initial Observations on a Pioneer Cohort: 1974 Women MBAs," *Sloan Management Review* 19, 2.

Grapard, U. (1995) "Robinson Crusoe: The Quintessential Economic Man?" *Feminist Economics* 1, 1.

Green, R. L. (1956) *The Adventures of Robin Hood*, Harmondsworth: Penguin Books.

Groenewegen, P. (ed.) (1994) *Feminism and Political Economy in Victorian England*, Aldershot: Edward Elgar.

Harding, S. (1991) "Who Knows? Identities and Feminist Epistemology," in J. E. Hartman and E. Messer-Davidow (eds) *(En)Gendering Knowledge: Feminists in Academe*, Knoxville, TN: University of Tennessee Press.

—— (1995) "Can Feminist Thought Make Economics More Objective?" *Feminist Economics* 1, 1.

Harrington, M. (1969) *The Other America*, New York: Macmillan.

Helburn, S. W. (1991) "Keynes's Idealism: A Critical Evaluation of Athol Fitzgibbon's Keynes's Vision: A New Political Economy," *Review of Social Economy* 49, 3.

—— (1995) *Cost, Quality, and Child Outcomes in Child Care Centers: Technical Report*, Denver, CO: Center for Research on Economic and Social Policy, University of Colorado at Denver.

—— (1999) "The Silent Crisis in US Child Care," *Annals of the American Academy of Political and Social Science* 563, May.

—— (2000) "Child Care Center Quality Differences: The Role of Profit Status, Client Preferences, and Trust," *Nonprofit and Voluntary Sector Quarterly* 29, 3.

Helburn, S. W. and Bergmann, B. R. (2001) *The Future Child Care: Improving Affordability and Quality*, New York: St Martin's Press.

Helburn, S. W. and Bramhall, D. F. (eds) (1986) *Marx, Schumpeter, and Keynes: A Centenary Celebration of Dissent*, Armonk, NY: M. E. Sharpe.

Helburn, S. W., Culkin, M., and Morris, J. (1991) "Quality and the True Cost of Child Care," *Journal of Social Issues* 47, 2.

Helburn, S. W. and Howes, C. (1996) "Child Care Cost and Quality," *The Future of Children: Financing Child Care* 6, 2.

Helburn, S. W. and Sperling, J. (1997) "ECON12 and the New Social Studies: Love's Labor Lost?" *Social Studies* 88, November/December.

Helburn, S. W., Sperling, J., Evans, R., and Lott, B. (1977) *Communist Economies*, Boston, MA: Addison-Wesley.

Jones, B. A. P. (1979) "Utilization of Black Human Resources in the United States," *Review of Black Political Economy* 10, 1.

—— (ed.) (1984) *New Perspectives on Unemployment*, New Brunswick, NJ: Transaction Books.

—— (1985–6) "Black Women and Labor Force Participation: An Analysis of Sluggish Growth Rates," *Review of Black Political Economy* 14, 2–3.

—— (1987) "From the Sixties to the Eighties: The Economic Status of Black Americans," in F. D. Jones (ed.) *Readings in American Political Issues*, Dubuque, IA: Kendall/Hunt.

—— (1988) "NEA Presidential Address: Economics Programs at Historically Black Colleges and Universities," *Review of Black Political Economy* 16, 3.

Kanter, R. (1977) *Men and Women of the Corporation*, New York: Basic Books.

Keynes, J. M. (1936) *The General Theory of Employment, Interest, and Money*, New York: Harcourt, Brace and World.

King, M. C. and Saunders, L. (1999) "An Interview with Marianne Ferber: Founding Feminist Economist," *Review of Political Economy* 2, 1.

Klamer, A. (1984) *Conversations with Economists: New Classical Economists and Opponents Speak out on the Current Controversy in Macroeconomics*, Totowa, NJ: Rowman and Allanheld.

Klamer, A., McCloskey, D. N., and Solow, R. M. (1988) *The Consequences of Economic Rhetoric*, Cambridge: Cambridge University Press.

Klein, L. R. (1974) *A Textbook of Econometrics*, 2nd edition, Englewood Cliffs, NJ: Prentice Hall.

Lange, O. (1993) *Economic Theory and Market Socialism: Selected Essays of Oskar Lange*, Aldershot: Edward Elgar.

Laslett, B. and Thorne, B. (eds) (1997) *Feminist Sociology: Life Histories of a Movement*, New Brunswick, NJ: Rutgers University Press.

Lloyd, C., Andrew, E. S., and Gilroy, C. L. (eds) (1979) *Women in the Labor Market*, New York: Columbia University Press.

Loury, G. C. and Coate, S. (1993) "Will Affirmative-Action Policies Eliminate Negative Stereotypes?" *American Economic Review* 83, 5.

MacDonald, M. (1995) "The Empirical Challenges of Feminist Economics: The Example of Economic Restructuring," in E. Kuiper and J. Sap (eds) *Out of the Margin: Feminist Perspectives on Economics*, London: Routledge.

Marshall, A. (1895) *Principles of Economics*, New York: Macmillan.

Marx, K. (1961) *Capital*, Moscow: Foreign Languages Publishing House.

Mayhew, A. (1980) "Schumpeterian Capitalism Versus the 'Schumpeterian Thesis'," *Journal of Economic Issues* 14, 2.

—— (1981) "Ayresian Technology, Technological Reasoning, and Doomsday," *Journal of Economic Issues* 15, 2.

—— (1983) "Ideology and the Great Depression: Monetary History Rewritten," *Journal of Economic Issues* 17, 2.

—— (1985) "Dangers in Using the Idea of Property Rights: Modern Property Rights Theory and the Neo-Classical Trap," *Journal of Economic Issues* 19, 4.

—— (1987) "Culture: Core Concept Under Attack," *Journal of Economic Issues* 21, 2.

—— (1989) "Contrasting Origins of the Two Institutionalisms: The Social Science Context," *Review of Political Economy* 1, 3.

—— (1994) "The Economic Development of the North Atlantic Community: Dudley Dillard and Economic History," *Journal of Economic Issues* 27, 2.

—— (1996) "Foreign Investment, Economic Growth, and Theories of Value: Evidence from Economic History," in J. Adams and A. Scaperlanda (eds) *The Institutional Economics of the International Economy*, Boston, MA: Kluwer.

—— (1998) "How American Economists Came to Love the Sherman Antitrust Act," *History of Political Economy* 30, supplement.

—— (1998) "On the Difficulty of Evolutionary Analysis," *Cambridge Journal of Economics* 22, 4.

—— (2001) "Human Agency, Cumulative Causation, and the State: Remarks upon Receiving the Veblen–Commons Award," *Journal of Economic Issues* 35, 2.

Meyer, J. R. and Kuh, E. (1957) *The Investment Decision: An Empirical Study*, Cambridge, MA: Harvard University Press.

Meyerowitz, J. (ed.) (1994) *Not June Cleaver: Women and Gender in Postwar America, 1945–1960*, Philadelphia, PA: Temple University Press.

Nelson, J. A. (1996) *Feminism, Objectivity, and Economics*, London: Routledge.

Olmsted, J. (1997) "Telling Palestinian Women's Economic Stories," *Feminist Economics* 3, 2.

Olson, P. (1990) "Mature Women and the Rewards of Domestic Ideology," *Journal of Economic Issues* 24, 2.

Peterson, J. and Lewis, M. (eds) (1999) *The Elgar Companion to Feminist Economics*, Cheltenham, UK: Edward Elgar.

Polanyi, K. (1944) *The Great Transformation*, New York: Farrar and Rinehart.

Polkinghorn, B. and Thomson, D. L. (1998) *Adam Smith's Daughters: Eight Prominent Women Economists from the Eighteenth Century to Present*, Cheltenham: Edward Elgar.

Pujol, M. A. (1992) *Feminism and Anti-Feminism in Early Economic Thought*, Aldershot: Edward Elgar.

—— (ed.) (1997) "A Special Issue: Expanding the Methodological Boundaries of Economics," *Feminist Economics* 3, 2.

Reagan, B. (1975) "Two Supply Curves for Economists? Implications of Mobility and Career Attachment of Women," *American Economic Review* 65, 2.

Reinharz, S. (1992) *Feminist Methods in Social Research*, New York: Oxford University Press.

Rima, I. H. (1969) *A Forum on Systems Management*, Philadelphia, PA: Temple University School of Business Administration, Bureau of Economics and Business Research.

—— (1984) "Involuntary Unemployment and the Respecified Labor Supply Curve," *Journal of Post Keynesian Economics* 6, 4.

—— (1990) "Beyond Studies in the Theory of Money – A Tribute to the Scholarship of Douglas Vicker," *Journal of Post Keynesian Economics* 12, 2.

—— (1991) *The Joan Robinson Legacy*, Armonk, NY: M. E. Sharpe.

—— (1994) "The Megacorp and Macrodynamics – Essays in Memory of Alfred Eichner: A Review," *Journal of Post Keynesian Economics* 16, 2.

—— (ed.) (1995) *Measurement, Quantification and Economic Analysis: Numeracy in Economics*, London: Routledge.

—— (ed.) (1995) *The Classical Tradition in Economic Thought*, Aldershot: Edward Elgar.

—— (1996) *Labor Markets in a Global Economy: An Introduction*, Armonk, NY: M. E. Sharpe.

—— (ed.) (2000) *Development of Economic Analysis*, 6th edition, London: Routledge.

Rivlin, A. M. (1971) *Systematic Thinking for Social Action*, Washington, DC: Brookings Institution.

—— (1982) "The Political Economy of Budget Choices: A View from Congress," *American Economic Review* 72, 2.

—— (1984) "Why and How to Cut the Deficit," *Brookings Review* 2, 4.

—— (1990) "Simulating Policy Alternatives for Long-Term Care: An Example of the Orcutt Approach," *Journal of Economic Behavior and Organization* 14, 1.

—— (1992) *Reviving the American Dream: The Economy, the States, and the Federal Government*, Washington, DC: Brookings Institution.

—— (1993) "Budgeting for Performance," *Government Finance Review* 9, 5.

—— (1997) "Statements to the Congress," *Federal Reserve Bulletin* 83, 9.

—— (1998) "Toward a Better Class of Financial Crisis: Some Lessons from Asia," *The Region* 12, 3.

—— (1999) "On Economic Literacy," *The Region* 13, 2.

—— (2000) "Seizing the Economic Opportunity," *Brookings Review* 18, 2.

—— (2001) "The Challenges of Affluence," *Business Economics* 36, 1.

Rivlin, A. M. and Timpane, P. M. (1975) *Ethical and Legal Issues of Social Experimentation*, Washington, DC: Brookings Institution.

—— (eds) (1975) *Planned Variation in Education: Should We Give Up or Try Harder?* Washington, DC: Brookings Institution.

Rivlin, A. M. and Weiner, J. M. (1988) *Caring for the Disabled Elderly: Who Will Pay?* Washington, DC: Brookings Institution.

Robinson, J. (1933) *The Economics of Imperfect Competition*, London: Macmillan.

Roll, E. (1992) *A History of Economic Thought*, London: Faber and Faber.

Rossiter, M. (1995) *Women Scientists in America: Before Affirmative Action 1940–1972*, Baltimore, MD: Johns Hopkins University Press.

Schlesinger, A. M. (1945) *The Age of Jackson*, New York: New American Library.

Shaw, L. B. (1978) *A Profile of Women Potentially Eligible for the Displaced Homemaker Program under the Comprehensive Employment and Training Act of 1978*, Columbus, OH: Center for Human Resource Research, College of Administrative Science, Ohio State University.

—— (1978) *Economic Consequences of Marital Disruption for Women in Their Middle Years*, Columbus, OH: Center for Human Resource Research, College of Administrative Science, Ohio State University.

—— (ed.) (1983) *Unplanned Careers: The Working Lives of Middle-Aged Women*, Lexington, MA: Lexington Books.

—— (1985) *Older Women At Work*, Washington, DC: Women's Research and Education Institute of the Congressional Caucus for Women's Issues.

—— (ed.) (1986) *Midlife Women at Work: A Fifteen-Year Perspective*, Lexington, MA: Lexington Books.

—— (1988) "Special Problems of Older Women Workers," in M. Borus, H. Parnes, S. Sandell, and B. Seidman (eds) *The Older Worker*, Madison, WI: Industrial Relations Research Association.

—— (2000) "Measurement and Analysis of Poverty," in J. Peterson and M. Lewis (eds) *The Elgar Companion to Feminist Economics*, Cheltenham: Edward Elgar.

Shaw, L. B. and Dex, S. (1986) *British and American Women at Work: Do Equal Opportunity Policies Matter?*, London: Macmillan.

Shaw, L. B. and Shapiro, D. (1987) "Women's Work Plans: Contrasting Expectations and Actual Work Experience," *Monthly Labor Review* 110, November.

Shaw, L. B., Zuckerman, D., and Hartmann, H. (1998) *The Impact of Social Security Reform on Women*, Washington, DC: The Institute for Women's Policy Research.

Simms, M. C. (ed.) (1988) *Black Economic Progress: An Agenda for the 1990s: A Statement by the Economic Policy Task Force of the Joint Center for Political Studies*, Washington, DC: Joint Center for Political Studies.

—— (1993) "Adolescent Pregnancy among Blacks in the United States: Why Is It a Policy Issue?" in A. Lawson and D. L. Rhode (eds) *The Politics of Pregnancy: Adolescent Sexuality and Public Policy*, New Haven, CT: Yale University Press.

—— (ed.) (1995) *Economic Perspectives on Affirmative Action*, Washington, DC: Joint Center for Political and Economic Studies.

—— (1996) "Making Policy Work for Black Women," in J. Malveaux (ed.) *Voices of Vision*, Washington, DC: National Council of Negro Women.

Simms, M. C. and Malveaux, J. (1986) *Slipping through the Cracks: The Status of Black Women*, New Brunswick, NJ: Transaction Books.

Simms, M. C. and Myers, S. L. (eds) (1988) *The Economics of Race and Crime*, New Brunswick, NJ: Transaction Books.

Simms, M. C. and Winston, J. A. (1997) "Is the Inner City Competitive," in T. D. Boston and C. L. Ross (eds) *The Inner City: Urban Poverty and Economic Development in the Next Century*, New Brunswick, NJ: Transaction Books.

Skidelsky, R. J. A. (1983) *John Maynard Keynes*, New York: Penguin.

Solow, R. M. (1993) "Feminist Theory, Women's Experience, and Economics," in M. A. Ferber and J. A. Nelson (eds) *Beyond Economic Man: Feminist Theory and Economics*, Chicago, IL: University of Chicago Press.

Strober, M. H. (1975) "Women Economists: Career Aspirations, Education, and Training," *American Economic Review* 65, 2.

—— (1984) "Toward a General Theory of Occupational Sex Segregation: The Case of Public School Teaching," in B. Reskin (ed.) *Sex Segregation in the Workplace: Trends, Explanations, Remedies*, Washington, DC: National Academy Press.

—— (1992) "The Relative Attractiveness Theory of Occupational Segregation: The Case of Physicians," *Proceedings of the 44th Annual Meetings of the Industrial and Labor Relations Research Association*.

—— (1994) "Rethinking Economics through a Feminist Lens," *American Economic Review* 84, 2.

—— (1997) "Balancing Act: Motherhood, Marriage, and Employment among American Women," *Journal of Economic Literature* 35, 4.

Strober, M. H. and Arnold, C. (1987) "The Dynamics of Occupational Segregation among Bank Tellers," in C. Brown and J. Pechman (eds) *Gender in the Workplace*, Washington, DC: Brookings Institution.

Strober, M. H. and Catanzarite, L. (1993) "The Gender Recomposition of the Maquiladora Workforce in Ciudad Juarez," *Industrial Relations* 32, 1.

Strober, M. H. and Chan, A. (1999) *The Road Winds Uphill All the Way: Gender, Work, and Family in the United States and Japan*, Cambridge, MA: MIT Press.

Strober, M. H., Fuller, K. A., and Cook, A. (1997) "Making and Correcting Errors in Economic Analyses: An Examination of Videotapes," *Journal of Economic Education* 28, Summer.

Weintraub, S. (1949) *Price Theory*, New York: Putman.

—— (1978) *Keynes, Keynesians and Monetarists*, Philadelphia, PA: University of Pennsylvania Press.

Williams, R. (1993) "Race, Deconstruction, and the Emergent Agenda of Feminist Economics Theory," in M. Ferber and J. Nelson (eds) *Beyond Economic Man: Feminist Theory and Economics*, Chicago, IL: University of Chicago Press.

Wrigley, J. (1995) *Other People's Children*, New York: Basic Books.

Zellner, H. (1972) "Discrimination against Women, Occupational Segregation, and the Relative Wage," *American Economic Review* 62, 1–2.

INDEX